Literary Daughters

By the same author

Jane Austen's Family
Jane Austen's England

LITERARY DAUGHTERS

Maggie Lane

ROBERT HALE · LONDON

Robert Hale Limited
Clerkenwell House
Clerkenwell Green
London EC1R OHT

British Library Cataloguing in Publication Data
Lane, Maggie, 1947–
    Literary daughters.
    1. Fiction in English. Women writers, 1778–
    1927. Biographies. Anthologies
    I. Title
    823'.6

ISBN 0-7090-3565-9

Photoset in Ehrhardt by
Rowland Phototypesetting Limited
Printed in Great Britain by
St Edmundsbury Press Limited,
Bury St Edmunds, Suffolk
Bound by Hunter & Foulis Limited

Contents

Illustrations

ACKNOWLEDGEMENTS

National Portrait Gallery: 1–2, 7, 9. British Museum: 3. National Gallery of Ireland: 4.
Captain G. E. Moulton-Barrett: 5–6. The Brontë Society: 8. Coventry City Libraries:
10. Houghton Library, Harvard University: 11. Amherst College Library: 12. Mrs Joan
Duke: 13. The Estate of Virginia Woolf and The Hogarth Press: 14.

To the memory of my sister
Julia Bartlett Thomas
1954–87

Acknowledgements

This book is offered as a work of interpretation, juxtaposition and synthesis, rather than of original research. I have therefore relied heavily on the biographers who have gone before me and whose thorough and scholarly studies I have sifted for just those relationships – and their literary consequences – which pertain to the theme of my work. In some cases – Maria Edgeworth's, for example – there was only one major biography to quarry. In others – notably that of Virginia Woolf – I found an abundance of approaches to her life (including her own). All the books which contributed to my understanding of the lives of my chosen women are listed in the Bibliography; to the authors of them all, I here acknowledge my profound debt.

Chiefly, however, I have worked from primary sources in the sense that I have thought it important to use the words of the women themselves – found in their letters, journals and so forth – to generate and support my observations. Quotations from these sources, often quite lengthy, have been incorporated into the text. This seemed to me essential on the twin scores of authenticity and interest. It saves me, I hope, from any accusation of fancifulness or bias, and it gives the reader, fresh and direct, the often complex feelings of these women about their fathers, in language which no lesser writer could hope to better.

I am therefore deeply grateful to the following publishers for permission to quote from copyright material: Oxford University Press (the letters and diaries of Fanny Burney and Maria Edgeworth, and the memoirs of Leslie Stephen known as *The Mausoleum Book*); John Murray (the 1830–31 diary of Elizabeth Barrett Browning); Basil Blackwell (the letters of Charlotte Brontë); Manchester University Press (the letters of Elizabeth Gaskell); Yale University Press (the letters of George Eliot); Harvard University Press (the letters of Emily Dickinson); Frederick Warne & Co (the letters and journal of Beatrix Potter); the estate of Virginia Woolf and the Hogarth Press (the letters, diaries, reminiscences, essays and novels of Virginia Woolf). Dr Juliet Barker of the Brontë Society was especially helpful in guiding me through the complex copyright laws governing posthumously published works such as letters and diaries.

The only one of my eight subjects whose letters have yet to be published is Beatrix Potter. My warmest thanks, therefore, are due to Judy Taylor, presently editing the letters for publication, for inviting me to examine them at her home. The other writer to whom I would like to record a debt of personal gratitude is Margaret Forster, who kindly pointed me in several very useful directions regarding Elizabeth Barrett Browning (her own biography of whom, promising to be a much-needed modern study in depth of the poet, unhappily for me will appear too late to contribute to my thoughts).

I am also grateful to all the galleries, libraries and individuals who granted permission to reproduce portraits in their possession. Full details appear with the list of illustrations.

Finally, to all the friends who encouraged me by thinking that the project sounded intriguing, I offer my appreciation, together with my hope that the result of my labours does not fall too far short of their expectations.

Introduction

In her perceptive essay on George Eliot, Virginia Woolf described her 'reaching out with "a fastidious yet hungry ambition" for all that life could offer the free and enquiring mind and confronting her feminine aspirations with the real world of men'.[1] This was the dilemma too of Virginia herself, and of every enterprising woman who went before. For them all, 'the real world of men' was encountered first in their fathers. This is why the father/daughter relationship has always been of crucial importance to any girl whose tastes and talents impelled her beyond the limited sphere of activity commonly allowed to her sex, and why it seemed to me a subject worthy of a book.

As the representative and embodiment of male authority, it was her father who established the framework within which a girl's ideas of herself, her duties and her options were formed. In reacting to whatever attitudes and expectations he brought to the relationship, she made her first negotiation with male power. His approval or disapproval, encouragement or discouragement, pride or disappointment, mattered vitally to her, not only on a personal level but in determining the place she claimed for herself in the world.

Every father/daughter relationship there has ever been is unique. Most, of course, have gone unrecorded. Those that are best documented belong to daughters who grew up to be writers. With their special insight into human nature and their powers of self-expression, they have probed and preserved the female experience, whether writing spontaneously in letters, more reflectively in journals and reminiscences or *refractively* in literary composition.

Drawing on these sources, I have set out to explore the complex father/daughter relationships of eight women writers: Fanny Burney, Maria Edgeworth, Elizabeth Barrett Browning, Charlotte Brontë, George Eliot, Emily Dickinson, Beatrix Potter and Virginia Woolf. With the exception of the fanatically discreet Beatrix Potter, they all referred to their fathers frequently in their writings, though only Virginia Woolf consciously analysed the relationship long after her father's death, coming back again and again to a subject which evidently obsessed her.

The significance of the father/daughter relationship in the lives of these eight women can hardly be over-emphasized. For them all it was the most important relationship of their first thirty or forty years; for many it remained so until the end of their lives, growing ever more profound as time strengthened the tie. None threw off the paternal influence painlessly.

Focusing on this one relationship in common, and juxtaposing eight diverse yet oddly echoing stories, offers a perspective not only on the individuals concerned but on the nature of the society in which they functioned. Thus it suggests one way of approaching the questions raised by any study of the early lives of creative writers. What exactly were the influences – social, cultural and familial – upon them? Were their emergent geniuses recognized or misunderstood? To what extent did the personalities and experiences of their formative years furnish material for the art of their maturity?

(These questions can, of course, be asked of a writer of either sex with equal validity, but it is my point that girls, whatever their background, have always been infinitely more subject to family pressures of every kind than boys. No matter how unpropitious the early circumstances of our male writers – the Dickens' poverty, for example, or the Hardys' obscurity – no physical or emotional restraint was wilfully imposed on them to prevent the full development and best use of their powers.)

On a wider level, other fascinating issues are raised. If even women of exceptional ability and character were so deeply in thrall to their fathers, it is irresistible to speculate about the silent majority, the millions of 'ordinary' women who had no imaginative outlet, intellectual passion or stomach for a fight. Were they cowed – or content? Did they suffer more or less than their articulate, gifted sisters?

It has often been remarked that writing has always been the one male preserve *relatively* accessible to women; it could be done at home, alone, with materials readily available, unlike most other arts and professions. The women studied in this book were therefore, in one sense, the lucky ones. In writing about them I have been deeply aware of all the other girls and women whose different abilities were frustrated, suppressed or subsumed in service to the male, and whose stories remain untold. The eight stories I have selected must therefore be seen on the one hand as representative of many millions of historic father/daughter relationships, and on the other hand as uniquely interesting, in that they record the experiences of women who were not only remarkable for their time but whose work lives and breathes (to use Emily Dickinson's words) for us today.

The relationships I have chosen to study cover a period of almost exactly a century and a half, from 1778, when Fanny Burney astonished her unsuspecting father by publishing *Evelina*, a best-seller, to 1927, when Virginia Woolf exorcised the inhibiting ghost of *her* father by dissecting his character in *To the Lighthouse*. Subversive, therapeutic, compulsive, escapist, a desperate cry for attention or bid for independence, writing by women during that period was rarely *wholly* the free and happy exercise of their creative talents which in a less patriarchal society it might have been. 'You can never imagine,' George Eliot makes Daniel Deronda's mother, a gifted musician, cry in anguish, 'what it is to have a man's force of genius in you, and yet suffer the slavery of being a girl.'

There were women before Fanny Burney who earned their living by the pen, but we have only scanty knowledge of their private lives. After Virginia Woolf, girls were not so exclusively confined to the home, and to a father's domination. The period covered by this study thus determined itself. During these 150 years, the position of daughters, above a certain economic level, changed hardly at all. They were consistently under-educated, expected to be obedient and submissive, to occupy themselves with trivia, to look to marriage as their only escape and to marry only with their fathers' consent. As unmarried, grown-up daughters, Beatrix Potter and Virginia Woolf were no more free to choose how to spend their time than Fanny Burney or Maria Edgeworth had been three or four generations before. Indeed, if there is any shift to be discerned, it is in the direction of greater control over daughters, as Victorian repressiveness replaced Georgian neglect. Halfway through the nineteenth century the imagined difference in capacity between the sexes was being emphasized as never before, with paterfamilias growing fulsome beards and women tight-lacing themselves into restrictive crinolines. It was as though the apparent omniscience of men and decorative helplessness of women had to be taken to their furthest limits before the impetus came to break down such absurd stereotyping. By late Victorian times, girls were beginning to glimpse opportunities undreamt-of by their earlier counterparts and to venture to protest at perceived injustice and discrimination. The male response was to exert authority more rigidly than ever.

Within the period studied, I know of only two major women writers in English on whom the influence of their fathers was *not* unduly great. One is Jane Austen, whose emotional independence from her parents (though she remained financially dependent on them all her life) is perhaps accounted for by her exceptional closeness to her many brothers and one sister. Between them, the congenial members of her own generation seemed to satisfy all the yearnings of her nature. From her mild-mannered father she took just the measure of love, approval, moral guidance and good example that she needed to establish a healthy, well-balanced personality. The only suffering she endured at his hands was when he took her to live in Bath against her will, perhaps with the ulterior motive of finding her a husband (she was twenty-five).

With respect to her creative life, he had applauded her youthful compositions – far from being a secret indulgence, writing began for her as a way to amuse her family – but he hardly took her aspirations seriously. His most important paternal duties, as he saw them, were to launch his six sons into a harsh economic world; in an age of 'patronage', he did not scruple to seek whatever advantage he could for them from distant connections in high places.[2] In comparison, his only known effort to establish professional recognition and a means of livelihood for his gifted daughter was once approaching a publisher with an early version of *Pride and Prejudice*. A rejection by return of post seems to have satisfied him, and he made no further attempt on her behalf. Jane did not publish anything until six years after her father's death. That she resented his not doing as much for her as for her brothers is unlikely, given her understanding of the way society operated, but not impossible; if so she certainly kept such 'wrong' thoughts firmly under control. Jane Austen owed a happy upbringing, and a private acceptance of her cleverness, to her father; she felt comfortable with herself largely because of him. With such a foundation, she was able to fend off in adulthood his conventional view that marriage and not literary fame must be her goal. Neither craving more love than he could give, nor angrily rebelling against his rule, there is no word so apt as 'detachment' to describe Jane Austen's attitude to her father. That, perhaps, is the mark of a mature personality – or a tribute to his skill and selflessness as a father. That she knew she was unusually lucky in this respect, the many unsatisfactory fathers in her novels testify.

The other exception is Elizabeth Gaskell, whose luck was of a different sort. In consequence of her mother's death when she was a baby, she was brought up by her aunts in Cheshire and did not see her father, whose home was in London, again until she was twelve. Thereafter she paid him annual visits, but intimacy was never re-established, and he died when she was nineteen. He had remarried quite soon after her mother's death, and his failure to receive her back into his home, and his subsequent absorption in his second family, came to be regarded by Elizabeth as deliberate and hurtful neglect of her. There is an element of wish-fulfilment in some of her portraits of loving fathers and daughters: Mr Hale and Margaret, Dr Gibson and Molly.[3] But even if she could not see it herself, hindsight shows that loss was surely gain.

Her wholly feminine upbringing, affectionately mocked and celebrated in *Cranford*, not only nurtured the quality of compassion which is so conspicuous in all her writing, it also made her self-reliant, confident, unafraid to fulfil every facet of her nature. Brought up neither to encounter male opposition at every turn nor to seek male approval for every action, in adulthood she sailed serenely into the open waters of life beyond the home, accepting it as both her right and her duty that she should participate in Virginia Woolf's 'real world of men'. Elizabeth Gaskell is one of the few Victorian women who led a truly well-balanced life, blending the roles of respected literary figure, social worker, minister's wife and devoted mother of four girls. Her heavy workload wore her out, and she died suddenly in her fifties, but if ever a life was lived to the full, to the benefit of others, to the satisfaction of herself and to the endowment of posterity, it was Mrs Gaskell's. A woman of great empathy with her friends, she yet found it hard to fathom Charlotte Brontë's habitual subservience to her father, simply because she herself was exceptional in never having learnt the same behaviour. The kind of love which underlay Charlotte's forbearance was beyond her experience or even her imagining.

The eight writers I have selected to study are merely the best known or best documented of many others of the period whose relationships with their fathers afford further intriguing variations on a theme. An interesting case was that of Mary Russell Mitford, who wrote to retrieve a fortune lost by her father at the gambling table, and kept on writing though he appropriated everything she earned. Two other writing Marys were mother and daughter. Mary Wollstonecraft spent much of her childhood trying to stop her father ill-treating her mother. His brutality and dissipation were among the factors that made Mary a staunch feminist long before her time. She bravely bore the ridicule of the male establishment for daring to express and live out subversive views on marriage, and her book *A Vindication of the Rights of Women* was the first to expose the injustices from which one half of the population suffered. There were many men who saw it as fair retribution when Mary Wollstonecraft died in childbed.[4]

Her daughter, who became Mary Shelley, author of *Frankenstein*, was brought up by the radical political writer William Godwin, in a remarkably equitable father/daughter relationship, tempered only by the vileness of the woman whom Godwin married under the mistaken notion that he was doing his best for Mary. The unconventional ideas which Mary absorbed from her free and easy conversations with her father attracted the young poet Percy Bysshe Shelley, and she eloped with him at the age of sixteen, only to be pursued all her married life by demands for money from Godwin, grown mercenary and a traitor to the principles which his daughter continued to preserve in all their idealistic freshness.[5]

That the society of the United States in the nineteenth century was just as unfavourable for female development as that of Britain is exemplified not only in the life of Emily Dickinson, one of the subjects of this book, but in that of her exact contemporary, Louisa Alcott, whom I had not space to include. These two girls, whose names were to become famous for their (very different) contributions to American literature, dwelt in no less subjection to their fathers than any ordinary English miss of the period. Emily Dickinson and Louisa Alcott were born within two years and a few miles of one another and lived out an almost identical lifespan. Growing up against the same Puritan, New England background, they reacted in opposite ways to the male domination they encountered in society at large and more immediately in their homes. While Emily Dickinson withdrew into a private world which she could control, Louisa Alcott attacked the public one – using her head, as she wrote, as a 'battering ram' against it.[6]

Bronson Alcott, her father, was a monster who believed himself a saint. Refusing out of principle to work for money, quarrelling with everyone who tried to help him, he subjected his wife and four daughters to extreme poverty and deprivation. To make it worse, he criticized them for their earthly appetites and even denigrated Louisa for the darkness of her hair and eyes, which he saw as a manifestation of sensuality and wickedness. While her sisters either gave up the struggle (Beth of *Little Women*) or cultivated their femininity to please him (Meg and Amy), Louisa, with no feeble spirit, determined to take over the male role in the family. 'Teach, sew, act, write, anything to help the family,' she vowed in her teenage diary; 'and I'll be rich and famous and happy before I die, see if I won't.'

Inevitably such aspirations brought her into conflict with Bronson, for though he cultivated passivity in himself, he retained in full the Miltonic idea of the father standing in place of God to his womenfolk. Louisa could neither shrug off his disapproval nor win his esteem, for driven by his own inadequacies into becoming active, strong and capable, she only intensified his pose of moral superiority. Though it was he who had set up the anxieties in her which could be quelled only by working, he could not love a daughter so alien to what his idea of a 'little woman' should be. In her mature years she made herself needed, but she could not make herself loved. Though she did at last achieve the financial security she had longed for, she was never a happy woman, never at peace with her own personality.

Nor is there any doubt that the book which brought her fame and money, *Little Women*, sickened her. It is of course her own story, diluted, sweetened and used to wash down a moral of dubious value. In her *alter ego*, Jo, Louisa became her father's 'little woman' in the end, dutifully subduing all that had made her one of the most original girls in fiction. Louisa's portrait of Bronson, moreover, replicates his own view of himself, saintly and too good for the world. Louisa wrote the book swiftly, almost unthinkingly, perpetuating the myths about her family which she had invented to make their situation bearable. A minor artist, she could not face the pain of telling the truth; but the consequence was that the book and its sequels, whose success should have brought her pleasure and self-esteem, became yet another source of dissatisfaction in a life warped by being lived almost wholly in reaction to her father. She survived him by just two days.

A greater writer who did strive to portray her father honestly in a novel was Rebecca West. *The Fountain Overflows* is her attempt to evaluate the complex relationships of her childhood, as poignant and imaginatively convincing as Virginia Woolf's similarly motivated *To the Lighthouse*. For Rebecca's father, though he left his family for good when she was eight, and died four years later, had an influence over her personality and her work which penetrated far into her long life.[7] A flamboyant, feckless Anglo-Irishman, Charles Fairfield was a chronic gambler and speculator, unfaithful to his wife and irresponsible towards his children, yet hero-worshipped and adored by them.

If *The Fountain Overflows* magnificently captures both his charm and cultivation, and his unreliability and detachment from the consequences of his actions, the problems of coping with this lovable but infuriating character recur in the fragmented autobiography which Rebecca worked at over the years and which was posthumously published as *Family Memories*.[8] 'His conversation was highly allusive and imaginative and witty,' she wrote, and of course she absorbed much from him. She believed that he was proud of her precocious cleverness and that she inherited from him the pleasure in ideas which 'was my perpetual anaesthetic and stimulant' and because of which 'I have not had such a bad life after all'.

But she also recalled 'with anger' his predilection 'for having sexual relationships with the women my mother employed, as servants or nurses or governesses, and with prostitutes', and the way 'the whole strength of his being was turned in a direction which led him away from his wife and children'. Artistically her father's effect on her life was undoubtedly good, but personally it was disastrous, causing her to seek a substitute father-figure in H. G. Wells, to distrust men and never to be able to establish a satisfactory relationship with a member of the opposite sex (not even with her son). Altogether, the insecurities Rebecca's father bred in her, as well as his positive legacy of wit and dash and optimism, must have been influential in her choice of defiant lifestyle and her development as a particularly robust writer. But defiance and robustness in a young woman are themselves symptoms of the end of an era of male supremacy. Born ten years after Virginia Woolf, living until our own times and participating fully and freely, as her talents qualified her to do, in 'the real world of men', unimpeded or unassisted by the attitude or interference of a father, Rebecca West's story, though important and fascinating, falls just outside the scope of this book.

'Whatever biography we open,' wrote Virginia Woolf (she was referring to biographies of Victorian women), 'we find almost always the familiar symptoms – the father is opposed to his daughter's marriage; the father is opposed to his daughter's earning her living. Her wish either to marry, or to earn her living, rouses strong emotion in him; and he gives the same excuses for that strong emotion; the lady will debase her ladyhood; the daughter will outrage her womanhood.'[9] Her observation could be a motto for this book, so well does it fit the experiences and the struggles, the emotional blackmail and the calls to sacrifice, made justly or unjustly in the name of love, described in the following pages.

Each of the eight relationships has a chapter to itself. Here I should like to consider them collectively, in order to discover what links there might be between them, what patterns and parallels can be discerned. In a broad overview, several distinct groupings emerge.

George Eliot and Virginia Woolf, for all their glittering talents and powerful intellects, would almost certainly not have written fiction at all had their fathers survived another ten years. It required nothing less absolute than their fathers' deaths for them to be able to establish the creative professional lives which fulfilled them. 'His life would have entirely ended mine,' Virginia acknowledged in her diary. 'What would have happened? No writing, no books; – inconceivable.'[10] The probability was even stronger in the case of George Eliot, reaching adulthood at the beginning rather than the end of Victoria's reign and wholly tied to her father's habits and household while he lived. Two of our most profound thinkers and innovative novelists, it is astonishing to realize how easily they might have failed to exploit their gifts. The loss to English literature is horrifying to contemplate; but how many other girls were there whose fathers did not die in time?

Indeed, Emily Dickinson can be seen as a victim of the sad and terrible truth that only death could liberate completely. So great a proportion of her life was lived under her father's autocratic rule that her unique contribution to poetry, though not stifled, *was* very nearly lost. That is to say, nothing could stop her writing, but had she been freed at twenty or thirty, like Virginia Woolf and George Eliot, instead of at forty-four, by which time her optimism had withered, might she not have found the confidence to publish (and thereby ensure the survival of) her work?

Of course, there were women who found sufficient confidence despite being kept back. Both Fanny Burney and Charlotte Brontë published without their fathers' knowledge. Both had been undeservedly overlooked, among their large and gifted families, in their earliest years. They had thereafter to contend with fathers who were, after the initial surprise that their daughters should be capable of publishing anything, exaggeratedly and sometimes embarrassingly proud of their literary achievements.

A reverse movement characterized the father/daughter relationships of Elizabeth Barrett and Beatrix Potter. They were alike in receiving early encouragement from their fathers, with whom they enjoyed a close childhood companionship. It was when each woman grew up, and wanted to develop her life along lines opposed to her father's wishes, that implacable coldness and sternness set in.

Whether coming to an appreciation of his daughter early or late, many a father was apt to be jealous of any other male influence upon her. Each of these last-mentioned women (Fanny Burney, Charlotte Brontë, Elizabeth Barrett Browning and Beatrix Potter) encountered bitter opposition when she wished to marry – despite being around forty years old at the time! It is an extraordinary fact that half the eight writers studied here married against her father's express will, *at a mature age.* Poor Beatrix Potter had to defy harsh parental opposition twice, at thirty-nine (but her fiancé died) and again at forty-seven.

Perversely, some of the fathers wished their daughters to marry as soon as they were of marriageable age, rather than pursue the life of the intellect. Pressure was put on Fanny Burney to accept an unwelcome proposal, and George Eliot was well aware that her failure to attract a husband was a source of shame to her father. Richard Lovell Edgeworth also tried to marry off Maria, though he himself so effectively absorbed the emotional energies of his famous daughter that there was none to spare for a romantic attachment.

Robert Evans and Leslie Stephen were the only fathers who did not live to see the success of their daughters (or even to know the names they would publish under, George Eliot and Virginia Woolf). Emily Dickinson, of course, published nothing in her or her father's lifetime. Of the other five fathers, only Rupert Potter was unmoved, attempting to ignore or belittle the growing fame of Beatrix. The remaining four were intensely proud: but it was a pride which led, almost without exception, to a wish to control, direct, interfere – even to assume the credit for what their daughters had done! Maria Edgeworth actually encouraged her father to guide her writing career, and no amount of 'help' from that quarter was too much for her. Fanny Burney tried dutifully to submit to her father's conviction that he knew best, despite her own superior judgement; Charlotte Brontë changed the ending of a novel to please her father, but this was nothing to the literary sacrifices Fanny Burney made. Well-intentioned though much of this paternal interference unquestionably was, their blanket assumption of automatic male superiority would be truly laughable, given the immense obstacles their daughters had already overcome (beginning with their own lack of encouragement!), if it were not that everything in the society of the time supported and justified this male view.

Besides, most of the fathers had reason to be proud of their own rise or place in the world, so perhaps we may allow them their conceit. Several had raised themselves from extremely humble beginnings, by either education or hard work or charm or some combination of these. If Charles Burney, Patrick Brontë and Robert Evans had not made those first difficult steps up the social and educational ladder, we would doubtless never have heard of their daughters.

It certainly appears that, to be exceptionally motivated herself, it was an advantage for a women to descend from an exceptionally motivated father, and that there is an important legacy of character to be traced here. The fathers in this study who were privileged by birth were scarcely less intent on personal achievement than the self-made men. Richard Lovell Edgeworth and Leslie Stephen tirelessly employed the intellectual gifts they had been born with: both were men of many parts and immense physical energy (Leslie's mountaineering exploits being a case of a man pushing himself to his limits for personal satisfaction). Rupert Potter, born to affluent circumstances, was the most idle of the eight, but even he pursued his hobbies with relish. Edward Barrett strove to retain the fortune he had inherited, and if it nevertheless was lost, he can hardly be called a weak-willed character. Edward Dickinson was engaged in a similar struggle, which in his case was crowned with success; he was a highly respected figure in his community.

Nevertheless, and with a couple of exceptions, these men were less concerned than most with the traditional male pursuits of money, power and status; or, at least, they tempered such pursuits by also seeking qualities of a more spiritual nature. Two writers, one musician, one clergyman, one estate manager, one country gentleman turned city merchant and two lawyers: the majority of them in their chosen careers showed some bias towards the artistic life congenial to their daughters; and, indeed, one of the lawyers – Rupert Potter – forsook his profession to devote himself to photography, an interest he passed on to his daughter. Fanny Burney, Maria Edgeworth, Charlotte Brontë, Beatrix Potter and Virginia Woolf all shared literary and intellectual tastes with their fathers, a source of genuine enjoyment and indebtedness.

It is time to enquire, perhaps, what part their mothers played in the development of these eight daughters. In fact, most of the mothers were either dead or ineffectual. Fanny Burney, Maria Edgeworth and

Charlotte Brontë all lost their mothers before they were ten, Virginia Woolf and George Eliot in their teens, and Elizabeth Barrett Browning in her early twenties. Their fathers were therefore the dominant parents in their daughters' lives, more especially since, before their deaths, these mothers had been much occupied with childbearing or their own ill health or the demands made on them by their husbands, to whom they were – without exception – wholly subservient. Only Emily Dickinson retained her childlike, demanding mother, and Beatrix Potter her cold and unsympathetic one, into their own middle age.

No fewer than six of the eight fathers lost at least one wife young from childbirth or excessive childbearing; some lost more than one. Only Mrs Potter, cleverly contriving to have only two children, and Mrs Dickinson, with three, managed to survive their husbands. What this premature loss of life did to the fathers' fears for their own daughters, as well as to the daughters' own conception of the perils of marriage and the inequality of the sexes on this most basic level of life, is interesting to speculate. 'Women seem to me to have the worse share in existence,' wrote George Eliot, referring in this instance to their biological rather than their social destiny.[11]

While Fanny Burney and Maria Edgeworth had to contend with much-disliked stepmothers, George Eliot and Virginia Woolf were themselves the product of second marriages, born at the tail end of extended families and in effect two generations younger than their fathers, with the consequent gulf in their ideas. Maria Edgeworth and Elizabeth Barrett, by contrast, were born to fathers scarcely into their twenties, who had hardly achieved the maturity necessary for the role.

Combined with the lack of effective mothering, the intellectual freedom accorded to all eight daughters by their fathers, if more by default than design, must have been instrumental in developing their imaginative and contemplative powers. Receiving minimal schooling, as girls and young women they largely educated themselves, from their fathers' or other libraries and resources available to them. Thus none was forced into a rigid mould, and all enjoyed the precious mental and physical liberty, roaming unrestricted in the countryside and in the world of books, which seem essential to the development of any creative writer, male or female. (The long, idyllic holidays in the country or beside the sea regularly taken by the Potter and Stephen families compensated Beatrix and Virginia for their immurement in London and were invaluable in stimulating their imagination.)

The obverse of this lack of formal education, however, was resentment when brothers, often less academically able, were unfairly favoured. Both Elizabeth Barrett Browning and Virginia Woolf felt sharp pangs of envy when brothers close in age, with whom they had hitherto intellectually held their own, were despatched to public schools to acquire knowledge denied themselves (though both girls insisted on studying the classics privately). Elizabeth, Virginia, Charlotte Brontë, George Eliot and Beatrix Potter all had minds which thirsted for learning and would have achieved the highest honours had their brothers' opportunities been extended to them. They were also envious of the *freedom* accorded to their brothers: the freedom to come and go from home, to choose their own lifestyle, to make their mark in the world. For all their advantages, however, not one of the twenty-nine brothers or half-brothers whom these eight women could muster achieved anything comparable to their celebrated sisters!

Certainly the ambition of these fathers was inherited or absorbed by a daughter, not a son. This so went against the normal expectation that it required some adjustment by both sides over a period of time. It was sometimes because of disappointment in his son or sons that a father would make much of a clever daughter, look to her for companionship and bask in reflections of her glory. This was the case with Fanny Burney, Maria Edgeworth, Elizabeth Barrett Browning and Charlotte Brontë. Disappointment is the product of the passage of time, however, so this reaction was ineffectual as early encouragement, manifesting itself more as an emotional demand upon a grown-up, already famous daughter.

One word that has been largely lacking from this summary is 'love'. For all the variety and complexity of the relationships studied, love is the continuum that binds them all, bestows on all their importance, subtlety and durability. A relationship that holds one back can be shrugged off if love forms no part of it on either side. All the fathers loved their daughters after their own lights and in conformity with the beliefs of their times, and though we might find their ideas of love faulty, negligent, self-glorifying or manipulative, their daughters were grateful for what they received. On the daughters' side, the emotion was more generous and unselfish. Every one of these women strove to please her father, to be what he wanted, often at great cost to herself. Conscious of that most unpleasant fact of all, the being indebted to another for the common necessities of existence, each found it hard to accept that she was justified in wanting to live her own life as she thought fit. It was by no means easy for any of them to subordinate the role of daughter to that of writer, independent thinker and free participitant in 'the real world of men'.

This question of financial indebtedness is not unimportant. Over and over again the letters and diaries of these women express the satisfaction – the joy, even – of having some money earned by herself; and for the fortunate few who eventually became self-supporting, the boost to their sense of integrity, and consequently to their freedom of action, was immense. The combination of obligation, helplessness and dependence suffered by all but a few girls and women habitually skewed their relationships with men, leading inevitably to subservience and self-effacement in all those who had a well-developed sense of duty. Money is unfortunately power, even in the most tender domestic relations; even when the man does not exert it, the woman of conscience is bound to feel it and to tailor her actions accordingly. If in the following chapters much emphasis seems to be put on the mundane subject of earnings, it is because it bears directly on personal relationships between women and the men who maintain them.

As to the direct influence of the strong personalities of these men upon our literary heritage, it manifests itself at many levels. Maria Edgeworth left an idealized portrait of her father. In the much more subtle and emotionally honest work of George Eliot and Virginia Woolf, the characters of their fathers are painstakingly and painfully examined. These great writers bring all the objectivity and insight of their maturity to the task of delicately separating out what was good and what was bad, what was beneficial and what was harmful to other people in their fathers' ways. Two of the best realized male characters in women's fiction, Adam Bede and Mr Ramsay, are the result of this need to understand and perhaps forgive. The more general themes of male oppression and the struggle of women to be allowed a voice were tackled not only by George Eliot and Virginia Woolf but by Charlotte Brontë, by Fanny Burney towards the end of her career and, in a most impassioned way, by Elizabeth Barrett Browning with her poem *Aurora Leigh*.

The knowledge that other women had encountered the same problems and had persevered, even triumphed, was immensely inspiriting to the later writers among the group. George Eliot was especially interested in the two whose publishing lives immediately preceded hers, Elizabeth Barrett Browning and Charlotte Brontë. Beatrix Potter's secret diary reveals how readily women writers sprang to her mind and how much she indentified with them during the long years when it seemed her whole life would be wasted at her parents' whim. The diary itself was modelled on that of 'my heroine, Fanny Burney'. The sense of a secret sisterhood was especially strong in Emily Dickinson. Publishing nothing in her lifetime, she held on to her belief in poetry's being her serious life's work partly by the inspiration she derived from the Brontë sisters, George Eliot and Elizabeth Barrett Browning. She knew enough about the latter's life to revel in the similarities with her own, as a poet confined to the house of her father, an autocrat whose preoccupations were property, inheritance and social standing.

Virginia Woolf's interest in the lives of many of her predecessors went as far as making them the subjects of some of the most sympathetic and admiring of her published essays. Her portrait of Richard Lovell Edgeworth is particularly disparaging (and comical),[12] while her indignation on behalf of Elizabeth Barrett Browning inspired a whole book, *Flush*. More widely, her contemplation of all the frustrated female talent which could *not* overcome the difficulties thrown in its way by men resulted in the masterly indictment *A Room of One's Own*, while her other feminist polemic, *Three Guineas*, examines 'the struggle with fathers in general, with the patriarchy itself'. It is in the work of Virginia Woolf, indeed, that the whole subject of the influence of fathers on daughters receives its most thoughtful treatment, just as it is in her life that that her own experience of this relationship is most deeply considered. In the present book, the chapter on Virginia Woolf comes last because she was born last, but it also makes a fitting climax to the seven other stories that have gone before.

The lives of these eight women, then, are bound together by unusual achievement, by their sense of their destinies as interwoven, by the common denominator of their contending with a powerful, much-loved father. The influence of their fathers on both their personal and creative lives is of the deepest significance and interest, whether we are considering them sociologically, as particularly articulate examples of eighteenth- and nineteenth-century womanhood, or artistically, as writers who brought their own life experiences to bear on some of the great novels, poetry and children's literature of the English language.

I

Fanny Burney
1752–1840

'Dear soul, how he feeds upon all that brings fame to Cecilia!'

When, at the age of twenty-five, Fanny Burney became an overnight sensation with *Evelina* – the novel that moved not only lending-library misses but men of the world like Dr Johnson and Edmund Burke to laughter and tears – her future seemed bright. She would go on to publish more and better novels, gathering fame and respect, money and honours, independence and fulfilment: all the good things to which few women had access but which her own unaided talents had already enabled her to taste.

That this was not the course her life took is attributable mainly to her father's interference. Dr Charles Burney had known nothing of *Evelina* until its publication, a fact to which much of its unspoilt, spontaneous charm is certainly owing, for Fanny had written her tale for her own delight, uninhibited by thoughts of its being read by the old, the wise or the judgemental. Now, overflowing with pride and always ambitious for the advancement of his family, Charles assumed full direction of her career. During the next ten or fifteen years he made a series of misjudgements, as he put pressure on her to produce another novel before she was ready, to abandon a promising attempt to write for the stage and to accept a position at Court which consumed her precious mental liberty, wrecking both her spirits and her health. If, in the aftermath of *Evelina*'s success, Fanny had been allowed to go her own sweet way, as she had for the first quarter of a century of her life, undirected by anything but her own integrity, not only her personal happiness but her literary reputation must have benefited.

These frustrating and under-achieving years for Fanny culminated in her father's last well-meant effort to control her destiny, as he attempted to prevent her marriage when she was forty-one. It was not her age but an alternative source of male support which then gave Fanny the determination to act according to her own judgement. Alone, she had never been able to overcome the idea that filial obedience should be unquestioning. In this she was actuated not only by her strict sense of duty but by her very real devotion to her father.

For Charles Burney was one of the most lovable of fathers. Indeed, if the test of a good father is whether even his step-children love him, he passes with distinction. He had six surviving children by his first marriage, two by his second, and three step-children brought under his roof by his second wife, Elizabeth Allen. The young Allens as much as the young Burneys were eager to acknowledge his 'kind indulgence', 'parental care' and 'affectionate conduct'.[1] It was a habit among all the branches of the family to record the incidents and emotions of their lives in journals or long letters to one another when apart. In all this body of writing there is scarcely one harsh reflection on Charles, but countless sincere tributes to his tenderness as a father. (And to prove that this was not mere discretion or respect on the part of the young people, it should be added that the case was far otherwise with the second Mrs Burney, who was frequently criticized on paper by *her* step-children, sometimes even by her own children.)

It was not only his family who loved Charles. As a musician and later a writer living in mid-eighteenth-century London, he mixed with all the famous personages of his time. His 'natural liveliness', 'general benevolence' and the 'rare unity of gaiety and feeling in his disposition', to use Fanny's words, readily won him the good opinion of new acquaintance, as well as the lasting friendship of those who knew him over a period of years.[2] 'My heart goes out to Burney,' wrote Dr Johnson; and Mrs Thrale, in whose drawing-room the great gathered, gave it as her opinion that 'no one is so much beloved as Burney'.[3]

This busy professional and social life left Charles little time for his family, but he had the gift of making each individual member feel important to him, and of bestowing whatever attention he could spare with genuine solicitude for their well-being. How then should Fanny, diffident, dutiful and female, have opposed the advice of such a father or disappointed him in any of her doings?

The ambition to rise in the world, the eagerness to seize any opportunity of advancement for himself and his family, from which Fanny was to suffer (though in fairness to her father it must be said that she and all her siblings derived many blessings from it too), had its origin in the insecurity of Charles Burney's start in life.

Born in 1726, he and his twin sister Susanna were the nineteenth and twentieth children of a charming but feckless actor-cum-dancer-cum-portrait-painter who had through his own improvidence slipped disastrously down the social scale. Virtually abandoned by his itinerant parents, Charles was left to the care of an 'uncultivated and utterly ignorant, but worthy and affectionate old nurse' who brought him up in her cottage four miles from Shrewsbury.[4] The devotion of this woman, the beauties of the Shropshire countryside, and the romantic old buildings of the city into which he walked daily when old enough to obtain an education from the free school there, retained a warm place in Charles's memory all his life. There was much in his boyhood to make him happy and hardy; but as he grew up, he became well aware that he had his own way to make in the world, that not only could his father do nothing for him but, worse, he had trifled away the fortune and social position of former generations of the family. To restore something of what he considered his rightful inheritance, raising himself by his own talents and ability to please, became Charles's conscious policy. The almost fawning snobbery and the chronic anxiety about money which between them provided the motivating forces for so many of the decisions of his long life were thus early embedded in his character.

He was well equipped to make a success of life. Like his father, he was excellent company, and judged so by his social superiors as well as by his equals; like his father, he possessed a host of minor talents waiting to be exploited; unlike his father, he also possessed steadiness and application. Despite being ambitious, Charles was sincere, sensitive and far from ruthless. He never in his life played a part; his desire to please was perfectly genuine and contributed to his lovable, almost vulnerable charm.

On leaving school Charles became a pupil of one of his much older half-brothers, James, who was organist at St Mary's Church in Shrewsbury. He had soon learnt all James could teach, and he was therefore thrilled to be offered an apprenticeship in London with the famous Thomas Arne, composer of the National Anthem, who noted the boy's gifts when travelling through the north-west of England. However, Arne's policy was to work him rather than to teach him, and Charles found himself bound to his master until the age of twenty-five, with no pay and no time to call his own. What he observed of Arne's cruelty and debauchery also sickened him, and before long he began to wish for his freedom.

About halfway through the apprenticeship Arne sold the remainder of it – sold Charles's services, in effect – for the sum of £300 to a young nobleman, Fulke Greville, who was looking for that then rare thing, a musician with gentlemanly manners, to become a member of his household. In Charles Burney he found what he had never expected to find. Practitioners of the arts, be they actors, painters, dancers or musicians, were at that time regarded as a species apart from men of education and culture and were normally only tolerated in good society for their entertainment value. It was a distinction of which Charles was acutely aware and which fuelled his determination to become a man of letters as well as a musician later in life; it also made him particularly sensitive about which of their talents his gifted children displayed.

His time as a favoured companion of Greville only added to his social polish and warmed his ambition. Another harsh fact of life understood by those seeking to advance in eighteenth-century Britain was that personal merit was not enough; it was the age of 'patronage' and 'interest'. Friends in high places were essential, and Charles assiduously cultivated all he could. His second daughter was to be named after Greville's young wife, Frances.

But it was his first daughter whose existence was the reason for his reluctantly ending his agreeable life with Greville – and just at the moment when the nobleman was proposing to set off on the Grand Tour and to take Charles with him. It must have cost Charles a great deal to give up this opportunity of travelling to Italy, with all its cultural and social advantages, but, like many an ardent and personable young man before and after, he had got a good girl into trouble and had to do the right thing by her. Esther Sleepe, who gave birth to little Esther a month before Charles married her, was by all accounts lovely of mind and person, and his passion for her never faltered throughout the twelve years of their marriage. Nevertheless, she brought him neither money nor good connections, and he may well have delayed asking Greville for his release – the articles of the transferred apprenticeship prohibited marriage – partly because he felt he should have done better for himself, partly because of his yearning for education and Europe. Fortunately for Esther, his honour prevailed; but it was perhaps due to his awareness of how very close he had come to leaving a virtuous woman in disgrace that Charles became in due course ultra-protective of his own daughters' reputations. This was to extend to his forbidding forty-year-old Fanny to have anything to do with the French writer Madame de Staël, because she was rumoured to have had a lover!

Charles was twenty-three when he thus found himself with a wife and child to support. He obtained the post of organist at a London church and added to his income by teaching and public performances, sometimes of his own work. As he recorded of this period in his *Memoir*, 'I now began to be in fashion in the city, as a master, and had my hands full of professional business of all kinds, scholars at both ends of the town, composition, and public playing.' After three years of this busy life, however, his health gave cause for alarm, and he was advised to leave London. With a great deal of reluctance he therefore accepted the post of organist in Kings Lynn, Norfolk, very much afraid that his influential friends in the capital would forget him and that he would sink for ever into the mediocrity of a provincial music master. His intention was to return to London as soon as he had recovered his health.

In fact, the family remained in Kings Lynn for nine years, happy years in which Charles allowed his ambition to sleep, while he enjoyed the society of his wife and growing family, and the respect of the local community. As happened wherever he went, he was soon 'held in the highest estimation for his powers of conversation and agreeable manners, which made his company much sought after by all the principal nobility and gentry of the neighbourhood'. This was recorded by the writer and agriculturalist Arthur Young, whose sister Dorothy and sister-in-law Elizabeth Allen, wife of the most prominent merchant of the town, Stephen Allen, became the intimate friends of Esther Burney, all three ladies sharing intellectual pretensions rare in women of that time.

Esther had borne three children before leaving London and had five more in Kings Lynn, of whom Fanny, born on 13 June 1752, was the first. In Kings Lynn also Esther buried three of her children, all boys. By 1760, when Charles decided that, in order to provide properly for his large family, he must relinquish the pleasant life in Norfolk and re-establish his career in London, much of Esther's own strength had gone, though her husband's had been fully restored by the country air. The birth of their ninth child in London in 1761 overtaxed what little strength remained, and the following year Esther Burney died of consumption. When ten-year-old Fanny heard the news, 'she was almost killed with crying', the woman who was looking after the young Burneys recalled.[5]

'All is lost and gone in losing her – the whole world is a desert to me!' Charles told Dorothy Young a month after his wife's death. Since his return to London he had begun to pick up the threads of his dropped career, and the future had appeared promising in every way. Now, for a time, all worldly success seemed empty and pointless without Esther to share it. But in due course he started to exert himself again, both professionally and domestically, for the sake of his children, who now became the chief object of his care. To make home seem like home again, even though its dearest figure was missing, to supply as much of a mother's tenderness as it was possible for a busy man to do, and to knit the family together with a strength that would defy whatever the world could throw at them, became as much Charles's resolution as to work untiringly for their benefit.

At the time of Esther's death the six children ranged in age from Hetty, who was thirteen, down to the baby Charlotte. James, a year younger than Hetty, had already gone away to sea; five-year-old Charles was the only other surviving son. In between the boys came the pair of sisters, Fanny and Susanna, who were, even in that affectionate family, exceptionally devoted to one another. In his desire to care properly for his children, their father was fortunate to have on hand, in London, both their grandmothers and an abundance of kind aunts, who were especially useful in bringing up the girls. Nevertheless, it was his mind and his personality which determined the tone of the Burney household and which made it a happy, lively and cultured place in which to grow up. His friends, drawn from the most creative layer of London society – most notably the actor David Garrick – added to the stimulating atmosphere in Poland Street.

Though unhappily deprived of a wise and sympathetic mother, the young Burneys enjoyed at least a compensatory degree of freedom during the next few crucial years of their development: for, without any kind of permanent female supervision and with a father who, while demonstrably anxious to do his best for them, yet was by necessity nearly always out of the house, they were left largely to their own devices. Like the young Brontës sixty years later, they were thrown by their motherlessness into a closer relationship with one another, and into a profounder reliance on their own mental resources.

This liberty to choose her own pursuits within the confines of a mutually supportive family suited Fanny, timid, thoughtful and observant as she was. Her gravity caused her to be known as 'The Old Lady' by some of her fathers' visitors to the house. No one but her sisters knew of her imaginative powers, her gift for mimicry, or the ease with which she could express herself on paper. So compulsive in her was the urge to write that she would not allow herself to do so in the morning, keeping it for a treat after a conscience-satisfying amount of sewing had been accomplished each day. By the age of fifteen she had accumulated enough manuscript to make a very impressive bonfire, when in a fit of self-denial she decided to burn it all and give up the pleasurable occupation for ever. Needless to say, she was soon making good the loss.

Fanny was also blessed by her situation within the family: neither the eldest nor the youngest, not musical like Hetty and Susan, not a boy whose career needed serious deliberation. Among the bright and gifted company of Burneys she seemed comparatively dull, and it suited her to be overlooked. 'She was wholly unnoticed in the nursery,' afterwards admitted her father, 'for any talents, or quickness of study.'[6]

If he was even aware that she was frequently to be found scribbling – and he may not have been, since he often did not return from professional engagements until eleven at night – he had as yet no idea that in her it was a gift, like music in some of the others, which it was possible to turn to account. Hetty's precocious ability he had already exploited; indeed, his own re-establishment in London was to some extent founded upon it. In April 1760, on the family's return from the provinces, ten-year-old Hetty had sung and performed on the harpsichord at a public concert, demonstrating her father's skills as a teacher and bringing him again into notice. Soon he had 'a long list of petitioning parents, awaiting a vacant hour, upon any terms that he could name, and at any part of the day', as Fanny wrote in her memoir of her father.

But Charles was aware that his income from teaching was precarious. If by any chance he should fall out of fashion or if, perhaps more likely, his health should give way from overwork, his children would be destitute. It was prudent to look about for alternative sources of income and at the same time to provide the family with as good an education as possible, 'to enable them to shift for themselves, as *I* had done', if all else failed. He was able to enlist some 'influence' on his sons' behalf. One nobleman of Charles's acquaintance, the Hon. Colonel Cary, helped obtain a good place on a frigate for the sailor, James; another, the Duke of Marlborough, in 1768 sponsored the entrance to Charterhouse of young Charles, who showed a more academic bent than his brother. As for the girls, French would seem a useful accomplishment if they were ever reduced to earning their own livings, and in 1764 Charles installed Hetty and Susan in a school in Paris for a period of two years. This move had the added advantages of reducing the expenses in Poland Street and of enabling him to take his long-wished-for journey on the Continent. Why Fanny was left out of the plan, when her younger sister Susan was included, is a mystery, unless Charles judged that her excessive timidity would render her miserable away from home. From his own point of view, at least, the journey was a success, for it led to the publication in 1771 of his *The Present State of Music in France and Italy: or, The Journal of a Tour through those Countries, undertaken to collect Materials for a General History of Music,* which launched him on his second career of writer, scholar and historian, with its attendant increase in status.

Meanwhile he had attempted to make his fortune rather more easily, by marrying a rich widow. His old friend from Kings Lynn, Elizabeth Allen, inherited £5,000 and other property on the death of her husband in 1763, and in the spring of the following year Charles proposed to her. Her response was to forbid him to write to or see her for twelve months, and it was this rebuff which probably decided him to go to France. The charm of his courtship, however, proved irresistible, and in October 1767 they were secretly married, against much opposition from her family, who thought she was throwing herself away on a penniless man with a large family to support. Ironically, just before the marriage, Mrs Allen lost a large part of her fortune when the merchant with whom she had invested it went bankrupt. It was too late for Charles to retract, and in any case, his bride had other desirable qualities – intelligence and good looks. He had to make the best of it by asserting that he had always been 'attached to the lady's person, not her property'. Three additional children were now brought under his roof, and soon the union produced two more, Richard and Sarah Harriet, stretching his resources yet further and adding to his financial anxieties. A larger house, in Queen Square, had eventually to be taken.

The young Allens and Burneys assimilated very well, but before long the second Mrs Burney's unhappy temper threw its gloom over the formerly happy household. She seemed to have an unbounded capacity for considering herself ill-used and fancying herself neglected and excluded by her step-children: an 'eternal jealousy of our affection and comfort from each other', in Fanny's words. She and the children were united only in preserving before Charles a semblance of harmony, for he could not bear his home to be the scene of sulks and quarrels, and none of them wanted to make him unhappy.

Peace returned to the house in London whenever Mrs Burney visited her relations in Norfolk, and then it was doubly valued and the cheerful personality of its master thrown into relief. In February 1769, for example, the 16½-year-old Fanny confided to her journal:

How delightful, how enviable a tranquillity and content do I at present enjoy! I have scarce a wish, and am happy and easy as my heart can desire. All are at Lynn but us three, Papa, Hetty, and I, so that I am very much alone, but to that I have no objection. I pass my time in working, reading and thrumming the harpsichord. If my dear Susette was here I should want nothing. I seldom quit home, considering my youth and opportunities. But why should I, when I am so happy in it? Following my own vagaries, which my papa never controls, I can never want employment, nor sigh for amusement. We have a library which is an everlasting resource when attacked by the spleen – I have always a sufficiency of work to spend, if I pleased, my whole time at it – musick is a feast which can never grow insipid – and, in short, I have all the reason that ever mortal had to be contented with my lot – and I *am* contented with, I *am* grateful for it! How strongly, how forcibly do I feel to whom I owe all the earthly happiness I enjoy – it is to my father! to this dearest, most amiable, this best beloved – most worthy of men! – it is his goodness to me which makes all appear so gay, it is his affection which makes my sun shine.

During the two years when Hetty and Susan had been abroad, and Charles just embarking on his literary career, it was natural that he should turn to neat, docile, sensible Fanny to be his amanuensis – a post she continued to fill as the volumes of his great work, *The History of Music*, were laboriously completed over a long period of his life. Fanny devoted many, many hours to this fair-copying, even when she had creative work of her own secretly on hand, always putting her father's demands on her before any other consideration. The first intimation he had that she possessed a comic gift of her own came in June 1769, on the momentous occasion of his being awarded a 'Doctor's Degree in Musick' at Oxford, when Fanny dashed off a set of humorous verses on the theme of his new dignity, five stanzas each ending with the precious words 'Doctor Burney'.

Her ability to describe scenes and set down conversations was sharpened by the constant practice of writing long journal-letters to absent members of the family, and especially to one old family friend, Samuel Crisp, who lived a retired life in the Surrey countryside and for whom letters from Fanny, or 'Fanniken', as he called her, constituted one of the chief delights of old age. Samuel Crisp was always ready with praise and judicious criticism; he had faith in Fanny's unique gifts before they were recognized by anyone else. On her part, she loved him perhaps better than anyone but Susan and her own father, and paid him the tribute of calling him 'Daddy Crisp'. This was to result, in due course, in her finding herself with *two* father figures to propitiate, but in these early years his encouragement was wholly beneficial. 'That I wish for the remnant of your evening concert, is saying nothing,' runs one typical note from him. 'You have learn'd from that Rogue your father (by so long serving as his amanuensis, I suppose) to make your descriptions alive, – send the remainder, therefore, without a moment's delay; – while still breathing and warm.'

'How close the Doctor kept Fanny to writing' – that is, copying *his* work – was well known in the family, but she voiced no complaint herself, being glad to contribute in that way to her keep. In 1770 Hetty married her cousin, another Charles Burney, but Fanny had no wish to exchange her father for a husband. 'He is all indulgence,' she wrote of her father to Samuel Crisp, 'and to quit *his* roof requires inducements which I am sure I shall never have. I never, never can love any human being as I love him.' This outburst was provoked by an unwelcome proposal of marriage from a certain Mr Barlow, whom she scarcely knew and certainly did not care for, in May 1775, as she approached her twenty-third birthday.

Though certain in her own mind, Fanny did not feel herself at liberty to decline the proposal without gaining her father's approbation for the step. At first it had appeared forthcoming, but when Mr Barlow wrote again, prudence exerted itself in Charles, to Fanny's terror:

My father looked grave, and asked me for the letter, put it in his pocket unread, and wished me good night. . . . The next day, a day the remembrance of which will never be erased from my memory – my father first spoke to me *in favour* of Mr Barlow, and desired me not to be *peremptory* in the answer I had still to write. . . . I scarce made my answer; I was terrified to death. I felt the utter impossibility of resisting not merely my father's *persuasion*, but even his advice. . . . I wept like an infant, when alone; ate nothing; seemed as if already married, and passed the whole day in more misery than, merely on my own account, I

ever passed in my life, except when a child, upon the loss of my own
beloved mother, and ever revered and most dear grandmother!

The episode ended with a touching *éclaircissement* between father and
daughter:

After supper I went into the study, while my dear father was alone, to
wish him good night; which I did as cheerfully as I could, though pretty
evidently in dreadful uneasiness. When I had got to the door, he called
me back, and asked some questions concerning a new Court-
mourning, kindly saying he would assist Susette and me in our
fitting-out, which he accordingly did, and affectionately embraced me,
saying, 'I wish I could do more for thee Fanny!' 'Oh Sir,' cried I, 'I wish
for nothing! only let me live with you.' 'My life!' cried he, kissing me
kindly, 'Thou shalt live with me for ever, if thee wilt! Thou canst not
think I meant to get rid of thee?'
    'I could not, Sir; I could not!' cried I; 'I could not outlive such a
thought!' and as I kissed him – Oh! how gratefully and thankfully! with
what a relief to my heart! I saw his eyes full of tears! a mark of his
tenderness which I shall never forget! 'God knows,' continued he, 'I
wish not to part with my girls! – only, don't be too hasty!'
    Thus relieved, restored to future hopes, I went to bed light, happy
and thankful, as if escaped from destruction. Sorry as I am for Mr B.,
who is a worthy young man, I cannot involve myself in a life of
discomfort for his satisfaction.

The life of comfort, to Fanny, was justifying her existence by being of
use to her father and pursuing the world of her own imagination in the
interim. Few young ladies in her position would not have been tempted, at
least, by Mr Barlow's offer, but already she knew that her most precious
possession was her mental integrity, which would almost certainly be
compromised by marriage to any 'ordinary' young man. At the time of the
proposal, she was well advanced with a novel. All through the early 1770s,
whenever there was a moment free for writing, she had been setting down
'scenes, situations, dialogues and incidents' long 'pent in her head'. Much
of the writing had to be done in the dead of night, while the rest of the
household slept. Afterwards passages were read aloud to Susan, just as
Jane Austen would later read her manuscripts to her sister Cassandra, and
in the same happy atmosphere of perfect understanding. Between Fanny
and Susan, an observer remarked, there seemed to be 'but one soul – but
one mind'.[7]
    As the long story neared completion, Fanny came up against the
question whether she should attempt to publish it. On an artistic level, she

must have been aware that it had merit – even if in her modesty she made no claim for its literary worth, she could not doubt its entertainment value. But on a personal level, there were strong inducements not to publish. It was thought that no 'nice' young lady would choose to expose her thoughts to the public. Novels, particularly novels by women writers, had a reputation for frivolity. No female novelist had yet emerged to gain the respect of a Richardson or a Fielding. 'An *Authoress* must always be supposed to be flippant, assuming and loquacious,' wrote Fanny sorrowfully. She shrank from braving the opinion of the world – the opinion, that is, of men; and yet, it once having entered her brain, she was unable to suppress the 'fantastic' wish of seeing *Evelina* in print.

The compromise was to publish anonymously. So serious was Fanny in this intention that she went to extraordinary lengths to preserve her secret, copying out the whole of the manuscript in a feigned hand, so that it would not be identified by the printers as having been written by the same person who had prepared Dr Burney's works for the press. Then, after a conference among the young Burneys, brother Charles was dressed up 'by the laughing committee, in an old great coat, and a large old hat, to give him a somewhat antique as well as vulgar disguise; and was sent forth in the dark of the evening with the first two volumes to Fleet Street, where he left them to their fate'.

The natural pride and delight which must have been Fanny's on having her manuscript accepted was tempered by two conflicting fears: the fear of doing anything so momentous without the approbation of her father, and the fear of bringing disgrace to his name if her novel should meet with ridicule, and it be known that he had countenanced its publication. There may also have been an unconscious desire to withhold from him the power of veto until it was too late. It was only when *Evelina* was in the very process of being set up in type that she blurted out her secret, begging her father not to 'demand a sight of such trash as I could scribble'.

'He could not help laughing; but I believe was much surprised at the communication. He desired me to acquaint him from time to time, how *my work* went on, called himself the *Père confident*, and kindly promised to guard my secret as cautiously as I could wish. I believe he is not sorry to be saved the giving me the pain of his criticism. . . . Yet I am easier in not taking the step, without his having this little knowledge of it, as he is contented with my telling him I shall never have the courage to let him know its name.'

Fanny's acceptance of his patronizing attitude to her 'work', and her own self-deprecating description of it, speaks volumes for the estimation in which anything performed by a woman was commonly held. Only by adopting the submissive posture could a woman get her own way and get away with it, in terms of retaining the approval of men.

Evelina, or a Young Lady's Entrance Into the World was published in January 1778. From the moment of its publication, Fanny's control of her own affairs began to slip away. Her fond belief that her privacy would be as safe afterwards as when the book 'was in my own bureau' proved naïve. *Evelina* was being talked about by 'all reading England', to use George Eliot's phrase, in a way that is not possible to imagine today. Its anonymity only intrigued people the more, with the result that '*every body* longs to tell *one* body!' the secret of the author's name. Her own father, in his pride, was the worst offender. At the Thrales' home in Streatham, where he heard *Evelina* praised in the warmest terms, and its author's identity much speculated about, he was quite unable to resist making the delightful and astonishing confession that, ' 'twas our Fanny's'.[8]

Charles himself had opened the first volume 'with fear and trembling, not supposing she would disgrace her parentage; but not having the least idea, that without the use of the press, or knowledge of the world, she could write a book worth reading'. Unable to bear the suspense of awaiting his verdict, Fanny had run away to Surrey and Mr Crisp; on her father's joining her there, he recorded, 'I thought she would have fainted, but I hastened to take her by the hand and tell her that I had read part of her book with such pleasure, that instead of being angry, I congratulated her on being able to write so well. This kindness affected her so much that she threw herself in my arms, and cried . . . till she sobbed.'[9]

Two days later Charles was proudly introducing Fanny to the circle at Streatham, and that was the end not only of her precious anonymity, or 'snugship' as she called it, but of her spontaneity as a writer. The interest taken in her by Mrs Thrale, Dr Johnson, Sir Joshua Reynolds and Edmund Burke was kindly meant, and very gratifying, but it was also intimidating. Everything she did, everything she wrote from now on would be subject to their scrutiny, their judgement, their appraisal.

Fanny was aware of her father's sensitivity about his position at Streatham, and all the more nervous on that account about appearing well. The arrangement that the Thrales had made with Charles, on discovering the conversational powers and agreeable manners of their eldest daughter's music master, was that once a week he should give Queeney her lesson, dine and stay the night, and for these services he should receive an annual stipend of £100. Since Charles's usual fee for a lesson was half a guinea, he was thus earning almost four times his normal rate, with an excellent dinner and the chance to shine in influential company thrown in. But to be paid to be a guest confined him, he knew, to the status of entertainer, and he was anxious to demonstrate both the gentility and the genius of his family. Indeed, Fanny's success was particularly opportune in restoring the respectability of the Burney name, for but a few months earlier it had been sullied by a scrape which sent young Charles down from Oxford in disgrace, and shortly before that shadowed by the elopement of the younger Allen step-daughter. These events were well known and sympathized with at Streatham; Charles thus stood sorely in need of a child he could be wholly proud of.

In every important respect Fanny was to prove herself an asset to him; she was to gain the sincere regard of all those at Streatham whose regard was worth having, and to become almost indispensible to Mrs Thrale. But that lady's first impression shows the ordeal to which poor shy Fanny was obliged to submit in deference to her father's wishes, and shows too that Charles's sense of social insecurity was not without grounds:

'His daughter is a graceful looking girl,' wrote Mrs Thrale in her journal, 'but 'tis the grace of an actress, not a woman of fashion – how should it? The Burneys are I believe a very low race of mortals. Her conversation would be more pleasing if she thought less of herself; but her early reputation embarrasses her talk, and clouds her mind with scruples about elegancies which either come uncalled for or will not come at all: I love her more for her father's sake than for her own, though her merit as a writer cannot be controverted.'

As she learnt to relax in their company, however, Fanny was able quietly but shrewdly to observe and evaluate and even enjoy this new set of beings. When they encouraged her to use her skill with dialogue to write a comedy for the theatre – Mrs Thrale, Sir Joshua Reynolds, Arthur Murphy and even Richard Brinsley Sheridan urging her on – she took their type of people as the characters for her play, which made fun of literary pretensions.

Fanny put many months of work into *The Witlings* and felt quite optimistic about it. She read one draft to Mrs Thrale, who was startled by the subject matter but generously praised the dialogue. Arthur Murphy, the actor, was impressed by her mastery of the technique of writing for the stage. Next Fanny sought the approval of 'Daddy' Crisp, eager to prove to him how unfounded had been his initial objections to her turning playwright, his belief that humour on the stage must proceed from coarseness of speech and *double-entendre*: 'I will never allow you to to sacrifice a grain of female delicacy for all the wit of Congreve and Vanbrugh put together,' he had warned. But Fanny was not allowed the quiet conference in Surrey she had hoped for: her father insisted on taking the manuscript there himself and debating its merits with Crisp. The result was that the two men agreed the play was dangerously offensive to too many people, and unladylike in the sharpness of its satire. Their verdict was that it must be reworked or abandoned. With the sting of her play forbidden, Fanny had no heart for the 'hard fagging' of rewriting it. Charles and Mr Crisp were relieved, the latter advising her to stick to novels, 'little entertaining elegant histories'. Fanny submitted.

The interference of Charles Burney and Samuel Crisp on this point perhaps had repercussions beyond its effect on Fanny herself. Had her play been successfully produced, had she established that it was possible to write with wit and humour and astringency but without coarseness for the stage, other women might have been encouraged to follow her lead, to the enrichment of English drama in the following century.[10] With her gift for dialogue, her acquaintance among theatrical people, and the comparative freedom of the age in which she lived, Fanny Burney was well qualified to set a precedent and to open doors for other women. As it was, literary women of the next 150 years simply did not see drama as a possibility; talents presumably lay wasted, and the Victorian stage remained both crude and lifeless. Some of the blame must be Fanny's, for choosing her subject tactlessly and throwing away an opportunity for herself and her sex; but the intervention of the father-figures in her life is certainly to be deplored.

What most distressed Fanny herself was the sheer waste of time, time that was hard to come by, with so many people now making demands on her. Mrs Thrale insisted on her company for weeks on end, whether at home in Streatham or on visits to Brighton or Bath. Never again would Fanny enjoy the leisurely genesis of an *Evelina*. Her father was soon pressing her to get on with another novel, while the success of her first was still fresh in the public's memory. The second great volume of his own *History of Music* was, he hoped, nearing readiness, and it would be a splendid *coup* if the new works of father and daughter could appear simultaneously.

Writing *Evelina* had been a joyful escape for Fanny, an act of inspired creation. 'You wrote it because you could not help it,' Mr Crisp said truly. The very reverse was the case with its successor, *Cecilia*. Written to satisfy her mentors, her second novel brought Fanny no enjoyment but much mental, even physical, stress.

'I go on but indifferently,' she informed Hetty in January 1781 from Surrey. 'I don't write as I did, the certainty of being known, the high success of *Evelina*, which, as Mr Crisp says, to fail in a second would *tarnish*, – these thoughts worry and depress me – and a desire to do more than I have been able, by writing at unseasonable hours, and never letting my brains rest even when my *corporeal machine* was succumbent.'

By the middle of the next month she was ill, and Mrs Thrale was indignantly telling Dr Burney that Fanny's 'anxious earnestness to oblige him had caused much of the illness we lamented. Why says he I did tease her to write while she was away that the book so long expected might at length be done.'

Fanny confided to Susan that she knew her father would be disappointed. 'He will expect me to have just *done*, when I am so behind hand. . . . I am *afraid* of seeing my father. Think of a whole volume not yet settled, not yet begun! & that so important one as the last! I cannot sleep half the night for planning what to write next day, and then next day I am half dead for want of rest!'

She returned to London but made little progress through the summer, what with her own poor health and 'many interruptions from ill management, inconvenience and ill nature' – that is, from her stepmother's troublesome ways. In August she nursed Hetty through a confinement and the death of the infant; in September she herself fell ill again. In November she was sent again to Surrey, with strict instructions to remain until her novel was finished. 'What shall I do with my Father,' she appealed to Susan, 'to prevent displeasure or cold looks on my return? – they would half break my heart, after the most kind letter he has sent me not to *budge* or *fudge*!'

The book roughly finished, she was allowed back to London for Christmas and for Susan's wedding to a sailor, Molesworth Phillips, on 10 January 1782. Then began the 'drudgery' of revision: 'so horribly aches my hand with copying'. By March the first volume was with the printer, and Fanny busy with the second and third. There was a constant sense of panic, insufficient time to polish and prune, the book being advertised in the newspapers before she had begun to copy or revise the fifth volume, and before she had even written an ending that satisfied her.

'I think I shall always hate this book,' she told Mrs Thrale. 'But for my Father I am sure I should throw it behind the Fire! – as, when he knew nothing of the matter, was the case with many of its predecessors; all, indeed, but *Evelina*.' Whatever her own misgivings about *Cecilia*, her father was 'quite infatuated with fondness for it, – not only beyond my most sanguine hopes, but almost beyond credibility'.

Cecilia was published on 12 June 1782, just two weeks after the second volume of Dr Burney's *History*. Meanwhile, in March, there had appeared in *The Morning Herald* a poem rhapsodizing about various 'Blue-Stocking' ladies and referring to Fanny with the words, 'Little Burney's quick discerning'. Fanny was distressed by the verses, but 'my father is so delighted, that, though he was half afraid of speaking to me at all about them at first, he carries them constantly in his pocket, and reads them to everybody!' Only after her father's death did she discover that he himself had been the author of that timely piece of publicity.

Evelina had earned hardly anything for its author; as a first novel, that was fair enough, but with the reading public desperate for another story from her pen, Fanny should have been in a good bargaining position. Her brother had negotiated the terms of *Evelina*; her father took over that task for *Cecilia*. On Fanny's behalf he accepted an outright payment of £250.

This struck Mr Crisp as a wonderful sum for a mere girl to earn for doing nothing much. 'If she can coin gold at such a rate, as to sit by a warm fire, and in three or four months (for the real time she has stuck to it closely, putting it all together, will not amount to more, though there have been long intervals, between) gain £250 by scribbling the inventions of her own brain – only putting down in black and white whatever comes into her own head, without labour. . . .'

In fact, *Cecilia* sold so well and made so much profit for the publishers and booksellers that Charles was proved not to have made such a wonderful bargain. From all sides Fanny was told that, 'I had behaved like a poor simple thing again, and had a father no wiser than myself!' After all her effort (despite Mr Crisp's impression of the ease of composition), it was depressing to feel cheated out of rightful earnings, but Fanny learnt her lesson and, when she next came to publish, was careful to make very different financial arrangements for herself.

If Fanny was aware of *Cecilia*'s inferiority, her reading public was not so discerning, and both individuals and reviewers were lavish in their praise. The *Critical Review* noticed the two Burney publications together, mentioning that *Cecilia* was by the 'daughter of the ingenious Doctor Burney, so well known in the literary world by his excellent *History of Music*'. On the whole the *History* was overshadowed by the novel, but Charles showed not a scrap of jealousy or resentment; to him the family was more important than the individual member, and whatever brought glory on the Burney name was to be welcomed. 'Dear soul, how he feeds upon all that brings fame to *Cecilia*!' wrote Fanny six months after publication; 'his eagerness upon this subject, and his pleasure in it, are truly enthusiastic, and, I think, rather increase by fulness, than grow satiated'.

After their exhausting labours, father and daughter were able to allow themselves a measure of relaxation. Charles, with his elastic spirits and ebullient temperament, revived quickly, as Fanny thankfully remarked. 'My father is all himself – gay, facile, and sweet. He comes to all meals, writes without toiling, and gives us more of his society than he has done many years.' Fanny herself, by nature less subject than her father to swings of mood and certainly less transparent, found it harder to recapture her youthful good spirits. Something fundamental to her personality had been violated, and she had lost for ever her carefree, trusting, optimistic attitude to life.

She was thirty when she published *Cecilia*; feeling her precious imaginative life to have been stolen from her and hurled into the public domain, she was readier now to contemplate the sanctuary that marriage represented. For many years, from 1783 to 1786 or even later, she entertained hopes of a certain clergyman whom she regularly met at the social gatherings of her circle. George Owen Cambridge, who was three years her junior, quickly won her 'solid good opinion for worth, honour, religion, morals and domestic virtues'. He appeared to enjoy her society and by his demeanour gave not only Fanny but their mutual friends the impression of wishing to 'engage her affections'; but, for 'no reason' as far as Mrs Thrale could see, the long-expected proposal never came.

The continual expectation and disappointment were no matter of indifference to Fanny, who sometimes found the wear on her spirits amounting to 'even torture'. No subject for a new novel presented itself during these years; plays were still prohibited; the urge to write was satisfied by long journal-letters to Susan. With the marriage of her youngest sister, Charlotte, early in 1786, all her full siblings had left home, and the prospect loomed of passing her middle years as the amanuensis of her father – now hard at work on the third volume of his *History* – and as the nurse and companion of an unloved stepmother. Fanny's resistance was thus worn down when a wholly uncongenial new direction in life was virtually forced upon her by her father.

In 1775 she had been capable of withstanding the attempt on her liberty in the shape of Mr Barlow, even when endorsed by her father; eleven years later, she was a changed person – better able to endure, less well able to fight – and she bowed to her father's wish that she immolate herself at Court.

Charles had long been craving royal recognition on his own account. The most recent of several disappointments to him had occurred in May 1786, when the post of Master of the King's Band became vacant. The Lord Chamberlain appointed a favourite without consultation with the King; there seemed general agreement, shared by the King himself, that Dr Burney had been badly used. Just three weeks later came what was intended for consolation: Fanny was invited to an audience with the Queen.

'The blow was struck on Monday – and hard it struck, and almost felled me,' she wrote to Hetty. She was offered the post of Second Keeper of the Robes. 'I can suggest nothing upon earth that I dare say for myself, in an audience so generously meant. I cannot even to my father utter my reluctance, – I see him so much delighted at the prospect of an establishment he looks upon as so honourable.' Neither she nor her father expressed, amongst all their emotions on the occasion, *surprise* at the appointment, and it may be that Charles had actually been able to drop a hint to Their Majesties through a friend at Court, Leonard Smelt.

'King George III and Queen Charlotte wished to make Dr Burney amends for the disappointment . . .' wrote one observer, Lady Llandover. 'Mr Smelt suggested the possibility of benefiting Dr Burney *through his daughter*.'[11] Smelt himself made it clear to Fanny that the honour was 'an intended and benevolent mark of goodness to her father himself, that might publicly manifest how little their Majesties had been consulted, when Dr Burney had again so unfairly been set aside".[12]

How then could Fanny decline an honour that had been actively sought for her by her father, and which he could see only in its most favourable light? She was to have £200 a year, and a footman and maid of her own, besides, of course, her keep. This was honourable provision for an old maid, who must otherwise be dependent on her father. On those grounds alone, it was impossible to one of Fanny's delicate conscience and strong sense of duty to refuse, unless he who must bear the cost of such a refusal backed her. But from Charles Fanny received no affectionate assurance that she would always have a home with him, no generous urging to consult her own wishes. Neither did George Cambridge come forward to rescue her by marriage, although Fanny made sure he was aware of her circumstances; only with this failure did she finally relinquish all hope of him.

Furthermore, the position at Court was represented to Fanny as a means of advancing her whole family. Charles foresaw recognition for himself, promotion for James, preferment for young Charles, all flowing from Fanny's intimacy with the royal household. Smelt himself assured her that, 'You may have opportunities of serving your particular friends – especially your father.'[13] Fanny could not dash these dreams without rendering herself liable to the charge of selfishness. To have declined the appointment, she told Hetty, would have been 'thought madness and folly – nor, indeed, should I have been *permitted* to decline it, without exciting a displeasure that must have made me quite unhappy'.

Fanny's distaste for the appointment was founded not on any foolish timidity but on a very clear perception of what it would entail. 'The separation from all my friends and connections is so cruel to me, – the attendance, dress, confinement, are to be so unremitting.' She dreaded the thought that she would be expected to solicit favours from Their Majesties; she was sufficiently well acquainted with the world, now, to know that petty jealousies and rivalries abound wherever there is power, and that, 'My situation will be thorny and dangerous.' Nor would there be any intellectual stimulation to make amends: the Court was known to be dull, stiff and formal. In fact, most of Fanny's hours were to be spent waiting outside the Queen's room or at her side; when she was required to do anything, it was to handle the elaborate and cumbersome dresses in which she had absolutely no interest. Her father seems never to have considered whether such occupation was worthy of his clever daughter's talents; as Macaulay said of him, 'He seems to have thought that going to court was like going to heaven; . . . that the exquisite felicity enjoyed by royal persons was not confined to themselves, but was communicated by some mysterious efflux of reflection to all who were suffered to stand at their toilettes, or to bear their trains.'[14] And the worst of it was that this was meant to be no two- or three-year tour of duty but a permanent position. She was expected to commit the remainder of her life to Their Majesties' service.

It was all settled very quickly, without the knowledge of the literary world, some of whom would almost certainly have protested. On 17 July 1786, just five weeks after the audience with the Queen, Fanny was escorted by her father to the Royal Lodge. She was pale and trembling: 'I could disguise my trepidation no longer – indeed I had never disguised, I had only forborne proclaiming it.' Her father, who after all cared deeply for her welfare and was but too blind, too much carried away, to consider how best to secure it, now experienced a moment's consternation. But Fanny, whose only consolation was the thought of pleasing her father, struggled to convince him that all was well. It was not difficult: 'His hopes and gay expectations were all within call, and they ran back at the first beckoning.'

His complacency and insensitivity to what Fanny was really feeling revealed themselves in a triumphant note to Smelt: 'Though I have been so fortunate as to marry three of my daughters to worthy and good husbands, I never gave one of them away with the pride and pleasure I felt on Monday', and in the letter of advice he wrote to Fanny herself two days later: 'I see – and what is still more important to you and me – *you* see, a very comfortable, magnificent prospect before you. Enjoy it in its full extent, and do all that your most warm and upright heart can dictate to make yourself useful and acceptable to your most excellent Royal Mistress, and I trust your life will be as happy, as well as splendid, as the most flattering dreams could suggest.'

The mixture of tedium and backbiting that Fanny had anticipated at Court turned out to be only too real. An additional source of unpleasantness was the jealous and tyrannical nature of the elderly German lady who was her immediate superior and constant companion. 'Nothing but my horror of disappointing – perhaps displeasing my dearest father, has deterred me, from the moment that I made the mortifying discovery from soliciting his leave to resign. But . . . kind, good and indulgent as he is to me, I have not the heart, so cruelly to thwart his hopes – his views – his happiness. . . .' she wrote to Hetty in a letter actually blotted by tears.

Only to her sisters did Fanny confess the full misery of her situation. Neither at the time nor later did she utter a word of reproach to her father. And yet her bitter comment on George Cambridge's attitude to her plight could with much greater justification have been applied to her father: 'He would prefer to see the person of whom he thought highest in the world, subdued into the saddest lot that destiny, without positive calamity, could frame for her! – know her doomed to confinement – dependence – and attendance, – banishment from her friends, – hardships to her health, and the tyranny and caprice and gloom of a companion notorious to the whole world for ill-nature!' It is impossible not to suspect that Fanny was unconsciously venting her feelings towards her father in this outburst. Her father, after all, had responsibilities towards her that Cambridge had not; and her father actively pushed her into the uncongenial life, while Cambridge merely failed to rescue her from it.

For four years Fanny bore it, while her health gradually deteriorated. During these years she kept a journal of her experiences intended for semi-public consumption rather than expression of her own feelings; and she found some time for creative writing, though the blank-verse melo-dramas she produced were almost wholly without any but therapeutic value, their gloomy tone reflecting the state of her spirits. By the spring of 1790 she was so utterly weary in mind and body that the longing to resign became overwhelming. But she would do nothing without her father's permission. Her sisters dropped what hints they could, compatible with Fanny's wish of not revealing the full truth to him; and men of the literary world, unhampered by filial delicacy, agitated on her behalf. Her release was 'the common cause of everyone interested in the concerns of genius and literature', William Wyndham told Charles, while Reynolds, Boswell and Walpole considered getting up 'a round-robin to the Doctor, to recall his daughter to the world'.[15]

By 28 May, when Fanny was given leave to join her father at West-minster Abbey for a performance of the *Messiah* – the longest period of time they had had together since her appointment – the necessary ground-work had been laid by others. Charles, intending only to give her pleasure, mentioned how the admirers of *Cecilia* regretted her present silence and seclusion; Fanny seized the opening and blurted out her longing for release. From being 'kind, gay, open', his mood plummeted: 'How was I struck to see his honoured head bowed down almost to his bosom with dejection and discomfort! – We were both perfectly still a few moments; but when he raised his head I could hardly keep my seat, to see his eyes filled with tears! – "I have long," he cried, "been uneasy, though I have not spoken, – but – if you wish to resign – my house, my purse, my arms, shall be open to receive you back!"'

In fact, it was to be another fourteen months before Fanny regained her freedom, so anxiously did Charles caution her not to be precipitate or to give Their Majesties grounds for offence. The recent events in France made him dread any appearance of disloyalty to the throne. He assured friends that only Fanny's poor health could induce her to give up her post and that, even so, 'she will risk the dying at her Majesty's feet to show her zeal', as he wrote to Arthur Young in February 1791.

Fanny determined to use those last months to test out her father's theory that her position in the royal household would give her the opportunity to benefit other members of her family. She had asked nothing and received nothing unsolicited hitherto; she was certain his hopes were unrealistic. Now she steeled herself to speak on her brothers' behalf; if she was unsuccessful, it would prove that her remaining at Court could be of no use to them – if successful, she would at least have done some good. It was a hateful task, and the result was negative, but at least she was easier in her conscience. Five years of very real suffering and loss of liberty had been based on a wholly erroneous conviction of her father's.

Throughout the spring of 1791 Fanny felt 'very unwell, low, faint and feeble'. The Queen was awaiting a replacement from Germany but was half inclined to insist that, if she granted her a holiday, Fanny would be well enough to resume her duties. While Susan warned that to give in to the Queen's wishes would mean the 'eternal sacrifice of what remains of health and of life, of comfort and of friends', Charles was torn between misgivings at incurring royal displeasure, 'which would make you and all of us uncomfortable for the rest of our lives', and real paternal fear that, 'like Agamemnon I had sacrificed you, my Iphigenia, to the state'. At last, on 7 July 1791, just ten days short of five years' service, Fanny was given her release in a 'gracious and amicable manner', to her father's great relief. She was awarded a pension of £100 per annum.

Fanny was thirty-nine when she left Windsor Castle for Chelsea College, where her father, as resident organist, now occupied a modest suite of rooms with Mrs Burney and Sarah. Her thirties had been a frustrating and miserable decade, wholly directed by and subject to her father's judgement. What were the prospects for her now, in her fortieth year, with her health and looks faded and her youthful muse, it seemed, departed? Not even the most optimistic of observers would have been able to predict the revolution that was to overtake Fanny's circumstances within the next two years, the romantic fairy-tale that was to become reality for her, and the completely different flavour of the second half of her long life, as she found the courage to live according to her own determination.

A leisurely tour of the West Country, ending with several weeks' visit to Bath in the late summer and early autumn of 1791, did much to recuperate Fanny's health. She returned to find her irrepressible father 'all goodness, gaiety and affection', just as once before she had found him bouncing back from adversity 'full of spirits, full of Handel, full of manuscripts, full of proof-sheets'. Whatever unintentional wrongs he had done her, it was impossible not to love and honour such a father.

1792 was devoted to family visits, and in January the following year

Fanny settled down for a long stay in Surrey, at the home of her beloved sister Susan. Here she was eagerly introduced to General Alexandre d'Arblay, one of a group of French *émigrés* who had sought temporary refuge in a neighbouring house. Susan's proficiency in French – denied, it will be remembered, to Fanny, who had now for the first time reason to regret her exclusion from the school in Paris – rendered her particularly useful and sympathetic to the interesting newcomers, and she was soon convinced of the justice of their politics, for they were neither monarchists nor revolutionaries but constitutionalists, dedicated to upholding the *limited* powers of the sovereign. This moderation, it was immediately apparent to both sisters, would be anathema to their father, a worshipper of royalty, who claimed to have spent his life 'fighting and scolding with Wickites, Foxites, Democrats, revolutionists, Jacobins and anarchists'.[16] Charles Burney was also a self-confessed Francophobe. Thus, even as she was falling in love with d'Arblay and observing the growth of his equal regard for herself, Fanny knew that this astonishing late chance of happiness would meet with opposition from her father.

By April there was an understanding, stopping short of an engagement, between the lovers, both of whom were past forty. In May Fanny engineered a meeting between d'Arblay and Charles. Her father began the interview in a mood unusual for him, 'full of reserve', but 'in a short time, his amiable nature took the reins from his fears and his prejudices, and they entered into literary discussions with all the animation and interest of old friends'.

However, Charles was not won over so easily. 'I cannot help foreseeing much future uncomfortableness, mortification, and privation, from the narrowness of circumstances, to persons deserving of a better fate, and who are likely to condemn themselves to a perpetual struggle with penury to the end of their days,' he wrote to a friend who intervened on their behalf. But it was not only poverty that he dreaded: any action which could be construed as disloyalty to Crown and country at such a delicate time simply horrified him and appeared totally unjustifiable. 'Indeed, if it were possible for them ever to reside in, or even to visit London, the alliance would probably shut my daughter out of that society in which she has hitherto been so earnestly sought. This, though unpleasant to reflexion, may be supported; but the displeasure of the Queen may have very serious consequences.' He summed up: 'If M. d'A. had any prospect of advancement or establishment here in any way likely to produce a sufficient income for his own subsistence, and there could be any means devised of procuring Her Majesty's favourable opinion, or at least toleration of this alliance, I should not hesitate in giving my benediction, and every assistance in my small power to a beloved child and an honourable and accomplished man.'

This letter was endorsed, more than thirty years later, by Fanny: 'In answer to these *apparently* most just, and *undoubtedly* most parental and tender apprehensions, Susanna . . . wrote a statement of the plans, and means, and purposes of M. d'A. & F.B., so clearly demonstrating their power of happiness, with willing economy, congenial tastes, and mutual love of the country, that Dr B. gave way and sent, though in trembling even to reluctance, a consent, by which the union took place the 31st of July in Mickleham Church. . . .'

Fanny was given away by her brother James, her father steadfastly declining to attend the ceremony. As Fanny told her brother Charles, 'My dear Father – alas! – from prudential scruples is coldly averse to this transaction – and my heart is heavy from his evident ill will to it – yet he has not refused his consent.'

Fanny had found the strength to break free from her father's influence, and though she was to continue to love him tenderly until his death, and to venerate his memory until her own, he no longer had power over her happiness. The remainder of Fanny's life was not uneventful, but it unfurled against the background of an emotionally satisfying, equitable and mutually supportive marriage, which made all the difference. Her father's approbation ceased to be of supreme importance to her, and even in adversity, even when 'assailed by many calamities – chiefly of separation and illness', she enjoyed the fundamental contentment of a nature in harmony with its mode of existence.

In December 1794, at the age of 42½, Fanny gave birth to a son, Alexander. The couple who had gladly chosen poverty for themselves were reluctant to inflict it on their son, and Fanny, the only possible bread-winner in that family, sat down to 'write, write, write' herself into a little fortune. (Their only other income was the pension which, contrary to her father's fears, had not been withdrawn; the General's hopes of gaining employment in England proved, as Fanny had known they would, 'cruel delusions'.) *Camilla, or a Picture of Youth* was published in 1796, bringing its author over £2,000, sufficient to build a home, Camilla Cottage, at Mickleham. Fanny, learning from her previous mistakes, published this third novel by subscription, to maximize her share of the profits. Because of her name, the sales were excellent, 'four times that of *Evelina*, and nearly double that of *Cecilia*'. One of the subscribers was Miss J. Austen of Steventon.

Like *Cecilia*, though for different reasons, *Camilla* was written under pressure and suffered from the effects of hasty composition. Fanny did not allow herself sufficient time at either end of the creative process – either for a leisurely gestation or for a thorough revision. As a middle-aged, married woman she was over-conscious of her duties to the reading public and apt to give way to the temptation to moralize. Her published prose – as opposed to her letters and journals, which were as lively as ever – never recovered from the inhibiting effects of celebrity. The book aroused a mixed response, but her father, who had been swiftly and completely reconciled to her marriage, most characteristically would hear no criticism of *Camilla*, flying 'like a tiger' to its defence.

In 1802 the long Surrey idyll came to an end when the d'Arblays took advantage of the Peace of Amiens to cross to France in an attempt to regain the General's property and were trapped by the resumption of war for more than a decade. The various exploits of her husband and son constituted Fanny's chief concerns during those years, her own courage being put to trial when she had to undergo an operation for breast cancer performed on her own bed without anaesthetic.

Naturally one of her anxieties was her father, now growing old, and the fear that she would never see him again. She felt terribly cut off from family news, for it was hazardous even for letters to get through. This long separation was for her 'a bitter stroke'. It would have comforted her to know that one of his grandchildren could describe Charles, in 1808, as 'young and gay as ever, reading and writing without spectacles . . . and cheerful and entertaining, and sprightly, and kind, as if he had been twenty-three instead of eighty-three'.[17]

Father and daughter were reunited four years later. Awaiting her arrival, he had walked about the room murmuring 'My honest Fanny!' and had given orders that he was to be alone when she was shown in. After her long absence she found him 'very much altered indeed – weak, weak and changed – his head almost always hanging down, and his hearing cruelly impaired'. He died in April 1814, in Fanny's presence.

Charles Burney's will was somewhat unusual. After remembering all his many children and grandchildren, he left the bulk of his money and the proceeds from the sale of his immense library to Hetty and Fanny, on the principle that, 'where education or professions were given to the sons, property that was personal rather than hereditary might without any injustice be given to the daughters'. Susan had predeceased him, and Charlotte was well provided for by her marriage, but both Hetty and Fanny had long made do on meagre incomes. 'His own design – heaven bless him ever! – has been to do what he himself thought strictly just by all: but particularly serviceable by Hetty and me. Blessed be his immortal spirit, Almighty God!' wrote Fanny.

Naturally her brothers, James especially, were inclined to feel themselves disinherited. During their father's lifetime neither James nor Charles had fulfilled his early promise, the middle years of each being stagnant periods in their careers, though honours came to them late: James was to die a Rear Admiral, Charles a Doctor of Divinity (and, as Fanny believed, on the point of gaining a bishopric). All his sons had brought a measure of shame to Dr Burney at one time or another: in his fifties James had left his wife and shockingly eloped with his much younger half-sister Sarah; Charles had been sent down from university for stealing books; and there was some unspecified scandal attaching to Richard, who lived in India. Only Dr Burney's daughters, with their 'rectitude that wanted no teaching', as he had observed of them at an early age, were above reproach.[18] Like many men, he had reacted to the unsatisfactory nature of his sons by bringing forward daughters who might otherwise have been undervalued.

In the same year that her father died, Fanny published her fourth and last novel, *The Wanderer*. Like its two immediate predecessors, it was written not out of joyous inspiration but for a non-artistic purpose, this time to finance Alex through Cambridge University. From the title, Fanny's reading public looked forward to revelations based on her experiences as an exile in France; in fact, its heartfelt subject was the difficulties of an unsupported female making her way in the world. 'Consider the situation of an unprotected woman!' as Mr Crisp had warned her when she turned down Mr Barlow's proposal. Since then, Fanny had had reason to do just that. In her voice of protest and preoccupation with this subject, which Anne and Charlotte Brontë were to make their own, Fanny was ahead of her times, but in her style and treatment she was old-fashioned, ponderous and dull, failing to win over her readers and adding nothing to her reputation.

From 1814 until the death of the General four years later, he and Fanny lived in happy retirement in Bath. Subsequently she moved to London, at the wish of Alex, and devoted the rest of her life to two tasks: sorting through the immense hoard of family papers, including editing and completing – indeed, virtually rewriting, with a daughter's pious anxiety to present a favourable portrait to the world – the memoirs of her father; and attempting to make something of her charming and clever but indolent and strangely childlike son. He predeceased her by two years; Fanny died in 1840 at the age of eighty-eight.

Mr Crisp had once likened Fanny to her father: 'indefatigable and ardent in all her pursuits'.[19] It was perceptive of him to notice the underlying resemblance, for superficially their temperaments could not have been more dissimilar. He was ambitious for fame, she intensely private; he loved the pleasures of society, she the intimacy of a few well-chosen people; he bounced back always the same from adversity, she learnt from it. In worldly wisdom and maturity of judgement she became the parent, he the child, but for many years she was forced to dissemble and subjugate her understanding. If Fanny had been less well pro-grammed to become the copybook daughter, she might have been a happier woman and a greater artist. As it was, she left one novel that is still well worth reading after 200 years, and three others that yield their nuggets of wit and good sense. In doing so, she fulfilled her father's ultimate ambition, that the name of Burney should be honoured and remembered long after they all were dead.

II

Maria Edgeworth
1768–1849

'Undoubtedly the wish to please my father is the first and warmest wish of my soul.'

Though seldom read nowadays, Maria Edgeworth has a secure place in the history of the novel. Her work was highly regarded in her own lifetime, and she succeeded Fanny Burney as the most famous woman writer of her day. In the early part of the nineteenth century, when exile and family preoccupations silenced Fanny's pen and when Jane Austen's novels were met with incomprehension or indifference, Maria's only rival for popularity was Sir Walter Scott, who confessed that he had been inspired to turn from poetry to novel-writing by Maria's stories of Irish life. It is generally accepted that Maria Edgeworth struck out a new path in fiction by initiating the regional novel. Not that all her work was set in Ireland: the public were equally warm in their admiration for her tales of fashionable London society and for the children's books (another innovation) with which she began her career. While Jane Austen had to wait for future generations to appreciate her genius, the lesser talent of Maria Edgeworth established her reputation and influence among her contemporaries.

The irony is that her success was achieved not through any of the usual compulsions to write: not from the delight of creation or the relief of self-expression; not as a means of escape, either imaginatively or literally, from the narrow confines of woman's sphere; not for money, independence or fame. 'It was to please my father I first exerted myself to write,' she stated in 1813; 'to please him I continued.'[1]

She never lost an opportunity to reiterate the theme. 'I shall work hard with the hopes of having something to read to my father,' she told a cousin in 1803, when she was thirty-five and a published novelist. 'This has always been one of my greatest delights and strongest motives for writing.'

Maria's 'inordinate desire to be beloved' by her father, which he, who must often have found it wearying, told her in 1811 was 'the defect of my character', sprang from the deep sense of insecurity which the circumstances of her early years created. To stimulate and retain his interest and affection became of fundamental importance to her and influenced everything she did.

But in the Edgeworth family it was not enough to be an ordinarily dutiful daughter. Maria would not have been noticed if that had been all she aspired to. For Richard Lovell Edgeworth had no fewer than four wives and a total of twenty-two children. With so much competition, Maria had to find some specially effective way of appropriating more than the slender share of attention that was fairly hers.

The damage done to Maria in infancy took a lifetime to repair. She was born on 1 January 1768, the third child of young parents who were rapidly becoming disenchanted with each other. Their marriage had been a rash mistake. Richard Lovell Edgeworth, born in Bath but heir to an estate in Ireland, was full of vitality and cleverness – the type of cleverness that assorts with ingenuity and curiosity rather than with solid study; and he had boarded, whilst a student at Oxford University, with the family of a lawyer, Paul Elers. One of Elers' daughters, Anna Maria, temporarily caught his fancy and, having dazzled her into falling in love, Richard felt bound in honour to propose marriage, although already aware that she could not offer him the intellectual companionship he desired in a wife. Their first child, also called Richard, was born in May 1764, before his father was twenty.

'I never passed twelve months with less pleasure or improvement,' Richard wrote of the first year of the marriage.[2] His choice of words is characteristic: brimming with mental and physical energy, interested in a thousand and one things, he detested waste of time and needed to feel that everything he did furthered the education of himself or others. 'Improvement' was the key word in his life and crops up repeatedly in his writings.

A second son, Lovell, was born and died in 1766; next came Maria, and two years later Emmeline, despite Richard's complaint that his wife 'lamented about trifles; and the lamenting of a female, with whom we live, does not render home delightful'. Not surprisingly, he escaped from it as much as possible to be with friends who shared his scientific and intellectual interests.

Most of these friends were male, but by no means all. At the Lichfield home of his closest friend, the somewhat eccentric Thomas Day, Richard made the acquaintance of two remarkable women. One was the poet Anna Seward (whose description of him as 'the lively, the sentimental, the accomplished, the scientific, the gallant, the learned, the celebrated Mr Edgeworth' conveys the attractiveness to women he was to retain all his life). The other was her friend Honora Sneyd, of whom Richard wrote, 'I was six and twenty; and now, for the first time in my life, I saw a woman that equalled the picture of perfection which existed in my imagination.'

Having lingered in Lichfield long enough to establish a mutual, though hopeless, passion, Richard tore himself away, not to return to his wife but to put an even greater distance between them. It was in Lyons, France, that he found diversion and occupation helping with an engineering project. He took the six-year-old Richard with him in an educational experiment whereby the boy was not to be subjected to conventional teaching but was to learn at random by mixing in adult company. On the part of the young father, this was an idealistic and ill-thought-out experiment which was to have unfavourable consequences and which was quite different from his later educational practices. It was inspired largely by Thomas Day, who, having proposed unsuccessfully both to Honora Sneyd and to her younger sister Elizabeth, fell back on the plan, propounded by Rousseau, of adopting an infant girl and bringing her up to be the perfect wife.

Perhaps intending to make another effort with his marriage, perhaps simply in want of the marital comforts which he could never long bear to be without, Richard eventually sent for his wife to join him in France. Maria had already learnt the lesson that fathers were more interested in their sons than in their daughters; she was now deprived of the only constant parent in her life, the little girls being left in the care of aunts. And when six months later Mrs Edgeworth returned home, she was pregnant again; in March 1773 she died of puerperal fever, ten days after giving birth to Anna.

As soon as he heard of his wife's death, Richard abandoned engineering and hurried back to England. His haste was not in order to comfort his children. Within three months of becoming a widower, he married Honora Sneyd.

Maria's first sight of her father, hitherto a stranger to her, made an impression which she was still recounting to younger members of the family in old age. As one recorded, 'Suddenly she heard a voice which she says she had a distinct recollection of thinking quite different and superior to any she had heard before – and the doors being opened she saw a gentleman in black and her imagination was instantly struck with the idea of his being sublimely superior to all she ever saw before.'[3] Thus began her hero-worship, born almost certainly out of panic that she had been deserted by everyone, a hero-worship that was never to diminish and which was seriously to retard her attainment of emotional maturity.

At 5½ years old, Maria had to get used to a new set of adults. In place of Mama, 'always crying' in her remembrance, and the ineffectual aunts, there were now a man of forceful personality and a stepmother of forbidding presence who were all-important in her world: a couple, moreover, wholly wrapped up in each other, with little time or patience for Anna Maria's children.

Honora was not unkindly disposed, but her standards were high and she found the elder children irredeemably spoilt by indulgence or neglect.

For the self-willed young Richard and the naughty, attention-seeking Maria, it was already too late. 'It is my opinion,' Honora wrote in 1776, when she had been a stepmother for three years and had two children of her own, 'that almost everything that education can give, is to be given before the age of five or six – therefore I think great attention and strictness should be shown before that age; particularly, if there is anything refractory and rebellious in the disposition, that is the time to repress it, and to substitute good habits, obedience, attention and respect towards superiors.'

These desirable qualities were singularly missing in the young Maria. Throwing tea in someone's face, cutting a sofa cover to bits and wilfully trampling on some new hotbed frames were among her attempts, totally misunderstood and counter-productive, to obtain the love and attention she craved.

'Yesterday Maria was talking of her childhood and saying how unhappy she was,' wrote one of her half-sisters some sixty-five years later. 'She remembered in Dublin getting out of a garret window on the window stool when she was about six years old and some passengers running and telling the maid of the child's danger and when the maid said as she took her in "Do you know you might have fallen down and broken your neck and been killed," Maria answered, "I wish I had – I'm very unhappy" – so piteous the idea of so little a child being so very wretched.'[4]

This incident occurred on the journey to the estate in Ireland, known as Edgeworthstown, which Richard Lovell Edgeworth had inherited some three years previously and which the high-minded Honora now persuaded him needed his personal supervision. Remote, self-sufficient Edgeworthstown was to become the centre of Maria's world – but not while her present stepmother was mistress and engrossing all her father's attention.

It was now that Richard began to develop theories of education that were both more sensible and more original than those he had tried out on his eldest son; and they emanated from Honora. As the family grew, she kept a register of each individual's intellectual growth and of his or her response to information and experience. The dearth of early reading material struck the Edgeworth parents, and together they worked out an ambitious scheme of what was wanted and began to produce the first textbooks themselves, textbooks in which children called Harry and Lucy ask questions and receive factual or moral answers.

These beginnings were to have important repercussions on Maria's later life, but for the moment she was excluded from the educational activity within the family. Both she and her elder brother were despaired of and sent back to England to school, though their father, now that he saw the true state of things at Edgeworthstown, could ill afford the fees.

Presumably Honora simply could not tolerate their presence. Maria was just eight when she endured yet another dislocation in her life, and she found herself among strangers again, at a school in Derby.

The letters she received there from her father were hardly calculated to allay her fears of being unwanted. His constant object was to improve those over whom he had influence, but his methods were crude and tactless. To be hectored on the subject of personal attractiveness, as Maria was at the tender age of ten, is sufficient to set up anxieties in even a less insecure personality. 'With a benevolent heart, complying temper and obliging manners,' her father wrote to her, 'I should make no doubt, that by your mother's assistance you might become a very excellent, and an highly improved woman. Your person, my dear Maria, will be exactly in the middle point, between beauty and plainness – handsome enough to be upon a level with the generality of your sex, if accompanied with gentleness, reserve and real good sense – plain enough to become contemptible, if unattended with good qualities of the head and heart.' Maria remained convinced that she was unattractive all her life.

Yet out of the crusts of such letters Maria was obliged to make a feast for her hungry soul. Many years later she wrote, 'I never can forget the delight and pride I felt in receiving letters from him when I was at school. The direction – the handwriting within – even the breaks, erasures and blots are present to me.'

On the advice of Maria's friends this passage was omitted, as being too emotional, from the *Memoirs of Richard Lovell Edgeworth* for which she had written it. So too was this: 'I had not for some years the happiness to be at home with him. . . . But even during the years that I was absent from him his influence was the predominating power in my early education. It is now above forty years ago, but I have a fresh and delightful recollection of his first coming to see me at school on his arrival from Ireland. I recollect the moment when . . . he stopped and said with a look and voice of affection which went straight to my heart, "Tell me my dear little daughter if there is anything you wish for or want – and remember what I now say – You will always through life find your father your best and most indulgent friend."'

Not only had separation and his own maturity increased Richard's fondness for his eldest daughter to what, perhaps, it ought always to have been, had he not been so young when he embarked on fatherhood and in the ensuing years so preoccupied by other relationships; but Maria had ceased to be an exasperating little girl. She had learnt to subdue her passions, to appear meek and helpless and grateful and obedient: reliable and proficient at doing anything she was told, but unable to act on her own initiative. This persona she was to adopt for the next forty years, and it was to have a profound effect upon what she wrote.

The first recorded instance of her father's setting Maria written work to do was when she was eleven: 'I send you part of an Arabian fable which I beg you to finish.' The following spring he desired her to write a story on the theme of generosity. Her eagerness to comply with his wishes was now in agreeable contrast to the attitude of her brother Richard, who had reacted differently to the mismanagement of their formative years, becoming more, not less, wayward and assertive. In fact, Richard never returned home to live but went to sea, made his home abroad, got into debt and was a thorough disappointment to his father. Here was a void for Maria to fill! She could surely aspire to combine the cleverness and usefulness of a boy with a girl's more amenable disposition. Her brother's defection showed her own loyalty and devotion in the most favourable light.

Another rival, by far the most powerful, for her father's affection, was removed from the scene when she was twelve. In April 1780, after a six-month illness, Honora died of consumption.

But if Maria entertained any hope of becoming the most important female in her widowed father's life, she was to be disappointed. Whenever one of his wives died, worn out by bearing his children, Richard Lovell Edgeworth had a successor already in mind. No other woman could quite take Honora's place in his heart; he talked of her all his life as his own true soul-mate and brought up all his children, even those of his later wives, to revere her memory and acknowledge her superiority of character and intellect. But he could not dispense with the comforts that could be supplied only by a wife, and such was his lifelong attractiveness to women that he never had to.

It had been Honora's own deathbed wish that he should marry her sister Elizabeth. Richard's opinion of Elizabeth when he had first met the Sneyd sisters was that she 'had much less energy of character, and was not endowed with, or had not then acquired, the same powers of reasoning, the same enquiring range of understanding, the same love of science, or, in one word, the same decisive judgement as her sister'. Nevertheless he proposed to Elizabeth at the end of the summer, and she, who had rejected at least one suitor – Thomas Day – with spirit, found the thirty-six-year-old widower with six children sufficiently desirable to accept.

Even during the engagement he was writing of his dead wife as 'the beloved, the unrivalled object of my affections. . . . For alas my mind turns in spite of every effort to Honora and to a wish of joining her.' But he had a long and happy life yet to lead, and many more children to beget. His third marriage took place on Christmas Day, and by the following March he could assure acquaintance, 'It is impossible that female gentleness and the strongest desire to please can be more apparent in any woman than in Mrs E.'

Meanwhile Maria was moved to a more fashionable school in London, where she endured 'all the usual torture of blackboards, iron collars and dumb-bells, with the unusual one of being swung by the neck to draw out the muscles and increase the growth, a signal failure'.[5] Her height never exceeded four feet seven inches. In London too she developed an eye complaint and was told by one doctor that she would go blind. Her father's reaction to the news was self-centred in the extreme; he had, he wrote to Maria, 'long been in a course of misfortune: the great loss which I sustained last year, disappointment from your brother, and several circumstances were almost too much for me; they have injured my health and now when your present mother's unremitting kindness, gentleness, attention and good sense begin to restore my mind to tranquillity, if you from whom I have lately expected much comfort and satisfaction should lose your health it will be the cause of a very severe relapse into my former uneasiness. . . .'

But these gloomy prognostications came to nothing. Indeed, Maria's life was about to be transformed. From the misery of school, ill-health and separation from her father she was suddenly plucked and at the age of $14\frac{1}{2}$ set upon an entirely new plane of existence.

Some time before Honora's decline the family had drifted back to England, but in 1782 Maria's father determined to return permanently to Edgeworthstown in order 'to dedicate the remainder of my life to the improvement of my estate and the education of my children'. Henceforward no young Edgeworth would be sent away to school. When the family crossed the Irish Sea in June that year, Maria was with them, her schooldays over. She suddenly found herself with a settled home, a congenial stepmother and regular access to her father: all she had now to do was to make herself indispensable.

There were several ways open to her. The most obvious was to assist in the education of the now rapidly expanding family. Honora had produced only two children – Honora and Lovell – but Elizabeth, despite less than robust health, submitted to a constant succession of childbearing. Four children were born in the first four years of her marriage, and eventually five more. All the family would gather round the long centre table in the library to do their lessons, read and draw every day.

This teaching duty, though earning Maria's keep as it were, did not involve her very closely with her father, but there was another occupation more promising in that respect. He had resolved to make a thorough survey of his property, to become acquainted with all his tenants and to regularize the chaotic terms on which the various holdings were let. That first summer he rode out daily; he often needed an assistant to take notes and to maintain the records and accounts at home. His eldest son was absent; his wife was otherwise occupied; it was the perfect opening for

Maria. Timid horsewoman that she was, she overcame her fears in order to accompany her father on these daily travels. Never, however, would she ride without him.

'Her father employed her as an agent and accountant,' wrote her third stepmother many years later; 'an employment in which she showed marvellous acuteness and patience', adding that it gave her 'habits of business and accuracy'.[6] By the aptitude which she unexpectedly showed for business, Maria proved how various could be women's abilities, how capable they were, given an opportunity, of contributing to the running of society. It is doubtful if she herself, with her emotional investment in dependence on her father, appreciated her achievement. But it is to the credit of Richard Lovell Edgeworth that he did not attempt to confine the females of his family to normal feminine work. He had gloried in Honora's 'masculine' intellect; he now encouraged Maria to exert herself in an unconventional sphere. Not that he unselfishly had in mind the development of their potential as individuals; it suited him to have a wife who could take an intelligent interest in his affairs, a daughter who could ably serve his interests. Nevertheless, compared with most men of his time, he was refreshingly free from prejudice.

Maria's unusual work for her father brought her further benefits. It 'let her into familiarity with the modes of thought and terms of expression among the people which she could in no other way have acquired'. Unconsciously she was laying up material for the Irish tales which were so to delight the public with their originality, realism and humour. Few women had access to this richness of experience, and again it was to her father that Maria, as she well knew, owed the factor that was to make her novels appealing to men as well as to women.

Since the death of the early masters of the novel, Richardson and Fielding, the form had been increasingly dominated by women – women writing for women – and had consequently rapidly lost prestige. Fanny Burney was perhaps the only exception to that belittling trend. It was the masculine input in Maria's work which drew the respect of men, including Walter Scott, who, inspired by her opening-up of possibilities to turn to novel-writing himself, gave the art form the necessary male boost which prepared it for the great Victorian practitioners of both sexes. It is valid to question whether, without the inadvertent participation of Richard Lovell Edgeworth, the English novel would ever have recovered its former status and gone on to such glory.

Writing itself was to be Maria's third and most enduring hold on her father's personal attention. By involving him at the ideas stage and by submitting all her written work for his correction and approval, she created for herself a unique means of access to his mind. It was he who first set her on that path, by giving her the task of translating the newly published *Adèle et Théodore: ou lettres sur l'education* by Mme de Genlis. The painstaking way she stuck to the work until it was completed, and her humility in attending to his criticism, equally delighted him, and he now began to find Maria a real object of interest as well as an asset to his household. 'I acknowledge with pleasure that your company and affection have contributed much to my felicity since you lived with me,' he wrote after eighteen months of the happy life at Edgeworthstown, words which must have been exquisitely sweet to one who had felt unwanted most of her life.

'My father's to come home tomorrow. Oh joy and jubilee!' wrote Maria with typical exuberance to an old school friend, Fanny Robinson, in December 1783. Richard was often in Dublin, for he had political and other interests which led him far beyond the domestic world which meant everything to Maria. She could never occupy the centre of his existence as he did that of hers. Nevertheless, it was gratifying when he referred to the almost completed *Adelaide and Theodore* as their 'joint endeavours':

My dear – I was going to say my dearest daughter – I received your letter with more pleasure than pride, and that is the humblest thing I ever said in my life – for indeed Maria I am not a little elated by the success of our joint endeavours to turn the vivacity of genius to the sober certainty of useful improvement. – What sincere satisfaction I shall feel in seeing you united to a man worthy of your merit – my whole mind has been turned to forming your character for the enjoyment and power of conferring permanent happiness. Indeed, were you to be disappointed in the reasonable and honourable hope of selecting from the mob of modern gentry one rational creature, who will esteem you as I do, yet the care that I have taken to form your character will not be thrown away – it will secure serenity in the evening of your life – and whilst I live will rivet the affection of a fond parent and a steady friend.

Much to Maria's embarrassment, her father was from this period always on the alert to find a husband for her. He was not in the least possessive. In the comfortable knowledge that he had an abundance of children, and an abundance of talents, he was ready and eager to share them with the world. 'He left me always at liberty to use or reject his hints,' Maria was to say of his contributions to her writing, and this was characteristic of his open-handed, if self-satisfied, attitude to life.

The next few years were a period of deep happiness to Maria, settled in Edgeworthstown, useful to the family, writing to please her father. She produced a play for the family to act, with a part written to suit each member; to do justice to Richard Lovell's gift of mimicry, she created for him a comic Irishman, a figure that was to recur in her fiction. She also spent much time writing down the stories which Richard told to amuse the family in the evenings, checking the details with him the following morning as they rode about together. These tales, known to them then as *The Freeman Family*, were to form the basis of her longest novel, *Patronage.*

This pleasurable and profitable apprenticeship suffered an interruption in 1791. The previous year Honora had died, aged sixteen, of the same complaint as her mother. Of all Maria's siblings, she had posed the most serious threat to her supremacy with their father, for young Honora had inherited her mother's perfections of character as well as her defects of health. After her death, Maria thought there could not be 'a kinder or more generous promise' than Richard's solemn vow, 'My dear daughters, I promise you one thing, I never will reproach any of you with Honora. I will never reproach you with any of her virtues.' Maria could breathe again.

And now the only other child of Honora, Lovell, seemed to be showing symptoms of consumption. Richard and Elizabeth decided to take him to England in search of a cure, entrusting to Maria a large share of responsibility for the younger children and the estate. When it came to such practical matters, Richard knew she was perfectly capable, but in her emotional dependence on himself she was immature. As he left, he put into her hands a bond for £500, and to her fulsome letter of thanks he replied from Eastbourne: 'I gave you £500 to make you independent for subsistence – I think every grown up person should by degrees be rendered independent as to the necessities of life – I shall always keep you dependent upon me for a degree of esteem, affection, entertainment and sympathy that you will find it difficult to obtain from any but a husband and to a good husband I will make over all my rich possessions in your heart. . . .'

He continued in this strain when he wrote next from Clifton, where he had decided to settle for the winter: 'Your letter of the 17th I received yesterday with very great pleasure – I do sincerely believe that you think all the kind things you say – and I do as sincerely wish to see your fondness and enthusiasm turned happily upon a proper object – I never see a gentleman of tolerable promise, that I do not immediately think of you. . . .'

He now decided, since their stay in Clifton was to be a lengthy one, that Maria should bring the younger children over to join their parents but that it would improve her chances of finding a husband if she herself could be given the advantage of a season in London. 'Most heavily shall I feel his absence if I am to spend the winter away from him,' wrote Maria to her aunt while this plan was in agitation. 'But I have had seven years of plenty.'

However, no one could be found to offer Maria a home in London, and it was arranged that she should go to Clifton after all. Even this plan was not without its attendant anxieties to the insecurity of her mind, as she revealed in a letter to her uncle written shortly after her arrival: 'All the phantasmas I had conjured up to frighten myself vanished after I had been here a week for I found that they were but phantoms of my imagination. As you very truly told me, my father was not a man for card parties etc and he is just as kind and fond of me as he used to be at home, as you prophecied.'

The Edgeworths spent two years in Clifton, to some effect, since Lovell did not develop tuberculosis. The other grown-up son, Richard, paid a rare visit to his family and managed to extract some money from his father to set up as a farmer in South Carolina, where he already had a wife. When he died in America four years later, his father wrote dispassionately, 'His way of life had become such as promised no happiness to himself or his family – it is therefore better for both that he has retired from the scene.' Richard Lovell Edgeworth was not a man to agonize over whether anything in his own treatment of his eldest son, either his early indulgence or the sternness that took its place on marriage to Honora, contributed to the weakness of his character. With so many children, one failure meant correspondingly less to him; Maria might with some justification have felt in perpetual danger of similarly being written off.

Only Maria of the original family reacted to the traumas of their childhood by obsessive clinging to her father. Emmeline and Anna both found husbands in Clifton. The twenty-year-old Anna accepted the proposal of the scientist Thomas Beddoes, thirty-three and 'uncommonly short and fat, with little elegance of manners', according to Humphrey Davy, who became his assistant in 1798.[1] Anna was almost certainly glad to escape from her father's dominant personality. Revisiting Edgeworthstown seventeen years later, she was struck by how he had mellowed, and thought he appeared 'in a much more amiable light' than when she had lived with him. Anna's marriage brought her into contact with the intelligentsia of Bristol in the 1790s, of whom Coleridge for a time was one; it was almost certainly from her that the story emanated, which he reported with some glee, that 'the Edgeworths were most miserable when children'.[8]

Their early misery, though a shared experience, does not seem to have drawn the family together. Maria was not especially close to her full sisters and was pleased enough when they left home. There was friction too between herself and Lovell, who once termed her 'that serpent in the house'. Only with the children of the third and fourth marriages, too far removed from her in age to challenge her pre-eminence with her father, was she able to form easy and even delightful relationships.

Even so, as Elizabeth Edgeworth's children grew, it was inevitable that more of their father's time and attention should be bestowed upon them. Maria's response was to apply herself more seriously to writing that would win his approval. From 1790 she was busy producing children's stories that fitted the educational theories first developed by Richard and Honora. 'I am very glad,' wrote Richard to Maria in 1791, 'to hear that you are inclined to increase our three volumes – I beg you to encourage this propensity as it will add exceedingly to your happiness and to mine.' No thought could have been better calculated to inspire her. During the Clifton years she wrote many of the stories which were later to appear in *The Parent's Assistant.*

The Edgeworths returned home in the autumn of 1793 to find a more than ordinarily disturbed Ireland. Richard was eager to play his part in setting it to rights, and Maria, naturally, believed him to have all the answers. Outsiders were more objective. One neighbour wrote grudgingly, 'Mr Edgeworth, "Dear Honora's" husband, has set up for the County, and though a man *far* from being liked in Society, yet from his great parts and independent principles, 'tis thought there could not be found among us an abler or better representative.'[9] The energetic and multi-talented young man who had found it easy to win friends and admirers had developed into a self-opinionated bore whom it was all too inviting to mock. From about that period are increasingly found references to him as tiresome, too talkative and altogether too pleased with himself. He was defeated at the election.

Richard's next obsession was related to the war with France. He promoted a scheme to set up a military telegraph but met with a succession of rebuffs so severe that he almost determined to leave Ireland for ever. As his secretary in all that business, Maria was witness to the corruption of government and commercial interest, magnified in her mind by her excessive partisanship of her father. The effect was to send her with renewed thankfulness back into the security of her own domestic circle, where the only disinterestedness was to be found. At the same time, apolitical though she was by nature, she began to entertain the ambition of vindicating and promulgating her father's ideas for reforming Anglo-Irish society, by the persuasive medium of fiction.

All the strands of her writing career had now been amassed, and she stood on the verge of publication. When it had seemed possible that she might venture into print with *Adelaide and Theodore* (in the event another translator forestalled her), Thomas Day had been horrified, sending her father 'an eloquent philippic against female authorship'. Richard had never shared that prejudice, and in 1795 he helped Maria to find a publisher for her *Letters for Literary Ladies*, a lightweight and uneven collection of which the first group, amusingly enough, was based on the correspondence of Edgeworth and Day on the very subject of 'female authorship'. The *Letters* give the impression of having been dashed off between more important work, and so they had. A year later Maria's simple, straightforward stories about lifelike children in recognizable settings, which she had been steadily accumulating since 1790, were published under the title *The Parent's Assistant.*

The title betrays to what extent the stories were designed to be part of her father's grand educational scheme. Richard and Honora, and later Maria herself, had observed in their own family the need for entertaining stories within the capabilities of children to read for themselves. Children's publishing was a new phenomenon, scarcely ten years old at this time, and hitherto practitioners had been rather heavy-handed with the moral and sparing with the light relief (as was Thomas Day's own famous *Sandford and Merton*). Maria fulfilled a need, and did so in an original way; her stories for children became immensely and deservedly popular.

Richard Lovell Edgeworth's scheme of education had three components: stories and textbooks, both designed for children to read themselves, under the parent's supervision, and an explanation of his theories written for the adult. This last was realized in *Practical Education*, which appeared in 1798 bearing both his and Maria's names. She later categorized their individual contributions to the work: 'The principles of education were peculiarly his, such as I felt he had applied in the cultivation of my own mind, and such as I saw in the daily instruction of my younger brothers and sisters during a period of nearly seventeen years; all the general ideas originated with him, the illustrating and manufacturing them, if I may use the expression, was mine.' Prodigal with ideas and theories, Richard lacked the application to transmute them into a solid work; diffident on her own account, Maria possessed the necessary diligence and attention to detail. It was a good working partnership. If Maria would never have appeared in print without the encouragement of her father, he certainly would never have published a book, or immortalized his name, without her hard work.

It was perhaps a little ironic that *Practical Education* was the work in which father and daughter collaborated most closely, since it was in many ways Richard's memorial to the beloved Honora. Having given her brainchild to the public with the help of Maria, Richard had no further interest in publishing on his own account. Henceforward Maria had to make a constant endeavour to involve him with her writing, especially as a new rival for his affections now appeared on the scene.

Elizabeth Edgeworth had been failing in health since 1791, when her daughter, a replacement Honora, was born. Nevertheless she went on to produce a ninth child, William, three years later. But by 1797 it was clear that she was seriously ailing.

Facing the prospect of widowhood for the third time, Richard Lovell Edgeworth, father of ten living children, might reasonably have been expected to spend the remainder of his life with the competent and devoted Maria as mistress of his household. Surely Maria, if she contemplated Elizabeth's death, must have presumed such would be the pattern of their future life together. Few would have supposed that Richard, having ruined the health of three young women by subjecting them to more frequent childbearing than their strength could endure, should consider, even before the last was in the grave, marrying a woman young enough to be his daughter and bringing yet another large brood into the world. Even a daughter less possessive than Maria would have been forgiven for finding the idea obscene.

Frances Beaufort was one year younger than Maria. Her father was a friend of Richard's, and she herself a friend of Maria's cousin Sophy Ruxton. A highly intelligent woman and a gifted artist, Frances had been invited to submit illustrations for a new edition of *The Parent's Assistant.* When Richard called to collect the drawings from her father's house in March 1797, he found Frances to be exactly the sort of intellectual, large-minded, calm and well-balanced woman he admired. He had not been unhappy in his third marriage, but as a partner Frances seemed to promise a repeat of the superior satisfactions of his second.

Frances, properly chaperoned by her mother, was invited to Edge-worthstown that summer, with the almost certain intention on Richard's part of getting to know her better with a view to making her his wife. His design went unsuspected by Maria, who otherwise would have been much more scratchy with their guest. The various characters in the household, and their relations with one another, thus came under the acute yet sympathetic gaze of an outsider, and the impressions Frances set down for her brother give a valuable glimpse of the Edgeworths at that time:

> The family are all you know chemists and mechanics and lovers of literature and a more united more happy more accommodating more affectionate family never yet came under my observation. . . . Our time was agreeably spent between reading and listening to Miss E. reading some of her own compositions, and walking – added to the lively conversation of Mr E., who knows more anecdotes and tells them better than anyone I know. . . . Mrs E. is still pretty though very ill and weak to the last degree: she is inclined to be cheerful and sometimes is comical. . . . Miss E. – the Maria – is little, being the same size as myself, her face is not pretty but very agreeable. She looks unhealthy-lively and has a sweet voice in speaking: her dress is neatness itself, and her manner pleasing to a degree that is equally distant from the affectation of concealing, or the vanity of displaying her talents. Next to her comes Lovell. He is a poet and a chemist, seems much attached to his father and kind to the younger children, but he is not like his father and yet methinks he tries to be like him – a bad plan, comparisons cannot be to his advantage.[10]

The signs were propitious for Richard. It is extraordinary that, at fifty-four, tiresome as he was generally found by casual acquaintance, he could seriously attract a young woman of sense and taste. Elizabeth Edgeworth died that November, and the following February Richard proposed to Frances and was accepted.

Maria was at first shocked and horrified, but her father took pains to talk her round. Frances too wrote to her placatingly, and Maria replied, staking her claim, 'If I may without presumption say so, my father's ideas, and mine, upon almost all subjects have so great a similarity, that I believe it to be morally impossible that I should not become attached to one who fixes his heart. – That heart is so large that, occupy as much of it as you will, dear Miss Beaufort, I need not fear that there should not be ample room enough left for me.'

Both the lovers went out of their way to give the jealous, anxious Maria the assurances she craved. By April she was reconciled to the match, telling Sophy Ruxton that she had completely changed her mind and now thought that Frances 'is exactly suited to my father, will increase his happiness a hundredfold and will never diminish his affection for me. Indeed, he never in his life showed me so much affection, so much confidence as he has done since he became attached to her.' An older and wiser Richard Lovell Edgeworth was more adept at handling Maria than when he had introduced the last stepmother but one.

Frances turned out to be just the mistress Edgeworthstown needed, a better counterpart to the forceful Richard than either the abrasive Honora or the self-effacing Elizabeth. The whole household benefited from her kind but firm presence. All her stepchildren quickly came to love and confide in her, and her own children, four daughters followed by two sons, grew into happy, well-adjusted individuals, stronger in both health and character than the previous batches of Edgeworths. As for Maria, she was very soon referring to Frances as 'next to my father, the friend I love best in the world'. It greatly eased the situation that, from about the time of this marriage, Maria's writing career gathered momentum; her most productive and successful decade was about to begin. With Frances soon occupied with childbearing and rearing, there could be no confusion of roles: each was important to Richard in her own way.

The two women were also united by some dramatic and disturbing events which occurred very soon after the marriage. Richard was waylaid by a mob and almost lynched for a French spy, and the entire household was forced to abandon Edgeworthstown for a few days. Maria gave thanks to heaven for the 'preservation' of her father, while he impetuously resolved to leave for ever an ungrateful Ireland, where he had resided so long 'from no other motive than a sense of duty and a desire to improve the circle around me'. The calm good sense of Frances and her father prevailed upon him to stay but, his thick skin finally punctured, he increasingly withdrew from public life and sought his happiness in the safe circle formed by his excellent wife, adoring eldest daughter and multitude of aquiescent infants.

With her duties as her father's amanuensis thus declining, Maria indulged in an extraordinary burst of creativity. She wrote further stories for children, slightly older children this time (keeping pace with the interests of Elizabeth's family), which were published as *Moral Tales* in 1801. The same year saw the publication of *Early Lessons*, which, as factual expositions, brought to completion her father's original tripartite educational scheme. Working on this textbook was uncongenial to Maria, and done only out of a sense of duty and to retain her father's involvement in her concerns. It left her imagination free, and she pleased herself rather than any one else by writing the two adult novels which really established her fame, *Castle Rackrent* (1800) and *Belinda* (1801).

Drawing together anecdotes of her father's and her own observations of the Irish tenantry, ranging over a large social spectrum and mixing humour with unsentimental realism, *Castle Rackrent* was something wholly new in fiction, and it delighted the reading public. *Belinda*, set in polite London society and containing a not very profound portrait of Richard Lovell Edgeworth in Mr Percy, the detached critic and independent-minded gentleman, was less original, but it established Maria's range and prevented her being typecast as a purely provincial novelist.

She had been working on the Irish story , at intervals, over many years, ostensibly for the private amusement of her own family, and she was at first doubtful whether to publish it. Her conviction that her educational writings were far more important and worthwhile than a mere novel could be emanated from her father. In her youth he had actually forbidden her to read Fanny Burney's new book, *Cecilia*. Now, in her maturity, she accepted without demur his opinion that, 'to be a mere writer of pretty stories and novelettes would be unworthy of his partner, pupil and daughter'. And long after his death, recoiling from what she saw as the vulgarity of another female novelist, she wrote, 'God forbid as my dear father said I should ever be such a thing as that – it was for want of such a father she has come to this.'

One of the devices Maria employed to skirt round her father's animus against novels was to deny that they *were* novels, offering them instead to the public as 'moral tales'. Another was flatteringly to use them as vehicles for his own political and social ideas. Not until seventeen years after his death did she venture to write a novel based on her own, wholly feminine, pre-occupations. A third device was to write novels only when not fully occupied by other work, and to lay them aside gladly when so directed by her father. But the greatest assistance in winning him round arose from his own ingenuity, ready invention and wide-ranging interests, for he became intrigued by the mechanics of plot-making and the components of storytelling. 'My father always says "Story! story! give me story! All works of fiction that last *must* have a good story."' Thus Maria had the satisfaction of working, as she thought, for the greater glory of his reputation, by promulgating his ideas; and at the same time of stimulating him to a continual response (which varied in degree from novel to novel but was never altogether withheld).

Richard's previous efforts to make Maria fulfil what he and every other person regarded as her female destiny had been unavailing, but he was about to have one last try. In January 1802 she celebrated her thirty-fourth birthday. Professionally she had achieved more than most women of her time, but in her private life she had failed in the common duty of every woman, the duty to attract an eligible proposal of marriage. Few prospective husbands were to be found in the Irish countryside; of the marriages that were made by Edgeworth daughters, none was to a man met in Ireland. Richard, deeply content with the services rendered him by his new wife, began to fret about getting some of the superfluous females off his hands. He decided to take the family abroad, frankly confessing that part of his purpose was to find husbands for Maria and for the eighteen-year-old Charlotte (the next eldest unmarried sister, Bessy, having succumbed the year before to the family complaint, tuberculosis).

Like so many other British travellers, the Edgeworths were encouraged by the Peace of Amiens to make Paris their destination. They had not been there two months when Richard's matrimonial scheme on Maria's behalf seemed, incredibly enough, about to be crowned with success. On 3 December Maria was alone in their lodgings, writing a letter to Sophy's mother, when, 'Here, my dear aunt, I was interrupted in a manner that will surprise you almost as much as it surprised me, by the coming in of Monsieur Edelcrantz, a Swedish gentleman, whom we have mentioned to you, of superior understanding and mild manners: he came to offer me his hand and heart!! My heart, you may suppose, cannot return his attachment, for I have seen but little of him, and have not had time to have formed any judgement, except that I think nothing could tempt me to leave my own dear friends and my own country to live in Sweden.'

Abraham Edelcrantz was a forty-six-year-old bachelor who had been commissioned by his king to travel through Europe looking for inventions that could be adapted for use in Sweden. Richard Lovell Edgeworth had struck up a swift friendship with him, for although the personalities of the two men could not have been more different – the Swede was reserved and unemotional – their tastes and interests were very similar. Now, exulting over the miraculous fulfilment of his plan, brushing aside all possible disadvantages in the one sure advantage of a husband at last for Maria, he warmly supported Edelcrantz's suit.

Her father's warmth, haste and carelessness were deeply hurtful to Maria. She found she was much less necessary to him than she had supposed. It astonished and distressed her that he appeared to entertain neither qualms about whether she could be happy married to a stranger and living in a land whose customs and language were unknown to her, nor regrets that if she accepted the proposal father and daughter would hardly ever see one another again. Later she called this episode 'the only subject on which we materially differed'. For five days he attempted to coerce her into an engagement.

Maria was aware that her admirer could not possibly know her well enough to feel for her that steady devotion which might have tempted her to face all the other drawbacks to the match. In an effort to soften or justify her refusal, or perhaps to test him, she told him of her extreme devotion to her father. 'He says he could never be contented to be loved next to a father,' she reported with satisfaction.

Nevertheless, staunch as was her resolve, Maria was shaken out of the equilibrium she had so painfully achieved during the past twenty years, thrown back to the turmoils of adolescence. Edelcrantz was the first man who told her he loved her and wanted to marry her; he was also likely to be the last. For someone of such tender feelings as Maria, perhaps for any woman, the subject could not be contemplated without emotion. The remainder of the holiday in France was spoilt for her. She was tearful or abstracted. And indeed for many years afterwards she was periodically beset by regrets or ponderings on what might have been. The longing for a loving, equal partnership, repressed all her life because its realization seemed so unlikely, was cruelly awakened by the unsatisfactory proposal of Edelcrantz.

Most of the family escaped from France just before the resumption of war which trapped the d'Arblays; but Lovell, who had been travelling alone, was also a victim, and he was interned for eleven useless, bitter, wasted years, which did nothing to help his already frail personality. In Ireland the renewal of the invasion scare induced the government to take Richard's telegraph more seriously, and he and his brother-in-law Francis Beaufort spent many months supervising the construction of a chain of telegraph stations from Dublin to Galway. It was his swan-song, in the realms of both science and public life. During his absence Maria settled down to write *Leonora*.

In April 1805 Richard suffered an attack of acute intestinal pain which set all Maria's terrors alight. 'Where should I be without my father? I should sink into that nothing from which he has raised me,' she wrote, though she was thirty-seven years old and an established author, hardly 'nothing'. She was still prepared to let him direct her career. 'I am now laying myself out for wisdom, for my father has excited my ambition to write a *useful* essay upon professional education,' she told Sophy in February. 'I have been so touched by his reason or his eloquence or his kindness or all together, that I have thrown aside all thoughts of pretty stories, and put myself into a course of solid reading.'

Professional Education, on the subject of training boys for the professions, took Maria three years to research and write, three years in which she denied herself the pleasure of writing fiction. Despite all this hard work on her part, only her father's name appeared on the title page, presumably because a man's name carried more authority on that subject. Self-deprecatingly Maria wrote, 'I am well repaid for all the labour it has cost me by seeing that my father is pleased with it and thinks it a proof of affection and gratitude – I cannot help however looking forward to its publication and fate with an anxiety and apprehension that I never felt before in the same degree – for consider my father's credit is entirely at stake! and do you not tremble for me, even when you read the heads of the chapters and consider of how much importance the subjects are and how totally foreign to my habits of thinking and writing.'

In a happy development Maria made double use of the 'careers' material she had so arduously researched, by incorporating some of it into her most ambitious novel, *Patronage*, which appeared in 1814 and whose characters were based on her father's old inventions, the Freeman family. Following the publication of three volumes of her *Tales of Fashionable Life* in 1809 and a further three volumes (containing the popular Irish story *The Absentee*) in 1812, *Patronage* thoroughly secured her reputation as a serious novelist. She was truly the 'celebrated author' that an 1810 visitor to Edgeworthstown, the Irish Solicitor General, Charles Kendal Bushe, found her. 'No pretensions, not a bit of blue stocking to be discovered,' he added, intending praise. As for her father, Bushe wrote perceptively, 'He talks a great deal and very pleasantly and loves to exhibit and perhaps obtrude what he would be so justifiably vain of (his daughter and her works) if you did not trace that pride to his predominant egotism, and see that he admires her because she is *his* child, and her works because they are *his* grandchildren.' Maria, he observed with equal acuteness, 'seems to have studied her father's foibles for two purposes, to avoid them and never to appear to see them'.[11]

Irritation with Richard Lovell Edgeworth was becoming the standard response. When, in the spring of 1813, the Edgeworths passed six weeks in London, Maria was fêted and lionized, but her father was tolerated only for her sake and was generally considered a tiresome old bore. Byron recalled, 'he was not much admired in London' and described how he 'bounced about, and talked loud and long'. Byron found Maria shy and unassuming: 'Her conversation was as quiet as herself. One would never have guessed she could write *her name*; whereas her father talked, *not* as if he could write nothing else, but as if nothing else was worth writing.'[12] And one of Walter Scott's correspondents, J. B. S. Morritt, sent him a picture that would have horrified Maria: 'Much as I should have liked to become acquainted with her the thing was impossible without taking her Papa into the bargain. Now of all the brood of philosophers I have yet seen, there is hardly one whom it seems more impossible to tolerate. There is a degree of Irish impudence superadded to philosophical and literary conceit, and a loquacity that prevents anyone being heard but itself which I never met in any creature to the same degree. He fairly talked down and vanquished all but the stoutest lion-fanciers of the blue-stocking.'[13]

The conviction which was to gather force in the literary world that all that was amusing and lighthearted in Maria's novels was attributable to herself, and all that was dull and tedious to her father, originated in that visit to London and in observation of their contrasting personalities. The following year John Ward, reviewer with the *Quarterly*, having just read Jane Austen's newly published *Mansfield Park*, wrote in a letter: 'She has not so much fine humour as your friend Miss Edgeworth, but she is more skilful in contriving a story, she has a great deal more feeling, and she never plagues you with any chemistry, mechanics, or political economy, which are all excellent things in their way, but vile, cold-hearted trash in a novel, and I piously hope, all of old Edgeworth's putting in. . . . By the bye, I heard some time ago that the wretch was ill. Heaven grant that he may soon pop off.'[14]

From 1814 Richard did indeed begin to lose the remarkable physical vigour for which he had always been known (his last, twenty-second child, Michael Pakenham Edgeworth, was born in 1812) and to suffer from a recurrence of abdominal pain. In 1815 Maria wrote that she found it hard to give her mind to any subject but her father's health. But he had expressed 'a strong desire that I should break from my state of idleness – and he cannot wish long in vain for anything in my power to do'. During the next two years she produced two novellas, *Harrington* and *Ormond*, published together in three volumes in June 1817. She made sure that her father, whose mind remained active to the end, was closely involved in the plotting and writing of these tales. He was also working on his own Memoirs. On 12 June 1817 he dictated to Maria a letter to his publisher informing him that he had written 480 pages of the Memoirs, which he entrusted Maria to complete. The following day he died, having assured her that 'no daughter since the creation of the world had ever given a father more pleasure'.

To Maria it was the end of 'the most delightful literary partnership of thought and affection that ever existed'. She could not find distraction for her grief in work, because writing – even reading – novels reminded her of her father too painfully. She especially doubted her own ability to write creatively again now that 'the all-powerful motive which brought out powers of which I was unconscious' was gone.

The awesome responsibility of presenting her father to the world by her revision and completion of the Memoirs hung over her head, and it was many months before she could settle to the task. The book did not appear until 1820. As the date of publication approached, she felt a 'terror' of seeing 'all that I hold most dear and sacred exposed to the public'. However, 'I *know* that I have done my very best – that I have done my duty without shrinking from any personal consideration and I firmly believe that if my dear father could see the whole he would be satisfied.'

He might well have been surprised, since in the excess of her filial piety she had revised what he had written far more thoroughly than he had intended, putting a favourable construction on everything possible. The book was not well received. The *London Magazine* wrote: 'We persist in thinking Mr Edgeworth's life a tiresome, vain, inglorious book . . . and his own account of his own jokes, who can bear it? His daughter may be pardoned her affectionate praise of him; but the public is not his daughter. He eulogises himself deplorably; and really, if we may judge from his own account, upon very slender grounds.' The *Quarterly Review* was also offensive, calling Maria's part in the work 'too rhetorically panegyrical – too pompous about trifles – somewhat too querulous – and as little amusing as the nature of memoir writing would permit her to be'.

Having completed her father's Memoirs, she devoted herself to completing his scheme for children's books. She wrote several more volumes in the *Early Lessons* series, and the four-volume *Harry and Lucy Concluded*, a scientific textbook requiring great application on her part. The characters Harry and Lucy, with their questioning minds, had been the creation of Richard Lovell and Honora half a century earlier and possessed deep significance for Maria, as the title she chose implies. 'I never could be easy writing anything for my own amusement until I have done this, which I knew my father wished to have finished,' she told her aunt in 1822.

She had two further reasons for hesitating to embark on a new work of adult fiction. It was at the early stages of an idea that she particularly felt the lack of her father's encouragement and reassurance. Despite her age, experience and achievements, she had little confidence in her own judgement. Somewhat pathetically, she attempted to cajole Walter Scott into providing the guidance she craved. 'I want you to tell me whether you think a subject promising which I am turning in my head for another popular or fashionable tale,' she wrote to him in October 1824. 'Throw me a few hints out of your abundance – above all hinder me from setting off on a wrong road if you think it would lead to nothing – I have lost him who used to judge for me and give richly.'

Furthermore, since her father's death, articles about her work had increasingly been used as an excuse to abuse Richard Lovell Edgeworth and to deplore his heavy-handed influence on her writing. Maria told Scott that this was the only line of criticism which had the power to hurt her: 'I should reproach myself for having brought it on by publishing again – I should say to myself – why could I not have avoided it by ceasing to write – or by writing only as I have done since 1817 children's books which no reviewer can ever think worth mentioning.' The tactless suggestion by the *North American Review* that year that she write a novel free of Richard Lovell's interference she termed 'a truly American proposal to a daughter to come out and dance a fandango on her father's grave to show him how much better she could do without him than with him'.

Without the reward of her father's attention to strive for, Maria simply had no motive to write powerful enough to combat those pressures and inhibitions. She had, however, other things to occupy her time and give her satisfaction. If her confidence in herself as a writer was shaken by Richard Lovell's death, her confidence in herself as a person unexpectedly blossomed. She, who had always protested that she needed paternal guidance in every aspect of her life, now assumed, equally and amicably with Frances, the role of head of the family. Together they sorted out the complicated financial affairs at Edgeworthstown and ran the estate in an exemplary fashion for the benefit of the heir, the inadequate, weak-willed Lovell.

Most importantly, in her fifties Maria was to enjoy her greatest social triumphs. Made more welcome than when an invitation to her had meant an invitation to her father, freed of his overpowering presence, she began to relax in company and to find her own voice.

In March 1819 Joseph Farrington wrote of Maria in his diary, 'She is now in great request, and passes her time at present in visiting families of distinction. When she was in England with her father three or four years ago, she was much sought for, but it was ascribed to curiosity to see a person much celebrated for her works. She is now invited by those who wish to have the pleasure of her conversation.' Three years later Isaac D'Israeli wrote to Byron, 'The literary comet in our *conversazioni* this season was Maria Edgeworth. . . . In her father's lifetime, when she came up to London, she was like a sealed fountain; but now, being on her own bottom, she pours down like the falls of Niagara.'[15]

The transformation was remarkable. Sydney Smith, wittiest of individuals himself, wrote of her, 'She does not say witty things, but there is such a perfume of wit runs through all her conversations as makes it very brilliant.'[16] A visitor to Edgeworthstown, the American George Ticknor, recorded his impressions: 'What has struck me most today in Miss Edgeworth herself is her uncommon quickness of perception, her fertility of allusion, and the great resources of fact which I can call nothing else but extraordinary vivacity.'[17]

This late unfolding of her personality at last resulted in a renewal of creativity. *Helen* was begun in 1830 and published in 1834, a full seventeen years since the death of her father and the publication of her last adult fiction. In the interval Maria had acquired the confidence to write to please herself.

Helen eschews the 'political economy' and facts beloved of Richard Lovell Edgeworth and concentrates on human relationships. It is considerably less didactic than anything Maria wrote with her father's approbation in mind. Characters in *Helen* possess weaknesses rather than vices and are observed with a more mature sympathy and understanding than Maria had shown herself capable of before. It is a book chiefly about women and women's concerns.

Moreover, having broken away from what her father regarded as important subject matter, Maria took the further bold step of exploring her relationship with him in fiction. Craving the approval of a revered parental figure had been the most powerful emotion within her breast for the greater part of her life; now at length she felt able to make it one of the themes of a novel. Maria actually told acquaintances that the character of Lady Davenant owed much to her memories of her father. By changing the sex of the all-powerful parent, however, she was able to be freer and more objective in her appraisal. Lady Davenant, all nobility and stern integrity, also held powerful echoes of Honora. She was perhaps an amalgam of Honora and the Richard Lovell Edgeworth of Honora's time, before he either mellowed or became ridiculous and while Maria was at her most impressionable and vulnerable age.

Maria had created Edgeworth-figures before, of course, notably Mr Percy in *Patronage* and Mr Percival in *Belinda*, but they had been godlike men, portrayed with unqualified admiration; their role in the plots had been to rescue grateful daughters from the plights their thoughtlessness had led them into. In *Helen* the parent/child relationship was much more subtle and more impartially examined. That Maria intended the effect of parental influence to be central to the understanding of the novel is evident from her reporting the response of an acquaintance: 'I must tell you that she discovered a moral in *Helen* which I certainly wished to impress but which few people except myself and my own particular family have ever noticed . . . that mothers, talented mothers should take care not to make their children afraid of them so as to prevent them from telling the truth and trusting them with their faults and secrets at a time when youth most want another's counsel and assistance. In short the moral of Lady

Davenant's character is that talents should make themselves objects of love not fear.'

Maria may also be acknowledging here – and it is significant that her 'particular family' had noticed her intended moral – the case of Richard Lovell Edgeworth's many other children, who feared rather than loved him. The boys, except Frances's last two children who were young enough to have escaped their father's influence, all turned out badly; the girls left home when they could, with a sigh of relief.

In *Helen*, published when the author was sixty-six, Maria simultaneously resolved the conflicts which had troubled her since her earliest years, and created a novel wholly reliant on her own taste and judgement. It was respectfully and in some places warmly received, but to many Maria Edgeworth was a name from the past, and a new generation of 'silver fork' novelists was more in touch with the fashionable mores of the day.

She was to publish nothing more. Her last fifteen years were spent peaceably at Edgeworthstown, where she died in 1849.

If Maria Edgeworth had not experienced first the neglect and then the gratifying collaboration of her father, she almost certainly would not have become a writer at all, and the history of the novel would not only have lacked one of its important links but might have dwindled or taken a different turn: such is the extraordinary dependence of female talent on male direction, interference, encouragement or inspiration.

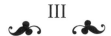

III

Elizabeth Barrett Browning
1806–61

'I have heard the fountain within the rock, and my heart has struggled in towards him through the stones of the rock.'

Of all the fathers known to us from the past, the one whose name is synonymous with tyranny must surely be Edward Moulton-Barrett. Ranks of stern Victorian patriarchs, exacting absolute obedience from their offspring, seem to stretch away behind this prime specimen of the type. It was a type recognized even in their own day. 'One of those tyrannical, arbitrary, puritanical rascals who go sleekly about the world, canting Calvinism abroad and acting despotism at home,' he was described as by a friend of Robert Browning just two months after his elopement with Elizabeth Barrett.[1]

Elizabeth's escape from her father's iron rule, from confinement, chronic invalidism and a climate that was killing her, to a renewal of health and youth and happiness with Browning in the sunshine of Italy, is one of the great love stories of all time. Had the lovers not been two of the most famous poets of their day, their story would still be irresistibly romantic. The fact that they were able to record the progress of their feelings in some of the most eloquent love-letters in the language has made it immortal. And Edward Moulton-Barrett's opposition is an essential ingredient of the plot.

But Elizabeth was both daughter and poet long before she was an actress in this sudden drama. The outward circumstances of her existence, and her rich inner life, were established without reference to what was to come. During all this time, the best part of forty years, her father's powerful influence on her worked for good as well as for bad. He encouraged her precocious talents and paid for the publication of her early poems. He singled her out of his eleven children for special attention and love. That love was to her both a comfort and a burden, but it was the main emotional involvement of her life, and it was a long time before she – reluctantly – came to see it as an imposition and a sham.

It seems fitting that Edward Barrett Moulton-Barrett derived his income, and therefore his ultimate power over his grown-up children (for it was economic dependence which kept most of them in his home), from slavery. He was born in 1785 into the Moulton family, resident holders of sugar plantations in Jamaica since the previous century. He was named for his maternal grandfather, Edward Barrett, owner of neighbouring and even more extensive plantations. With his younger brother, Samuel, he was eventually to inherit both estates, hyphenating the two surnames together.

From his earliest years Edward had reason to distrust the sexual appetites of the male. He watched his mother suffer as his father, a cruel and licentious man, took mistresses among the slaves. Edward's reaction was to exert a rigid control over his own feelings. Thousands of his generation did much the same, creating the repression of the Victorian era from their disgust at the loose living of their forebears. Edward Moulton-Barrett's was merely an extreme case within the general trend.

When he was seven, his mother brought her children to England to be educated, mainly by private tutors. Edward tried Harrow for a few months but was allowed to leave when it was not to his taste; later the same thing happened at Cambridge. Old before his time, he could not tolerate the thoughtless high spirits of his contemporaries. He was already being described as 'difficult, insensitive, self-willed and isolated'.[2]

At nineteen he fell in love with Mary Graham Clarke, the clever, beautiful, gentle daughter of a business associate of his family. His legal guardian at first opposed his marrying at so young an age, but when he came to know Mary, he capitulated, saying only that she was 'far too good' for him.[3] Edward thus early found a proper outlet for his own sexual drive. Their children began to arrive at regular intervals, the first, Elizabeth, named for 'Granny Moulton', being born on 6 March 1806, before her father had attained his majority.

Mary was five years Edward's senior and hardly likely to have held him in fear and awe, at least at first. Her letters to her mother, especially those written in the early years of her marriage, show a serene and happy temperament, well suited to bear with little rubs and deriving much satisfaction from the task of bringing up her family. Yet in after years Elizabeth was to suggest that the milkiness of her mother's nature had been 'turned' by the thunder of her father's. It seems likely that, while Edward passionately loved his wife – and was to miss her unbearably after she was gone – he did from time to time inadvertently hurt her, in the way that an imperious, basically selfish man can hardly fail now and then to hurt a tender-hearted woman whose whole peace of mind is at his mercy.

Mary's letters to Elizabeth herself, while always speaking with due affection of 'dear Papa', do hint at the flaw in his character which was to develop so dramatically when things started to go wrong with his life. He was unable or unwilling to consult even a beloved wife about his plans, whether they were as important as purchasing a property or as trivial as taking a journey. Repeatedly leaving her in the dark as to his intentions, he thus twisted their relationship out of true. Well qualified by her intelligence and thoughtfulness to be a supportive helpmeet, she was denied the exercise of her judgement and forced into a position of childlike subservience. Possibly the immature husband thought that only by such measures could he impose a proper male authority on an older and perhaps wiser wife. At any rate, the pattern was established which was likewise to dominate his relationship with all his children when they grew up.

Early in the marriage Edward demonstrated his determination to go his own way. The couple lived first in a rented house in Durham, where Elizabeth and the next two children were born. Edward, however, longed to be master of his own property – despite the rather precarious state of his finances, which, dependent on so many factors beyond his control, such as the trade in Jamaica, legislation over slavery, mismanagement at a distance, and family disputes, ought to have made him cautious. 'You give a lamentable account of the prospects for next year,' he wrote to his lawyer towards the end of 1807; nevertheless he proceeded to take out loans.[4] Mary, whose family connections were all in the north, had no say in where her new home should be, let alone how much should be paid for it. In the spring of 1809, after months of searching in all parts of England, Edward offered £24,000 for Hope End, an estate of nearly 500 acres on the borders of Herefordshire and Worcestershire. Wearily Mary wrote to her mother, 'I well know that it will be a satisfaction to all parties, when Edward gets happily settled in a place to his wishes.'[5] *His* wishes; hers were not taken into consideration.

The expense did not stop there. The existing Queen Anne house, which had been quite good enough for the previous owner, Edward converted to stables and offices. To accommodate his family, he then set about building not a solid, sober mansion such as became his character and situation in life but an extraordinary, frivolous, flamboyant pile somewhat reminiscent of the Brighton Pavilion. 'We lived in a Turkish house my father built himself,' Elizabeth told Browning, 'crowded with minarets and domes, and crowned with metal spires and crescents.'[6] What much-repressed quirk in Edward's spirit led him to build in the same style as the rake Prince Regent, whose character was the very antithesis of his own?

At Hope End were to be spent Edward Moulton-Barrett's happiest and most creative years. His good humour was totally dependent on his being in absolute control of every aspect of his life. In refashioning Hope End according to his own whims and fancies, and exercising autocratic rule over his domain and the people in it, his nature found deep satisfaction. So much did he crave this power base that he shut his eyes to the shifting sands on which it was built. He invested not only his money, and borrowed money, but his heart in Hope End. 'Even now,' Elizabeth was to write ten years after the family had left it, 'I never say "Hope End" before him. He loved the place so.'[7]

Hope End took six years to complete. Neighbouring families were invited to view the finished effect in 1815 and, as Mary Barrett told her mother, 'most lavish they were of admiration for the house and furniture, which are indeed very *unique* and striking'. (Having offered up their tribute to Edward's creation, the neighbours were seldom invited to invade his domain again.)

Nothing was too good for Hope End. It was decorated not merely with opulence but with extravagance; Mary said the interior reminded her of the Arabian Nights. The balustrades were of brass, the doors of mahogany inlaid with mother-of-pearl, the walls of crimson flock wallpaper or covered with huge paintings of foreign scenes. The effect must have been of brilliance, sparkle and colour – particularly as the central staircase was lit by a huge glass dome – as different as could be from the family's later dreary residence in Wimpole Street.

Edward was no less lavish with his spending out of doors. A subterranean passage led from the house to the grounds, which, besides the deer park, featured ponds, cascades and grottoes, a kiosk, a summer cottage and an ice-house, a great walled kitchen garden and a magnificent hothouse.

It was a self-contained little paradise, where Edward reigned supreme and Elizabeth grew up shielded from all the harsher aspects of life. Her position as eldest in the family suited her perfectly. Intellectually precocious, physically adventurous, bossy and wilful, she was the undisputed leader of her siblings. At the age of three, she was already 'reigning in the nursery and being renowned amongst the servants for self-love and excessive passion', as she later confessed.[8]

There was more than a touch of her father in her. Perhaps that was part of her appeal to him, for in a little girl it seemed to present no rivalry. He began his paternal career with the usual prejudice in favour of sons. When a boy was born one year after Elizabeth, he wrote to the manager of his Jamaican estates that, 'The Negroes ought I think to have a holiday and some money distributed. . . .'[9] No such celebration had attended the arrival of the first-born, a mere daughter! After young Edward, always known as Bro, came Henrietta, and then Mary (who died in infancy). 'Mary has got another girl,' wrote a family friend when this third daughter was born, 'to the great disappointment of everybody.'[10]

Nevertheless, Edward seems to have delighted in his eldest daughter's forwardness and not to have attempted directing her against her will into a more conventional feminine mould. She was never forced to learn to sew, for example, because she hated it; but, most unusually for the time, she was permitted to share the Greek and Latin lessons of Bro. While he was something of a dullard, Elizabeth (whose family nickname was Ba) quickly outstripped him as a classical scholar. Neither Bro nor his father on his behalf appeared to resent this usurpation of masculine supremacy. Far from being made to suffer for her exceptional tastes and talents, Elizabeth was petted, encouraged and admired.

The record of her childhood attainments is impressive. She began reading adult books at the age of four, and by her middle teens was familiar with the Greeks and Romans, Shakespeare, Pope and 'all modern authors who have any claim to superior merit and poetic excellence', as she wrote at the time. She devoured not only poetry, drama and fiction but history, philosophy and metaphysics, this last forming her 'highest delight' when she was twelve. Her father allowed her the free run of his library, except for one shelf where resided such 'immoral' novels as *Tom Jones*.

Writing, which was compulsive with her from the moment she could guide a pen, equally met with his approbation. A poem written when she was six was rewarded by a banknote addressed to 'The Poet Laureate of Hope End'. The title gave her much more pleasure than the 10 shillings. She went on to compose verse tragedies, with equal facility in either French or English, which were acted out in the nursery, to the applause of her admiring parents.

Her mother encouraged her gifts quite as much as her father, and some sort of game was established wherein Mary pretended to be Elizabeth's publisher, and work was submitted to her. Mary was almost certainly of a more intellectual cast of mind than Edward, and it was from her mother that Elizabeth inherited her interest in philosophy and her skill in judging character. Edward's abilities, in any sphere of life, were mediocre; he had never excelled at anything, even managing money. The apogee of his career was, perhaps, when he was twice elected, in 1812 and 1814, as Sheriff of Herefordshire. But he did not really seek public honour or public responsibility; he was happiest as the undisputed ruler of his private little kingdom.

A portrait-painter staying in the house to paint the children gives an interesting glimpse of how Elizabeth appeared to strangers: 'The eldest . . . is a girl of about eleven years old, and possessing an extraordinary genius. She has a command of language and ideas that is quite marvellous and her versification is sufficiently varied and harmonious. She has all the ingenuous simplicity and airy volatility of spirits of the most sprightly of her age and sex. Her brother though by no means deficient has no chance in competition with her. She is idolized by her parents and yet such is the excellence of her disposition that I think she is not in the least danger of being spoilt.'[11]

At that age, Elizabeth herself confessed, her attention was wholly given to 'the ambition of gaining fame. Literature was the star which in future prospect illuminated my future days. . . . I was determined to gain the very pinnacle of excellence.'[12] That recollection was written when she was just fourteen and already sufficiently confident of her destiny to keep a record of her progress towards it. Her father shared, perhaps inspired, her confidence, for that year too he paid for a privately printed edition of an epic poem she had written in the style of Pope's *Iliad*, called *The Battle of Marathon*.

In a man with so many sons – eventually there were eight boys and three surviving girls – this cultivation of a daughter's genius showed an admirable breadth of mind and a courageous disregard for convention which Elizabeth inherited in good measure. The remainder of the children were unremarkable and undefiant. Their father enjoyed playing cricket with them on the lawn, but they made fewer demands on his attention than Elizabeth, with her mixture of brilliance and perversity. He merely laid down the law to them, and they, on the whole, obeyed. (Bro was good-natured but lazy, Henrietta scatty and Arabel meek. Among the younger boys only Charles, known as Stormie, shared his eldest sister's love of classical learning, but he suffered from a nervous stammer and was so embarrassed by it at university that he left before taking his degree, 'much to Papa's vexation'. George, the only son to achieve any worldly success, became a lawyer, unimaginative and self-righteous.)

Whenever a favour was required by the children, it was Elizabeth who was deputed to wheedle round her father. Several notes exist, written at intervals over the years, in which such small favours are asked. From their wording it is apparent that Papa's 'frown' was already a matter of dread but that there was a good chance he would 'smile' on their wishes instead. His character was already enigmatic. He was dictatorial, but he was also playful and affectionate, or they would not have dared to address him by a nickname, 'Puppy'.

While Mary lived to hold the family together, and while the children were too young to wish for liberties they could not have, they seem to have enjoyed a happy and sheltered life. No one contended with Elizabeth for first place in the affections and esteem of family and new acquaintance alike. For Elizabeth wanted to be first in everything – not only in cleverness but in goodness and in being loved. And such were her charms and brilliance that she succeeded. It was not only her parents who favoured her above the others: her 'Granny Moulton' and her uncle, Sam, were to leave her, and only her, substantial sums of money in their wills.

'Much more wild and much more mad than the others,' Elizabeth acknowledged herself. 'I was always of a determined and if thwarted violent disposition.' She later remembered almost with disbelief how she had frequently 'upset all the chairs and tables and thrown the books about the room in a fury'.[13] At the age of eight, through sheer force of character, she contrived to be included in a trip to Paris that her parents had intended to take alone. Neither of them attempted to discipline her. It was left to a long-suffering servant to tell her that people sometimes found her disagreeable. The knowledge astonished her, but she was too intelligent not to examine her conduct in the light of that revelation, and to set herself to remedy her faults.

Her conscience was as highly developed as her other faculties, and her later childhood was a perpetual struggle to subdue her impulsive nature. 'I am now fourteen,' she wrote, 'and . . . my character has not changed – It is still as proud as wilful as impatient of control as impetuous but thanks be to God it is restrained. I have acquired a command of myself which has become so habitual that my disposition appears to my friends to have undergone a revolution. . . . My mind has and ever will be a turmoil of conflicting passions.' At the age of twenty-five, though her self-control now rarely slipped, inwardly, she knew, her mind was unchanged. 'So very exacting and exclusive and eager and headlong – and strong – and so very, very often wrong.'

Elizabeth's strength was physical as well as mental. Despite the many hours spent reading and writing, she was far from being a sedentary child and ran and rode about the country with delight. It was when she was fifteen that she suffered the first attack of her lifelong malady. For several months she was in such pain that her frantic parents hardly left her side. Her case was not understood by her doctors, but the description of her symptoms by one of them is of interest:

It began with a pain in the head, which continued at intervals for seven weeks – the pain then attacked various parts of the body. The suffering is agony – and the paroxysms continue from a quarter of an hour to an hour and upwards . . . there are generally three attacks in the day and none during the night – very considerable debility and consequent nervous irritation, producing smallness and feebleness of the pulse – pain, and weakness in the back, which will not allow her sitting up, without support by pillows, and she is always rendered worse by exercise. . . . The mind has ceased in a great degree to engage in those investigations and pursuits which formerly constituted its greatest delight, and there appears to be a degree of listlessness perceptible to those around her, even where the affections are concerned.[14]

It is thought now that Elizabeth's case was a form of tuberculosis, susceptible to long periods of remission but always present in the background and liable to be brought on by nervous excitement: a real illness, and the one from which she eventually died, but influenced by her subconscious. Was it coincidence that the first attack occurred at a crucial point in her development, at a time when she had suddenly come up against the fact that as a woman her life was going to be unfairly restricted? Just a few months before, thirteen-year-old Bro had gone away to Charterhouse, depriving Elizabeth of the Greek and Latin tutor she had shared with him. 'Alas! our pursuits will no longer be the same!' she wrote at the time. There was to be no school, no university for Elizabeth. The pleasant hours spent doing exactly what she wanted and what she excelled at were coming to an end. She was reaching an age when she might be expected to help her mother, whose own health was failing, with the running of the house and the upbringing of the many little ones. Certainly Elizabeth's symptoms can be read as a punishment or a threat to her doting parents: 'See what happens if I don't get my way!' After several months, during which they hardly left her side, she seemed to recover fully and to resume a normal life, 'bounding' up and down the surrounding hills with her usual vigour, but she had tasted the power of invalidism, which was henceforth to be an option, an escape route, at her disposal.

An undated story by Elizabeth, many details of which relate to her own life, is revealing of her adolescent attitudes: 'Beth was a poet herself – and there was the reigning thought – No woman was ever before such a poet as she would be. As Homer was among men, so would she be among women. . . . Beth was also a warrior. . . . Poor Beth had one misfortune. She was born a woman. Now she despised nearly all the women in the world except Madame de Staël – She could not abide their littlenesses called delicacies, their pretty headaches, and soft mincing voices, their nerves and affectations. . . . One word Beth hated in her soul – and the word was 'feminine'. Beth thanked her gods that she was not and never would be feminine. Beth could run rapidly and leap high. . . .'[15] To find that the pressures to be feminine might be stronger than she could resist was for Elizabeth a rude awakening from the childhood idyll which had been fostered to some extent by an indulgent father careless of the conventions.

His own idyll too was slipping away from him. Bro's departure in 1820 and Elizabeth's illness in 1821 marked the beginning of an increasingly unhappy decade. The property in Jamaica which Edward and Samuel Moulton-Barrett had inherited and from which they drew their income was badly managed in their absence, but worse than that, the Barrett part of the inheritance was disputed by another branch of the family and, after a lengthy legal battle, the case was decided in 1824 in Edward and

Samuel's disfavour. Dependent now on just the Moulton property to support the lifestyles to which they were accustomed, the brothers knew that one of them must go over to Jamaica to try to improve the management of the estate. Both were reluctant, but the wishes of the elder and more autocratic brother prevailed, and it was Samuel Moulton-Barrett who sailed in 1827. (There had a little earlier been a breach between the brothers which Elizabeth had helped to heal; in a letter to her beloved uncle Sam she discreetly but favourably compared the openness of his character with that of her father.) Meanwhile Edward made what economies he could, withdrawing Bro and the next boy, Sam, from Charterhouse in 1826 (thereafter none of the Barretts was to attend school) and spending more of his own time in London handling the family's mercantile affairs.

In 1826 too, Elizabeth formed the first of several relationships with older men, based on a sharing of intellectual interests but emotionally intense because it was her nature to be so, which were to arouse her father's barely concealed jealousy and provoke no small amount of sarcasm in him. He himself could not satisfy her craving for learned conversation; since the dismissal of the tutor, no one at home could meet her at her own level.

Elizabeth had been contributing poetry to magazines since the age of sixteen, and in 1826 her father paid for the publication of her book entitled *An Essay on Mind, and other poems.* It was read and admired by Hugh Stuart Boyd, a writer and classical scholar who lived in a cottage in Malvern, less than five miles from Hope End; he sent Elizabeth his own books and invited her to call. For a whole year Edward Barrett forbade the visit, on the grounds of impropriety; it was the first time Elizabeth's wishes had not been fondly indulged by her father and marked a definite shift in their relationship. Indeed, it was a portent to all his hapless children of what his attitude would be when any of them developed a friendship with a member of the opposite sex.

Elizabeth and Boyd at first contented themselves with corresponding on the literary and classical matters that were dear to them both. Boyd had to rely on his wife or daughter – neither of whom was in the least intellectual – to take down his dictated replies to Elizabeth, for he was blind. He had vast quantities of Greek poetry stored in his head, and many works of scholarship still waiting to be written. His craving for an intelligent amanuensis led him at last to make a pathetic appeal to Elizabeth's father, who grudgingly gave his consent to a visit, provided she was chaperoned by Bro.

Elizabeth now developed what can only be called an infatuation for this blind, pedantic, egoistic married man who was twenty-five years older than she. Her former determination to get her own way was now exerted again in his favour, until her father grew accustomed to the fact that she was forever making her way over to Malvern, with or without a chaperone. Hours and hours of her time were spent working for Boyd, who, fond of her though he must have been, certainly took advantage of her tendency to hero-worship him. Edward Barrett was not pleased (neither was Mrs or Miss Boyd) but the situation had slipped out of his control, and the best he could do was throw minor difficulties in his daughter's way, such as keeping her short of the loose change needed to pass through the turnpike, and never letting her know in advance when the pony trap might be available. These measures only served to increase Elizabeth's determination and to heighten her pleasure in successfully accomplishing a visit. She perhaps gained a false estimate of her power to oppose her father, for on his side defeat in the battle of wills bred greater reserves of determination for use on future occasions.

Elizabeth suffered no shortage of physical stamina when there was a pleasurable end in view. Often she would walk the five hilly miles to Malvern and borrow a donkey to get back. To reach Ruby Cottage on foot necessitated a steep scramble down a bank which led to the Boyds' garden: 'I ran, I slipped, rolled, presto prestissimo, to the bottom. Got into Mr Boyd's room, and got scolded for being out of breath.'[16]

Edward Barrett never deigned to visit the Boyds at Ruby Cottage in all the five years Elizabeth was an intimate there. In 1830 she was permitted to stay at the cottage for 2½ weeks, a rare concession. She recorded that on her return she was met by her father with the remark, ' "So you have condescended to come back at last." And when I told him how happy I had been, the reply was – "I do not doubt *that*. I am only afraid that you will find it impossible to tolerate us, after Mr Boyd." '[17]

Meanwhile, in 1828, during a visit to Cheltenham, occurred the death of Mary Barrett, which reinforced her husband's feeling that everything was going against him. It has been suggested that a measure of remorse and guilt attended Edward's grief at his wife's death. Certainly, if he felt that an inability to control his desires had hastened her decline, for she had endured pregnancy and childbirth twelve times, the last at the age of forty-four, his utter aversion to the idea of marriage for any of his children becomes somewhat easier to comprehend. In the intensity of his self-pity, he shut up her rooms exactly as she had left them, and never mentioned her name in front of the children again. This was the first serious manifestation of the withdrawal that was to bewilder and then alienate the hearts and minds of all his family.

At twenty-two, Elizabeth might have been expected to take over the running of the house and the supervision of the children, of whom the youngest, Octavius, was only four years old. However, she made it quite clear that the only duty she could possibly undertake was teaching the little boys their classics. Her father did not force the issue and was still sufficiently indulgent towards her to refrain from making it a question of duty. Instead, an unmarried sister of Mary Barrett was invited to join the household, that Elizabeth might retain her freedom.

The relationship with Boyd sustained Elizabeth through this difficult period of her father's 'reserve in matters of suffering' and her own reluctance to assume the responsibilities of womanhood, for which she may have suffered in her conscience. She needed to be reassured by her father that she was still the remarkable individual he had encouraged and praised, with a destiny far different from most women's. But he was estranged from her by jealousy and disapproval of Boyd, and in any case was soon to be deeply preoccupied by other troubles.

Financial ruin was hastening towards him. By 1831 he was threatened with foreclosure on Hope End. Knowing that the loss of his home was inevitable, he was yet determined to keep the children in ignorance almost until the time came to pack their things. Elizabeth was twenty-five, Bro nearly twenty-four, but he would neither confide in them any knowledge of the disaster nor consult them about where they were to go. 'In all the bitter bitter preparation for our removal, there was never a word said by any one of us to Papa nor by him to us, in that relation,' Elizabeth afterwards recalled.[18]

It was almost as if, by not speaking about anything unpleasant, Edward could persuade himself it had not happened. It had been the same with the loss of his wife; it was to be the same whenever a potential suitor came into the life of any of his children. He had done his best to ignore the existence of Mr Boyd, and many years later, when he became aware that Robert Browning was calling at his house, he acted as though, by avoiding meeting him himself and by never mentioning him, he effectively annulled the threat which Browning presented.

With respect to the loss of Hope End, this attitude was of course far more productive of anxiety in his children than an open acknowledgement of their difficulties would have been. He probably did not intend it to be so, but supposed he was sparing them distress. 'I dread much the effect on my dear children in tearing them away from all their most happy associations,' he wrote to his brother in Jamaica. Yet to their faces he could make no such affectionate admission. Taken into his confidence, there can be no doubt that they would have supported and reassured him, but he chose to bear the pain alone, believing that he had failed in his duty to promote the material welfare of the family. Later Elizabeth said that his fortitude in leaning on no one during the crisis was one of the things she admired about his character. Yet the children suffered un-necessary anguish from his silence, as they were left to hear from servants that Hope End had been advertised for sale. Even when prospective purchasers came tramping through their rooms, Edward made no communication.

In a journal kept at that time, Elizabeth frequently recorded her estimations as to whether 'Papa' was in 'good spirits' or 'bad spirits' at mealtimes, the nervous response of the children to whichever it happened to be, and their building hopes or indulging fears as appropriate.

The testiness of Edward's temper, as well as the fondness for his children which lay so well concealed underneath, was well illustrated by one seemingly trivial episode recorded in the journal. 'After dinner,' Elizabeth wrote on 17 June, 'Papa unfortunately walked *after* me out of the room . . . the consequence of this was a critique upon my down-at-heel shoes; and the end of that was, my being sent out of the drawing room to put on another pair.' And two days later, 'Sent upstairs again, on account of a hole in my stocking. Shoes and stockings have got me into scrapes lately.' (She was a grown woman of twenty-five!) This was 'the last evening with dearest Papa', as he was about to set off for London – though, of course, confiding nothing in his children as to what he hoped to achieve there. His departure only added to their uncertainties. On 21 June Elizabeth wrote: 'I found a parcel directed by Papa to me. Opened it in a fright. Six pairs of black silk stockings sent by him from Cheltenham, and one line in pencil from him, to say that he intended to sleep there and proceed to London on the next day. My own dear kind Papa! – How very kind to think of me and my pedestals at such a time! – How I ought to love him! – *ought!* – how I *do*!' The profession does not altogether sound convincing.

It was not until 23 August of the following year, 1832, that the Barretts finally left uncertainty, Hope End and the carefree memories of childhood behind them. Without consultation, Edward chose the South Devon resort of Sidmouth for their next home. In her own concerns, Elizabeth was not unhappy in Sidmouth, where the sea, the red cliffs and the rolling green countryside offered her much the same mental breathing-space as the Malverns. A friendship with an impassioned local preacher, George Hunter, helped to put Mr Boyd's part in her life into perspective, but this time she had the gratification of feeling that her admirer (he was another married man) was keener than herself.

Now several of the young Barretts were reaching the stage of romantic attachments, and they did not have the discretion of their elder sister, to fall in love only with unattainable people. Unpleasant scenes arose, as their father began to make it clear that he would never countenance the idea of marriage for any of his children. Elizabeth, full of sympathy, took their side and attempted to intervene on their behalf. She had always been the one to get round their father, but now all her efforts were unavailing. 'I was repulsed too often – made to suffer in the suffering of those by my side

– depressed by petty daily sadnesses and terrors,' she later admitted to Browning. There were 'dreadful scenes' because Henrietta had 'seemed to feel a little' for a man, whom she had given up 'at a word – yet how she was made to suffer', Elizabeth recalled. 'I hear how her knees were made to ring upon the floor, now! I have tried to forget it all – but now I must remember.'

Her sense of being specially loved by and influential with her father, and the respect his conduct through the Hope End crisis had inspired, were thus eroded at Sidmouth. She had struggled to love a difficult man, to appreciate his good qualities, to be a dutiful daughter. Met with unkindness and injustice, she gave up. All the children now began to develop what Elizabeth termed 'the vices of slaves': sullen outward submission to their father, deviousness and deceit in snatching what happiness they could behind his back.

Edward was spending more and more of his time in the City, and in a move to keep his family under his surveillance, as well as to curtail expenses, after three years at Sidmouth he announced that they were to take a house in London. Elizabeth's spirit rebelled, but she had no choice but to follow him to an environment she was persuaded would be detrimental to both her physical and her mental well-being. At twenty-nine she was as much subject to her father's direction as when she had been a little girl. It was not, in her case, a matter of economics. Alone of the eleven children, she was financially independent of her father, a fact which was to be of crucial importance when she fell in love with Browning. 'Granny Moulton', who had died in 1830, had left her namesake stocks and shares which brought her an income of £300 or £400 a year. This was controlled and administered by Edward, but Elizabeth could of course have requested that it be put into her hands, as indeed she was later to do. The sum was quite sufficient for a single woman to live on; it could have supported her sisters, too, in modest comfort. But in 1835 for unmarried daughters with a parent still living to establish their own household was something which was only be to dreamed of – hardly that.

Yet at this stage in her life Elizabeth was still resourceful, determined and boiling with repressed indignation on her own and her siblings' behalf. It brings into question how much she was able to control her physical condition, which was of the utmost usefulness to them all. At Sidmouth she had enjoyed unbroken, robust health. Two years in the fogs and confinement of London, with the strain of eleven adult or adolescent children living constantly under their father's watchful eye, reduced her to an invalid. In the spring of 1838, shortly after the family moved house from Gloucester Place to their final home in Wimpole Street, she burst a blood vessel in her chest. For some time she had been suffering from a persistent cough and general debility. The doctors warned that she might not survive another winter in London and prescribed the sunshine of southern Europe.

Edward refused to let her go. Her health was not so important as to retain her under his control. Once one child was allowed her liberty, others might begin to strain at the leash. Elizabeth did not show her strength, but neither did she submit. She worked deviously. Backed by her doctors, her brothers and sisters and an aunt who lived in Torquay, she wrung from him the compromise of permitting her to return to the mild climate of South Devon, under her aunt's protection.

Escorted by Bro, Henrietta and George, Elizabeth made the journey to Torquay by boat in August 1838. She remained there for three years, while brothers and sisters came and went. Their movements were at the mercy of their father's will, of course, yet it was sweet to snatch these occasional periods of liberty. Torquay was therefore a relief from immediate tyranny, while Edward's real power remained unchallenged. Elizabeth especially delighted to keep Bro with her as much as possible, and he, with no profession and always the adoring younger brother, was happy to dance attendance on her. His disposition was refreshingly different from their father's, 'generous and serene'.

Elizabeth also became attached to the local doctor, another older married man. His sudden death in October 1839 was the first of the griefs, building up in intensity, which were to devastate her at Torquay. Her second brother, Sam, who had been sent out to Jamaica, died there in February 1840. She received the news like 'a bodily blow'. Edward ordered the return to London of Bro. Elizabeth pleaded for his being allowed to stay, and her father sternly replied that, 'Under such circumstances he did not refuse to suspend his purpose, but that he considered it to be *very wrong in me to exact such a thing.*'

At that period in her life, Elizabeth was fully prepared to thwart her father's will in matters great as well as small, if she could. Bro too had fallen in love. 'You have heard of Arabel's and Brosie's separate romances,' Elizabeth wrote to her brother George in June. Edward made it quite clear that, if any of his children married, they would be cut off from allowance and inheritance alike. 'In a storm of emotion and sympathy on my part, which drove clearly against' her father's intentions, Elizabeth tried to make over her own income to Bro. Edward won that battle. But a tragedy was about to happen that for the next five years was completely to alter the balance of Elizabeth's relationship with her father.

On July 11 Bro went out in a small boat with three companions. The sun shone, the sea was smooth, but they never returned. Three weeks later Bro's body was cast ashore.

Of course, Elizabeth blamed herself. Bro would not have been in Torquay but for her selfish insistence. She had been properly punished for pitting her will against her father's. Like many religious people, she refused to see death and suffering as the arbitrary and incomprehensible workings of fate. She must look for God's purpose in everything. The loss of Hope End she had sometimes fancied was retribution for loving Mr Boyd too much. Now, by taking Bro away, God had evidently meant to chastise her for her wilfulness. Poor Bro had had to be sacrificed that Elizabeth might be shown the way to spiritual perfection. In one sense this commonly held interpretation of life's sorrows humbled its upholder, but fundamentally it was more comforting than to accept that disaster struck indiscriminately and without producing ultimate good.

The lesson was that her father knew best and that it was her duty to obey him. He probably drew the same lesson himself. This new coincidence of thought and the mutual desire to preserve what was left of the family after the loss of the two eldest sons did more than draw Elizabeth and Edward together: it made them, until Browning chanced to cross the threshold, all in all to one another.

'My only full contentment can be in doing in his own full pleasure,' Elizabeth assured her friend Mary Russell Mitford. 'You will understand that my poor most beloved Papa's *biases* are sacred to me, and that I would not stir them with a breath.' To her brother George she wrote that, 'All that remains to me of earthly happiness seems to me dependent on my return to Wimpole Street.'

It was fourteen months before she was pronounced fit to travel; but when, after a ten-day journey in a carriage fitted with extra springs and a bed that pulled out 'like a drawer out of a table', she was carried up to her room in Wimpole Street, she was met with nothing but tenderness by her father, a fact which sealed her new feelings of love for him. 'He was generous and forbearing in that hour of bitter trial,' she wrote in defence of her father to Browning, 'and never reproached me as he might have done and as my own soul has not spared – never once said to me then or since, that if it had not been for *me*, the crown of his house would not have fallen. It would have been *cruel*, you think, to reproach me. Perhaps so! – yet the kindness and patience of the desisting from reproach, are positive things all the same.'

Elizabeth believed she had little time left on earth, and no earthly wishes; she had made herself, indeed, 'pure of wishes'. That being so, there was nothing to come between herself and her father; she would submit, and joyously, to anything he decreed. Yet the situation was more subtle than that. The whole history of their relationship, from her adolescence on, was one of struggle for supremacy between two strong wills. At different times Elizabeth used different weapons: now, discarding the crude instruments of stubbornness and rebellion which had proved no match for male power, she adopted a subtler tactic, putting herself so very much in the right that the moral victory was hers.

She could not understand why, after Bro's death, 'an unnatural tenacity to life prevented my following my beloved, quietly, quietly as I thought I would'. Her constitution was more indestructible than she supposed, as events were to prove. So indeed was her will. But she was content to go along with the doctors' advice and immure herself in that famous third-floor bedroom at 50 Wimpole Street, forbidden exercise and air, with only her books, correspondence and poetry for occupation. And, of course, doing nothing, she got weaker and weaker.

There is no evidence to suggest that Edward encouraged her to take to her bed or to remain there, out of possessiveness or a desire to keep her helpless, as some people have thought. On the contrary, the remarks of his on the subject of her illness which survive seem to show a suspicion of *maladie imaginaire.* He was fond of declaring that part of Dr Chambers' job was 'to reconcile foolish women to their follies'. More seriously, 'Papa says sometimes when he comes into this room unexpectedly and convicts me of having dry toast for dinner, and declares angrily that obstinacy and dry toast have brought me to my present condition, . . . that if I *pleased* to have porter and beefsteaks instead, I should be as well as ever I was, in a month!'

Apparently unresented by Elizabeth, Edward's remarks show some discernment. Her only avowed ambition was to be of comfort to her father, to try to make up to him somehow for the loss of 'the crown of his house'. But unconsciously was she punishing him by fading away in his presence, stubbornly fixing herself in Wimpole Street when she might have improved her health elsewhere? In effect she was demonstrating that she would rather die than leave him or incur his displeasure. Her death would then be his responsibility; her devotion could not be faulted. It was she who had engineered the return from Torquay and, for all her vaunted submission, she successfully resisted suggestions that she should winter in Clifton or in Wales. Miss Mitford, who knew what was possible in that household, told another correspondent that Miss Barrett was 'so obstinate as to pretend that there is no difference between the air of Wimpole Street and that of the country'.

Certainly nothing could have been more unhealthy than Elizabeth's chamber, which she never left during the winter and which Arabel shared with her at night. To prevent the draughts which were thought to be so threatening to the invalid, paper was pasted tightly round the crevices of the windows, which were not opened from October to May. Ivy outside and blinds within excluded daylight. A fire was kept burning night and day during the winter months. The oxygen replenished itself only by eluding human vigilance. Dusting and sweeping were forbidden once the room was sealed up for the winter, lest dust in the atmosphere irritate Elizabeth's lungs. It settled on the room's surfaces undisturbed. 'At last we come to walk on a substance like white sand,' Elizabeth told Miss Mitford, 'and if we don't lift our feet gently up and put them gently down, we stir up the sand into a cloud.' She added, 'The spiders have grown tame – and their webs are part of our domestic economy.' Even her spaniel, Flush, was afraid to explore under the bed.

Elizabeth had a personal maid to attend to all her needs. A double door shut out not only the draughts but the life of the rest of the house: its responsibilities and conflicts as well as its pleasures. 'Flush's breathing is my loudest sound, and then the watch's tickings, and then my own heart when it beats too turbulently,' she wrote to Mr Boyd. She took opium to quiet her heart.

Every evening her father would pray at her bedside, 'with one of my hands held in his and nobody besides him and me in the room'. This, for four years, constituted bliss for Elizabeth. 'God knows,' she wrote afterwards, when she was planning her escape, 'that I had as much joy as I imagined myself capable of again, in the sound of his footstep on the stairs, and of his voice when he prayed in this room – my best hope, as I have told him since, being, to die beneath his eyes.'

Elizabeth Barrett at least enjoyed the possession of that essential 'room of one's own' which was denied unnumbered potential women writers through the centuries. Isolation and inactivity were good for her poetry, if not for her emotional and bodily health. In 1844 she published a collection of poems which, building on the reputation she had already established with a previous volume in 1838, now marked her as one of the principal women of letters in the country. In those two collections Elizabeth abandoned pedantic imitation and found her own voice, with a fine disregard for convention, whether in rhyme and metre or in the subjects thought fit for poetic handling. With such poems as 'The Cry of the Children' she displayed the same power to move people, the same humanity, that were loved and admired in the novels of her contemporary, Dickens. Like the best literature always, her poetry was alive to and a little ahead of the thinking of the time. It brought her both popularity and critical acclaim. 'A deep-hearted and highly accomplished woman', *Blackwood's* called her, adding somewhat patronizingly that she possessed 'a wider and profounder range of thought and feeling, than was before felt within the intellectual compass of any of the softer sex'.

The 1844 *Poems* were dedicated to her father: 'You who have shared with me in things bitter and sweet, softening or enhancing them, every day'. She gloried to record in print that her love for him was 'the tenderest and holiest' affection of her life, that life itself having been 'sustained and comforted by you as well as given'. She ended the dedication by approaching as close as she could to the total submission of infancy: 'Somewhat more faint-hearted than I used to be, it is my fancy thus to seem to return to a visible personal dependence on you, as if indeed I were a child again.'

It is ironic that it was the publication of the 1844 *Poems* which, by bringing Elizabeth the correspondence, the visits and the growing love of Robert Browning, released her from this emotional thrall to her father. Browning's love was generous, just, mature, unselfish and conducted on terms of perfect equality. It opened Elizabeth's eyes to the degrading nature of the 'love' that existed between her father and herself. At the same time, of course, it plunged her into the necessity, sooner or later, of openly defying him on a point wherein he was accustomed to exercise his will with a degree of autocracy exceptional even for him.

Ever since she had reconstructed her relationship with her father following the death of Bro, one factor had been particularly important in securing for Elizabeth a special place in his esteem. 'Once I heard of his saying of me that I was "the purest woman he ever knew," – which made me smile at the moment, or laugh I believe, outright, because I understood perfectly what he meant by *that* – viz – that I had not troubled him with the iniquity of love-affairs, or any impropriety of seeming to think about being married.'

Why Edward should have been so set against any of his children's marrying is perhaps the most unfathomable aspect of his complex personality. Many Victorian men abhorred licentiousness in their children, but Edward almost encouraged it (in his sons, at least) by denying them a respectable sexual life. To wish to preserve the virginity of daughters is perhaps comprehensible; to hope to preserve that of sons quite mad. This 'peculiar wrongness', as Elizabeth called it, was the most cruel and irrational aspect of her father's behaviour; 'one laughs at it,' she wrote truly, 'till the turn comes for crying'.

Most of the children had had their turn, but Elizabeth, though suffering with them, had not for a moment imagined that this was an area likely to cause conflict between her father and herself. Even when she had been young, healthy and beautiful, 'of a slight, delicate figure, with a shower of dark curls falling on either side of a most expressive face, tender eyes, richly fringed by dark eyelashes, a smile like a sunbeam and such a look of youthfulness' (as Miss Mitford described her at thirty), she had neither desired nor expected to marry. In her childhood she had heard two married women (one her mother perhaps?) agreeing that 'the most painful part of marriage is the first year, when the lover changes into the husband by slow degrees'. At twenty-five she dreamt she was married, and woke up to the immense relief of finding herself single. Cynically, she regarded most marriages as 'the growth of power on one side and the struggle against it, by means legal and illegal, on the other'. She was much too clear-sighted to take all her views from her own family; she must have seen tyrannical husbands all around her. 'I understand perfectly, how as soon as ever a common man is sure of a woman's affections, he takes up the tone of right and might . . .'

Believing herself, then, personally immune to romance, and with her restored sense of holding first place in her father's affections, Elizabeth, while continuing to sympathize deeply with her brothers and sisters in their trials, had from the time of Bro's death gradually arrived at a position in which she was apt to humour her father's foibles. 'My dear naughty Papa', she called him in 1843 when describing to Miss Mitford some social transgression on his part, adding comfortably, 'We never any of us can "reason high" with him, as Adam did with the angel Gabriel, in relation to anything done or undone – he is master as he ought to be!'

This attitude was plainly ridiculous in an intelligent woman, and it could not withstand the breath of fresh air which Robert brought into the Wimpole Street chamber. He first wrote to Elizabeth in January 1845 and first visited her that May. From this time Elizabeth began to take a more critical view of her father. In July a party of her brothers and sisters spent the day at White-Knights, Miss Mitford's country cottage; this innocent expedition had to be kept secret from Edward, though one cannot imagine why he should object – and Miss Mitford hinted to Elizabeth that he was too strict with his children. Elizabeth seemed to find relief in replying honestly:

> Yes – there is an excess of strictness. Too much is found objectionable. And the result is that everything that *can* be done in an aside, *is* done. . . . Dear Papa's wishes would be consulted more tenderly, if his commands were less straight and absolute. We are all dealt with alike, you know – and *I* do not pretend to more virtue than my peers. Nevertheless I could not, I think, have let that pleasure pay for the pain – the anxiety and fear – of the day at White-Knights, as they did: and as it was, I was in a complete terror the whole hours of their absence, I do admit to you, and in agony, when our grand Signor's step sounded on the stair just ten minutes before Arabel appeared in my room.

If a picnic could cause such anxiety and fear, how much more the knowledge that Robert was courting her under her father's roof! In all the sixteen months during which he was a regular visitor to Wimpole Street, father and suitor never met. Edward was in the City during the daytime, and Robert had always left by his return – except for one memorable occasion when a thunderstorm detained him, and the two men were together in the house (albeit on different levels of it) for an hour. Edward disliked being introduced to any of his children's friends, preferring to ignore their existence and to convey his disapprobation thereby. Robert, accustomed to the common civilities of life, was astonished that Elizabeth's father did not take the trouble of being introduced and of offering a few words of gratitude for his visiting and amusing his invalid daughter!

In the letters which the lovers exchanged almost daily between visits, Elizabeth now began to explore her feelings for her father, explaining and justifying him to Robert – and to herself – where she could, and preparing Robert for the opposition which at first he could hardly believe they would encounter – or that manly openness on his part would not overcome. She first wrote on the subject on 25 August 1845:

> Every now and then there must of course be a crossing and a vexation –. but in one's mere pleasures and fantasies, one would rather be crossed and vexed a little than vex a person one loves; and it is possible to get used to the harness and run easily in it at last; and there is a side-world to hide one's thoughts in – and the word 'literature' has, with me, covered a good deal of liberty as you must see: real liberty which is never enquired into – and it has happened throughout my life by an accident (as far as anything is accident) that my own sense of right and happiness on any important point of overt action, has never run contrariwise to the way of obedience required of me; while in things not exactly *overt*, I and all of us are apt to act sometimes up to the limit of our means of acting, with shut doors and windows, and no waiting for cognisance or permission. Ah! – and the last is the worst of it all perhaps! to be forced into concealments from the heart naturally nearest to us; and forced away from the natural source of counsel and strength! – and then, the disengenuousness – the cowardice – the 'vices of slaves'! – and everyone you see, all my brothers, constrained *bodily* into submission – apparent submission at least – by that worst and most dishonouring of necessities, the necessity of *living*, every one of them all, except myself, do you see?
>
> But what you do *not* see, what you *cannot* see, is the deep tender affection behind and below all those patriarchal ideas of governing grown up children 'in the way they *must* go!' and there never was (under the strata) a truer affection in a father's heart – no, nor a worthier heart in itself – a heart loyaller and purer, and more compelling to gratitude and reverence, than his, as I see it! The evil is in the system – and he simply takes it to be his duty to rule, and to make happy according to his own views of the propriety of happiness – he takes it to be his duty to rule like the Kings of Christendom, by divine right. But he loves us through and through it – and *I*, for one, love *him*!

However, circumstances were about to arise which forced on Elizabeth's consciousness the conviction that her father did *not* love her as she
had thought, did not even love her enough to put her health before his own
wishes. With Browning's encouragement and belief in her ability to get
well, the therapeutic influence of his love, and a semi-conscious desire to
make herself fit to be his partner if she could, Elizabeth had walked up and
down stairs, and even out of doors, during the summer. Her doctors
agreed that she had made a remarkable, though still only partial, recovery
and that, to consolidate the effect through the colder months
approaching, it was essential that she winter in Italy. A brother and sister
would accompany her; it was tacitly understood that Browning would
meet her abroad; by September Pisa was being mooted.

Edward could not forbid Elizabeth to go, but he could make his strong
displeasure felt. First he would not discuss the subject; then, when
pressed by Elizabeth to give the word of consent without which she could
not be happy, he withheld it. Pettishly, he accused everyone in the house
of undutifulness and rebellion, Elizabeth not excepted. She told him that,
though she was ready to sacrifice her health to his wishes, she wanted to be
absolutely clear what those wishes were. He refused to walk into this trap.
'I might go my own way, he said – *he* would not speak – *he* would not say
that he was not displeased with me, nor the contrary: I had better do what I
liked: for his part, he washed his hands of me altogether.'

'I feel aggrieved of course and wounded – and whether I go or stay that
feeling must last – I cannot help it,' she told Browning sadly. He replied
with an outburst of sympathy, indignation, astonishment that there could
be any such father living, and with exhortation to 'do your duty to yourself;
that is, to God in the end'. He had already, some time before, proposed
marriage to Elizabeth, and she had silenced him, feeling she would be a
burden to him; now he wrote, 'You are in what I should wonder at as the
veriest slavery – and I who *could* free you from it, I am here scarcely daring
to write. . . . I would marry you now and thus – I would come when you let
me, and go when you bade me. . . .'

The despair into which her father's behaviour had cast her, and the
contrast between his selfishness and Robert's generosity, broke the last
reserves in Elizabeth. 'Henceforward I am yours for everything but to do
you harm,' she replied. 'None, except God and your will, shall interpose
between you and me.' If the chains of ill health could only be broken, she
would not allow other emotional or pseudo-dutiful chains to keep her
from Browning.

Edward now almost ceased to communicate with Elizabeth, sending a
message through George 'that I might go if I pleased, but that going would
be under his heaviest displeasure'. He was evidently terrified that more
than a yearning for Italy was stirring Elizabeth to insurrection. Yet

his wholly inadequate, immature and counterproductive response was silence and withdrawal. He discontinued the evening visits which had once been their most exclusive bond. 'To show the significance of those evening or rather night visits of Papa's – for they came sometimes at eleven, and sometimes at twelve – I will tell you that he used to sit and talk in them, and then *always* kneel and pray with me and for me – which I used of course to feel as a proof of very kind and affectionate sympathy on his part, and which has proportionably pained me in the withdrawing. They were no ordinary visits, you observe, and he could not throw me further from him than by ceasing to pay them – the thing is quite expressively significant.'

In the face of this opposition, and giving as her main reason reluctance to involve her brothers and sisters in more trouble, Elizabeth relinquished the hope of going to Italy. She was not yet quite strong enough, either bodily or mentally, to defy her father absolutely. Nevertheless, her father's despotic conduct over 'the Pisa business', as the lovers came to refer to it, had far-reaching consequences. (But not on Elizabeth's health: luckily the next winter in London was mild.) It brought her to agree to a secret engagement, and it shattered her image of her father. 'The bitterest "fact" of all is,' she told Robert on 14 October, 'that I had believed Papa to have loved me more than he obviously does: but I never regret knowledge – I mean I never would *un*know anything – even were it the taste of apples by the Dead Sea – and this must be accepted like the rest.'

It was a long time before Robert became thoroughly convinced that his suit, if openly acknowledged, would not be acceptable to Elizabeth's father. Elizabeth knew better. 'We should be able to meet never again in this room, nor to have intercourse by letter through the ordinary channel. I mean, that letters of yours, addressed to me here, would infallibly be stopped and destroyed – if not opened. And then, I might be thrown out of the window or its equivalent.' Ten days later she added that her father 'would rather see me dead at his foot than yield the point: and he will say so, and mean it, and persist in the meaning'.

Aware how extreme such a statement must seem, she forced herself in the letter of 27 January 1846 – almost exactly a year since Browning had first written to her – to review the whole of her relationship with her father, attempting to explain it to the man she hoped to marry, and to order it in her own mind.

> I believe, I am certain, that I have loved him better than the rest of his children. I have heard the fountain within the rock, and my heart has struggled in towards him through the stones of the rock, thrust off, dropping off, turning in again and clinging! Knowing what is excellent in him well, loving him as my only parent left, and for himself dearly,

notwithstanding that hardness and the miserable 'system' which made him appear harder still, I have loved him and been proud of him for his high qualities, for his courage and fortitude when he bore up so bravely years ago under the worldly reverses which he yet felt acutely – more than you or I could feel them – but the fortitude was admirable. Then came the trials of love – then, I was repulsed too often – made to suffer in the suffering of those by my side – depressed by petty daily sadnesses and terrors, from which it is possible however for an elastic affection to rise again as past. Yet my friends used to say 'You look broken-spirited' – and it was true.

Then came Bro's death.

God seemed to strike our hearts together by the shock; and I was grateful to him for not saying aloud what I had said to myself in my agony, '*If it had not been for you*'! And comparing my self-reproach to what I imagined his self-reproach must certainly be (for if *I* had loved selfishly, *he* had nøt been kind), I felt as if I could love and forgive him for two (I knowing that serene generous departed spirit, and seeming left to represent it) and I did love him better than all those left to *me* to love in the world here. I proved a little my affection for him, by coming to London at the risk of my life rather than diminish the comfort of his home by keeping a part of his family away from him. And afterwards for long and long he spoke to me kindly and gently, and of me affectionately and with too much praise; and God knows that I had as much joy as I imagined myself capable of again, in the sound of his footsteps on the stairs, and of his voice when he prayed in this room; my best hope, as I have told him since, being, to die beneath his eyes. Love is so much to me naturally – it is, to all women! and it was so much to me to feel sure at last that he loved me – to forget all blame – to pull the weeds up from that last illusion of life: and this, till the Pisa business, which threw me off, far as ever, again – farther than ever. . . .

Robert and Elizabeth formed an agreement to marry secretly at the end of the summer, when she should be at her strongest, and to make their home in Italy. 'Do you know I am glad,' she wrote in April, 'I could almost thank God, that Papa keeps so far from me – that he has given up coming in the evening – I could almost thank God. If he were affectionate, and made me, or *let* me, feel myself necessary to him, how should I bear (even with reason on my side) to prepare to give him pain? So that the Pisa business last year, by sounding the waters, was good in its way – and the pang that came with it to me, was also good. He feels! – he loves me – but it is not to the *trying* degrees of feeling and love – trying to me.' She remained susceptible to the occasional token of kindness on her father's part. One day in May, 'Papa brought me some flowers when he came home – and they went a little to my heart as I took them. . . . If he had let me I should have loved him out of a heart altogether open to him. It is not my fault that he would not let me.' And in July she reported that, 'Twice or three times lately he has said to me "my love" and even "my puss", his old words before he was angry last year – and I quite quailed before them as if they were so many knife-strokes. Anything but his *kindness*, I can bear now.'

She did not have a great deal of it to bear. More typical was this scene in August, following a thunderstorm which had delayed Robert's departure from the house:

> Dearest, he came into the room at about seven, before he went to dinner – I was lying on the sofa and had on a white dressing gown, to get rid of the strings – so oppressive the air was, for all the purifications of lightning. He looked a little as if the thunder had passed into him, and said, 'Has this been your costume since the morning, pray?'
>
> 'Oh no,' I answered, 'Only just now, because of the heat.'
>
> 'Well,' he resumed, with a still graver aspect (so displeased he looked, dearest!) 'it appears, Ba, that *that man* has spent the whole day with you.' To which I replied as quietly as I could, that you had several times meant to go away, but that the rain would not let you, – and there the colloquy ended. Brief enough – but it took my breath away.

What a tone to take with a forty-year-old woman! Did he suspect Browning of courting his daughter? Elizabeth thought not, and that indeed he was always the last to suspect his children of entertaining lovers, implacable though he was when he did find out: 'a curious anomaly' of his nature, she felt. It would be more consistent to suppose that he battened down such suspicions until forced to acknowledge their truth – just as he had with the impending loss of Hope End. If anything is certain about this deep, unhappy man, it is that he was unable to cope with life except on terms laid down by himself. His anger when either people or circumstances thwarted him was the anger of an outraged toddler who has not yet accepted that the world does not bend to his will. And his methods of coping with life had also hardly risen above that of the toddler: sulks and tantrums; silent withdrawal alternating with outbursts of wrath.

In the end the elopement (though Elizabeth shrank from the word) was precipitated by an action of his which was typically dictatorial. 'This night, an edict has gone out,' she wrote hurriedly to Browning on 10 September: the family were to move to the country for a month while the house in

Wimpole Street was cleaned and decorated. From the country, flight would be almost impossible. Browning's response was to go for the licence the next day.

Fourteen, nearly fifteen happy years of marriage lay before Elizabeth Barrett Browning. (Her middle name as well as her maiden name was Barrett, so she remained 'E.B.B.', to her husband's satisfaction. He was surely the least possessive of men.) Those years brought her the pleasures of his devoted companionship, of motherhood, new friends, travel, an increase in strength and health, and fulfilment of her poetic gift. *Sonnets from the Portuguese*, a sequence exploring her love for Browning written during their courtship but not shown to him until some years afterwards; *Aurora Leigh*, a long polemic 'novel' in verse on the subject of the plight of women, and on their right to establish a creative and unconventional life; and *Casa Guidi Windows*, exploring contemporary Italian politics, all brought her much acclaim and proved the remarkable extent of her range. She was even mooted as a possible Poet Laureate in 1850 – a distinction that never has been bestowed upon a woman. Amazingly, perhaps, she survived four miscarriages and a first childbirth three days after her forty-third birthday. Her defiance of her father was certainly supremely justified by the outcome, and never for a moment did she regret it.

Nevertheless, she deeply wished for a reconciliation. Two days before she left Wimpole Street, preparing to write the letter of explanation to her father that was perhaps (she certainly felt so at the time) the hardest thing she ever had to write, she told Robert,

> I will put myself under his feet, to be forgiven a little – enough to be taken up again into his arms. I love him – he is my father – he has good and high qualities after all: he is my father *above* all. . . . Surely I may say to him, too, 'With the exception of this act, I have submitted to the least of your wishes my life long. Set the life against the act, and forgive me, for the sake of the daughter you once loved.' Surely I may say *that*, and then remind him of the long suffering I have suffered – and entreat him to pardon the happiness which has come at last.
>
> And *he* will wish in return, that I had died years ago!

She was right. Edward wrote just once to her, disinheriting her, casting her off from his affections and giving her warning that henceforth she was to him as dead. (The only other two of his children who subsequently married in his lifetime, Henrietta and Alfred, were treated exactly the same.) No reply was made to Elizabeth's many later letters of supplication. Her failure to be reconciled was the one distressing circumstance of her new life. She showed an astonishing lack of pride, even of reason, in her attitude to him after she was married. 'I love him very deeply,' she told Miss Mitford in 1850. 'When I write to him, I lay myself at his feet.'

In the summer of 1851 the Brownings, accompanied by their two-year-old son, named for his father but known as Pen, made their first return visit to England. For part of the time they rented a house near Wimpole Street, that they might visit and be visited by Arabel. The visits *to* Wimpole Street could, of course, be made only while Edward was in the City. On one occasion Elizabeth stayed so late in Arabel's room that she heard her father return home. 'I heard Papa come up stairs, go down again, talk and laugh – I, in a sort of horror of fright and mixed feelings,' she told a friend. 'It made me very sad all evening after, and Robert was not pleased, and called it "imprudent to excess."' On another occasion Edward caught a glimpse of the golden-haired Pen – his only grandchild at that date – laughing with George in the hall. 'Whose child is that, pray?' he asked George. 'Ba's child,' replied George, whereupon Edward turned abruptly away without a word.

Elizabeth was unable to be so close to him without making one last effort. She wrote to him, and so did her husband, a letter 'so generous and conciliatory everywhere, that I could scarcely believe in the probability of its being read in vain', as Robert said. The reply, addressed to Robert only, was of a 'violent and unsparing' nature and enclosed a packet of all the letters Elizabeth had sent in the five years of her marriage, not one of which had even been opened. 'He said he regretted to have been forced to keep them until now, through his ignorance of where he should send them,' wrote Elizabeth. So there's the end.'

Edward Moulton-Barrett died in 1857, unreconciled to his eldest daughter, who survived him by just four years. His influence on the greater part of her life had been extreme – encouraging her talent and her individuality in childhood, when he was proud of her; stifling her spirit in early adulthood, when she threatened to set up her will in rivalry to his; rewarding her with an unhealthy, selfish, demoralizing love when she became suitably quiescent; throwing a fearsome shadow over her courtship and marriage. No action of her life, while she remained in England, was taken without reference to him. It required extraordinary force of character and intellect to remain uncrushed by such a father; Elizabeth possessed them and in the end attained the emotional independence and personal happiness which his 'love' would have denied her. His influence on her poetry, while indirect, was more thoroughly beneficial, for through her determination, in all but one phase of their relationship, to resist injustice and repression, Elizabeth emerged a stronger woman, her human sympathies enlarged: it made of her a better artist than if she had been pampered all her life as the precocious 'Poet Laureate of Hope End'. Which is not to deny the value of that early indulgence and liberty; both that and its reverse were required to make a poet whose wide learning was matched by her capacity to feel. Edward Moulton-Barrett by no means always did the best for his eldest daughter's happiness but, inadvertently, he did the best for Elizabeth Barrett Browning's art.

IV

Charlotte Brontë
1816–55

'When we have but one precious thing left, we think much of it.'

In two generations, the family of Brontë rose from illiteracy and obscurity to the highest levels of literary achievement and renown. Charlotte, Emily and Anne Brontë all built on the foundations laid by their remarkable father. All inherited his questing intellect, his moral fearlessness and his iron self-discipline. But it was only in his daughter Charlotte that Patrick Brontë's burning ambition reappeared. Had it not done so, it is unlikely that any of the sisters would have been heard of.

Charlotte's life began by being a disappointment to her father, a third daughter when he longed for a son. Branwell arrived fourteen months later to steal the limelight. 'My poor father naturally thought more of his *only* son than of his daughters,' Charlotte wrote after her brother's death.[1] There is no discernible resentment in her words. It is one of the ironies of the Brontë story that their father persisted in looking to his son to achieve something glorious, long after it had become apparent that Branwell was incapable of sustained work or of any self-control whatsoever, while all the time he – Patrick – had three genius daughters on his hands. But if it is ironic, it is hardly surprising, still less blameworthy. Patrick Brontë was merely responding realistically to the times. The relative ease with which a man of ability could carve a career for himself, joined to Branwell's extrovert personality and boyhood brilliance, justified the entire family's expectation that it would be he who added lustre to their name.

Nor was Charlotte even especially favoured among the daughters. Maria, the eldest, so extraordinarily clever and companionable, so capable of discussing politics on his own level with Patrick when still a child, occupied that place in his heart, from the death of Mrs Brontë to that of Maria herself four years later at the age of ten. Much later, it was Emily to whom he became especially close, in the undemanding, unpossessive way that befitted her nature, when she remained at Haworth to keep house while her sisters went away as governesses. At this period Patrick taught the physically courageous Emily how to shoot, and she became something of a substitute – and more satisfactory – son. As for Anne, the baby of the family, self-effacing, frail and deceptively gentle, she was to the end 'My *dear* little Anne'.

It was when they had all gone, all save Charlotte, that she and her father had to be everything to each other: to such an extent that he opposed her marrying and clouded her last years with conflict. With an accession in his appreciation of her qualities came an accession in his wish to control and cherish her. Because she lived the longest, because she pushed the hardest, because she experienced all the changes that came with fame and with being sought in marriage, Charlotte's relationship with her father underwent more vicissitudes than that of either of her sisters.

In his old age, Patrick Brontë rather relished his reputation for eccentricity. 'Had I been numbered among the calm, sedate, concentric men of the world,' he wrote, 'I should not have been as I now am, and I should in all probability never have had such children as mine have been.'[2]

He was born in a two-roomed, mud-floored Irish hovel, on St Patrick's day, 1777, the first of the ten children of Hugh Prunty or Brunty, subsistence farmer and owner of just three books. Patrick began his working life in his early teens as a linen-weaver, continuing to educate himself in his off-duty hours; by the time he had reached the age of sixteen, his acquirements were impressive enough to obtain for him the post of teacher at the local Presbyterian church school. While Patrick taught the sons of farmers and shopkeepers, the local minister taught *him*, for he had attracted the patronage of Thomas Tighe, a Cambridge graduate, who gave him classical and theological instruction and allowed him the run of his library. Quite when Patrick conceived the ambition to emulate his cultured friend, to read for a degree at Cambridge and to take holy orders, is unknown, but after nine years of working in the school by day and pursuing his own studies by night, he was ready to set off on his quest for a better life. With just £7 in his pocket, he made his way to Cambridge and was entered at Tighe's old college, St John's, on 1 October 1802.

As a little child, Charlotte must have loved to hear this history of her father. There could be no dreams of Cambridge for her, but still she could draw inspiration and encouragement from his successful struggle against the odds and apply them to her own restricted circumstances. Nearly forty years after her father's great adventure, intensely involved in a plan of her own to better the prospects of herself and her sisters, she wrote, 'Papa will perhaps think it is a wild and ambitious scheme; but who ever rose in the world without ambition? When he left Ireland to go to Cambridge University, he was as ambitious as I am now. I want us all to go on. I know we have talents, and I want them to be turned to account. . . .'

At Cambridge, Patrick's hard work and serious attitude – unusual at a time when the majority of undergraduates were men of easy circumstances out to enjoy themselves – earned him the award of several 'exhibitions', though the value of them all put together was less than £10 a year. He had been entered at St John's as a sizar, the lowliest of the three ranks of undergraduates, which meant that he was entitled to deductions in his expenses in return for a certain amount of domestic service rendered. Through the mediation of a Cambridge clergyman, Henry Martyn, he was also in due course offered financial assistance from the Church Missionary Society's fund, and by no less a person than William Wilberforce. In a letter which illustrates not only the strong impression which Patrick's unusual story made on his contemporaries but his honesty, his complete lack of avarice and his sense of vocation, Martyn wrote to Wilberforce in February 1804:

> I availed myself as soon as possible of your generous offer to Mr Brontë and left it without hesitation to himself to fix the limits of his request. He says that £20 per annm. will enable him to go on with comfort, but that he could do with less. He has twice given me some account of his onset to college, which for its singularity has hardly been equalled I suppose since the days of Bishop Latimer. He left his native Ireland at the age of 22 [*sic*] with seven pounds, having been able to lay by no more after superintending a school some years. He reached Cambridge before that was expended, and then received an unexpected supply of £5 from a distant friend. On this he subsisted some weeks before entering St John's, and has since had no other assistance but what the college afforded. There is reason to hope that he will be an instrument of good to the church, as a desire of usefulness in the ministry seems to have influenced him hitherto in no small degree. . . .[3]

That letter was endorsed by Wilberforce, 'Martyn about Mr Bronte. Henry Thornton and I to allow him £10 each annually.' It will be noticed, incidentally, that Patrick's surname had arrived at a halfway stage of gentrification; the diaeresis was yet to come.

Patrick was to continue to live frugally and to work diligently all his life – an example followed by his daughters but not, disastrously, by his son. By such means, in 1806, he realized his two ambitions: he obtained his degree and was ordained into the Church of England. However poor he might remain, he had achieved the status of gentleman, and his daughters would be born into the educated middle class.

His first curacy was in Essex, where he fell in love with the niece of his landlady, Mary Burder. She returned his affection, and an engagement was entered into, but her relations withheld their consent. Meanwhile a quarrel developed, in which Patrick, hurt no doubt by the suggestion that he was not good enough for Mary, seems to have accused her of standing in the way of his career. As a red-headed Irishman, he possessed a hasty temper, which was usually but not invariably held under rigid control; even in his old age, Charlotte described how the veins in his forehead started up like whipcord when something angered him. The breach with Mary became complete when he moved to a new curacy in Shropshire, but the affair was to have its repercussions fifteen years later.

From Shropshire Patrick progressed to Yorkshire, where he was to hold four successive appointments and to spend the rest of his long life. Though he took his profession extremely seriously, devoting both mental and physical energy to it to an uncommon degree, his ambitions were not solely clerical: they were literary, too. Between 1811 and 1818 he published, at his own expense, four slim volumes, two each of poetry and prose. As can be deduced from their titles, *Cottage Poems*, *The Rural Minstrel*, *The Cottage in the Wood* and *The Maid of Killarney* were aimed at simple people; their purpose was instruction and edification. They display little literary merit; whether Patrick was satisfied with them and ceased to write because he had nothing more to say, or whether he was so *dissatisfied* that he gave up in disgust, can only be conjecture.

What is certain is that his writing years coincided with the happiest, most fulfilled and optimistic years of his personal life. Some people write for therapy, to escape misery or depression in flights of imagination or in sheer, absorbing work. (The quality of the work produced need bear no relation to its therapeutic effect.) Both Anne and Charlotte Brontë come into this category, especially Charlotte, after the death of her sisters; she admitted as much. Their father's case seems to have been the reverse, or at least, if he did take up his pen creatively in the long, lonely years that were to follow his one enchanted decade, he decided that the results were not worth preserving. But it seems more likely that he lost the will to write when sorrows overwhelmed him.

In December 1812 Patrick married Maria Branwell, a well-educated lady twenty-nine years old, from Penzance in Cornwall. The couple made their first home at Hartshead, where their daughter Maria was born late in 1813, to be followed by Elizabeth in February 1815. They then moved to Thornton, a little market town with a lively social life, where they made several friends, notably the Firth family. At Thornton four more children were born in quick succession: Charlotte in April 1816, Patrick Branwell (a son at last!) in June 1817, Emily Jane in July 1818 and Anne in January 1820. One month later, the Archbishop of York signed the order appointing Patrick Brontë perpetual curate of Haworth; the happy Thornton days were almost over, although he did not know yet that he would have reason to repent them. In April, when Mrs Brontë appeared to have recovered from the birth of her sixth child in as many years, the family made the move to the isolated moorland parish which was to play such an important part in their story.

The perpetual curacy – equivalent to incumbency – of Haworth was decidedly promotion for Patrick. It was his for life and carried a stipend of £180 per annum and a good parsonage house. The religious history of the parish was inspiring, for the famous evangelical preacher William Grimshaw had been its incumbent half a century before; his reputation was something to live up to. In 1820 Haworth contained 5,000 parishioners, not only in the village but scattered over the moors in farms and hamlets; this was an exciting challenge to Patrick, for he prided himself on being able to walk forty miles in a day. He was forty-three years of age when he arrived in Haworth, the end of the long, hard road which he had traversed from his humble beginnings in Ireland to his establishment as a respected clergyman, with a parish of his own. Whether his ambition was satisfied with Haworth, it is impossible to tell. For the next forty years he was to devote himself unstintingly to its moral and physical welfare, while his extraordinary family flourished and faded about him.

First to sicken was his wife. Taken dangerously ill in January 1821, she died after seven months of agonizing pain, leaving her grief-stricken husband to the 'innocent yet distressing prattle' of his 'small but sweet' family.

It was Patrick's philosophy that, while affliction sent by God must be borne uncomplainingly, the individual had a duty to strive to alleviate his own suffering. He was an energetic, passionate man, with a need for physical love. Accordingly, during the next two years, he approached no fewer than three young women with a view to marriage. Miss Elizabeth Firth, though she looked on him kindly, was already interested in another clergyman; the sister of the rector of Keighley scorned the 'idea of marrying somebody who has not some fortune, and six children into the bargain'; and his old flame, Mary Burder, was unexpectedly able to take her revenge by refusing him some fifteen years after he had (in her view) jilted her. Three rebuffs were all he could bear; coming on top of the loss of a dearly loved wife, they drove him in on himself; he became self-contained, aloof, stern. Though with his Irish charm he had made friends easily in his youth, he was to make not a single new friend from now on. The effect on his children was unfortunate. Though they were variously, over the years, to find ways into his heart, access was no easy, assured thing.

So Patrick resigned himself to perpetual widowerhood, and his dutiful sister-in-law, Elizabeth Branwell, resigned herself to perpetual exile from the climage and society of Penzance. She had arrived during her sister's illness to supervise the children and the housework and never returned to her much-favoured Cornwall. The rigid habits of both these unfulfilled people became the fixed poles around which the bright stars of the six young children swam.

In his desolation, Patrick derived his chief comfort from the companionship of little Maria, who possessed, he fondly recalled many years later, 'a powerfully intellectual mind'. To Charlotte, too, Maria became now the focus of her love, and of her yearning to be loved. At the age of just 6½ Maria stepped into her mother's shoes, and did so with an astonishing measure of success. It was not that she was motherly in a practical way; her mind was too abstracted and elevated for that, and at school she was often to be accused of untidiness. Elizabeth, the next sister, whom Patrick described as possessing 'good solid sense' – and who answered the question, 'What was the best mode of education for a woman?' 'That which would make her rule her house well' – was more conventionally maternal. But it was Maria who most satisfied the emotional and intellectual cravings of a family who cared little for conventional comforts. The calibre of her mind can be judged from her answer to the question, 'What was the best mode of spending time?': 'By laying it out in preparation for a happy eternity.' Maria must have been nine at the oldest, Elizabeth just eight, when they answered those questions of their father's and 'made a deep and lasting impression' on his memory.[4]

The following year, both were dead. Their short sojourn and disproportionate sufferings at the Clergy Daughters' School at Cowan Bridge have been immortalized by Charlotte in *Jane Eyre*, in which the character of Helen Burns is a portrait of Maria. With his high value for education, judging it to be 'the best, the most intrinsic, and abiding fortune' that any parents could give their children, Patrick must have thought the newly established school, with its subsidized fees, just the thing for his large family of girls, who would have to earn their own living when he was dead. It was a tragic mistake; perhaps Maria and Elizabeth would have died anyway, from consumption, but the privations of Cowan Bridge certainly hastened their decline. Maria was sent home to die in February 1824, Elizabeth in May; on the very day the second victim reached home, and Patrick realized what was happening, he set off to snatch back Charlotte and Emily, saving them, at least.

This second blow, this second removal of his dearest object on earth, further hardened Patrick, and it would be many years before he allowed another daughter to mean as much to him as Maria had. Though now the eldest of the family, Charlotte did not inherit the special confidence which Patrick had reposed in Maria. She was to refer to herself many years later as having been 'the weakest, puniest, least promising of his six children', and certainly all Patrick's expectations were now centred on Branwell. Indeed, when, after Charlotte's death, he tried to 'state some things respecting the development of her intellectual powers' to help Mrs

Gaskell with her biography, he found that, 'a difficulty meets me at the very commencement, since she was from a child, prone to say very little about herself and averse from making any display of what she knew'. Taking her lead from her father, the little girl projected all her 'aspirations and ambitions' on her brother.

Most of Patrick's time was devoted to parish business and study. For all his gifts of intellect, he was no dreamer, and he took a very practical interest in medicine and health, for the benefit not only of his own family but of the parishioners generally. He made extensive notes from his own experience in his copy of Graham's *Domestic Medicine*, in an attempt to record which cures worked and which did not. He was to take a very active part in improving the water-supply at Haworth, in the face of much local opposition and lethargy. He never minded whom he offended, if he thought he was acting for the general good. One of his household rules was that his children must wear only wool or silk, and for good reason: during his first twenty years at Haworth, he wrote, 'I have performed the funeral service over ninety or a hundred children, who were burned to death in consequence of their clothes having taken fire and in every case I have found that the poor sufferers had been clothed in either cotton or linen.'[5] The same fear of fire prevented his having any curtains in Haworth parsonage – shutters kept out the intense cold – until Charlotte, as sole survivor, was allowed her way in the matter, and some very handsome crimson curtains were hung. 'It did not please her father, but it was not forbidden,' her friend Ellen Nussey remembered.[6]

Two other 'eccentricities' of Patrick's which attracted some censure were his habits of eating his dinner alone in his room and of sleeping with a pair of loaded pistols at his side, which had to be discharged the next morning. Neither of these habits did anyone any harm, and his children simply grew up accepting them as part of their father's character. If he had been more conventional, less reliant on his own judgement, they would not have enjoyed the degree of freedom which he allowed them, remark-able in a nineteenth-century clergyman's family. As he explained the matter himself, 'Being in early life thrown on my own resources – and consequently obliged under Providence to depend on my own judgement and exertions, I may not be so ready as some are to be a follower of any man or a worshipper of conventionalities or forms.'[7]

Largely left to their own devices by a busy father, one whose philosophy was that it was character-building for them to be allowed much mental and physical freedom, the children therefore 'formed a little society amongst themselves – with which they seemed contented and happy', he believed. But that his children amused and interested him is evident from the set of questions he posed, of which Maria's and Elizabeth's answers have already been given. (The high moral tone of the household, showing that the children were allowed liberty, not licence, is also apparent from both questions and answers.) Anne, aged four, was asked what a child like her most wanted, and answered, 'Age and experience.' Of Emily, Patrick enquired what to do with Branwell when he was naughty. She replied that he should be reasoned with and then, if still naughty, whipped. Branwell, evidently already naughty beyond control and encouraged to believe himself superior because of his sex, was asked how to tell the difference between the intellects of men and women, and replied: 'By considering the difference between them as to their bodies.' Charlotte's question was what was the best book in the world. 'The Bible.' 'And the next?' 'The book of Nature.' In fact, the very questions show how well Patrick differentiated between the personalities of his still very young children.

This then was the atmosphere of the home in which Charlotte dwelt without interruption or further grief from her eighth to her fifteenth year. Aunt Branwell kept the girls in order and taught them the very necessary art of sewing – they had to make and repair virtually every stitch they wore – but the children seem to have derived little mental stimulation from her. For that they were indebted partly to the Yorkshire servant Tabby, with her fund of local stories, partly, of course, to the thoughts and feelings inspired by the moors themselves. But their greatest debt was undoubtedly to their father: his talk, his library (to which they were allowed free access), the newspapers and periodicals he took, and the toys he gave them – most notably the famous box of twelve wooden soldiers which inspired the creation of two imaginary kingdoms, Angria and Gondal, with their associated plays, stories and poetry, exercising and developing the Brontës' literary talents until they were ripe to embark on the novels of their maturity.

From January 1831 to May 1832 Charlotte enjoyed a second, happier experience of school, from which she emerged richer not only in learning but in friends. With two girls of her own age, Ellen Nussey and Mary Taylor, she commenced a lifelong friendship at Roe Head. In the summer of 1833, Ellen paid her first visit to the parsonage and found Patrick, at fifty-six, already 'venerable with his snow-white hair. . . . His manner and mode of speech always had the tone of high-bred courtesy. He was considered somewhat of an invalid, and always lived in the most abstemious and simple manner.' His habits had a comforting regularity: 'He assembled his household for family worship at eight o'clock; at nine he locked and barred the front door, always giving, as he passed the sitting room door, a kindly admonition to the "children" not to be late; half-way up the stairs he stayed his steps to wind the clock. . . .'

Though during their father's lifetime the Brontë girls were assured of a home and maintenance, his death would deprive them instantly of both.

Patrick had never been completely well, he told an old friend, since he left Thornton and, as Ellen noted, he was already regarded as an invalid, his health often giving genuine cause for alarm. It was essential to be prepared; and the Brontë sisters were never ones to shirk unpleasant facts. And so, after a childhood which, although marred by the tragedy of Cowan Bridge, had been otherwise composed of an almost perfect (for her) blend of liberty and learning, Charlotte was now obliged to face the realities of the world, in which the only way for an educated woman to earn her own living was by teaching in a school or as a private governess. Both had their degradations and their long hours of drudgery. With admirable self-denial she set about bending her proud spirit and her soaring imagination to this necessity.

Besides, there was Branwell to launch on his great career. 'All the household entertained the idea of his becoming an artist, and hoped he would be a distinguished one,' recalled Ellen. Though Patrick had the highest possible regard for a university education, and though Branwell's grasp of the classics was more than adequate to secure one, the fond father allowed the son of many – too many – talents to choose his own path, and it was to be art. Funds were scraped together for Branwell to study in London. Charlotte was prepared to sacrifice years of her own life to help him on. She wrote to Ellen that she had determined to leave home now, 'knowing I should have to take the step sometime . . . and knowing also that papa would have enough to do with his limited income, should Branwell be placed at the Royal Academy'.

In fact, Branwell never presented his letters of introduction, lacking even that much courage; he squandered all the money entrusted to him on drink and returned home within days, claiming he had been robbed. There could be no greater contrast with his father's hard-won and triumphant entrance to Cambridge.

Subsequently Branwell was to set up as a portrait-painter in Bradford; to pester magazines with ill-judged, arrogant offers to write for them; to become a clerk on the new railway system; and to go as a private tutor in the family where Anne was already governess. All these beginnings came to nothing or ended in disaster, not through bad luck but through lack of diligence, through dissipation and drink. While Charlotte grew disillusioned, Patrick was never to fail in tenderness and tolerance towards 'my brilliant and unhappy son'. Only when Branwell had drunk and drugged himself into an early grave could Charlotte, after years of stony-heartedness, match her father's Christian spirit of forgiveness and 'weep . . . for the wreck of talent, the ruin of promise, the untimely dreary extinction of what might have been a burning and shining light'.

While she was enduring her own uncongenial and self-enforced

occupation, her personal ambition, however hard suppressed or subli-
mated to her brother's, did not quite sleep; she could not have supported
life without some vestige of hope, some dream. We get the clearest
impression of her father's longstanding attitude to her literary yearnings
from a letter which she wrote early in 1837, in the extremity of her despair.

Ironically enough, it was her reunion with Branwell, she home for the
Christmas holidays of 1836, he now jauntily recovered from the humiliation of the London episode, which spurred her to write to the poet Robert
Southey, enquiring whether there was any possibility of a woman's
earning a living from writing, and enclosing some of her poetry. At the
same time Branwell wrote to Wordsworth, a letter which so disgusted him
that he never answered it. Charlotte's letter was evidently of an altogether
more prepossessing character and drew a kindly if discouraging response
from Southey:

> The day dreams in which you habitually indulge are likely to produce a
> distempered state of mind; and, in proportion as all the ordinary uses of
> the world seem to you flat and unprofitable, you will be unfitted for
> them without becoming fitted for anything else. Literature cannot be
> the business of a woman's life, and it ought not to be. The more she is
> engaged in her proper duties, the less leisure she will have for it, even as
> an accomplishment and a recreation. To those duties you have not yet
> been called, and when you are you will be less eager for celebrity. You
> will not seek in imagination for excitement, of which the vicissitudes of
> this life, and the anxieties from which you must not hope to be
> exempted, be your state what it may, will bring with them but too
> much. . . .

To this Charlotte, whilst accepting humbly enough the advice
contained therein, felt impelled to reply,

> . . . I am not altogether the idle, dreaming being it [her first letter]
> would seem to denote. My father is a clergyman of limited though
> competent income, and I am the eldest of his children. He expended
> quite as much upon my education as he could afford in justice to the
> rest. I thought it therefore my duty, when I left school, to become a
> governess. In that capacity I find enough to occupy my thoughts all day
> long, and my head and hands too, without having a moment's time for
> one dream of the imagination. In the evenings, I confess, I do think, but
> I never trouble anyone else with my thoughts. I carefully avoid any
> appearance of preoccupation or eccentricity, which might lead those I
> live amongst to suspect the nature of my pursuits. Following my father's
> advice – who from my childhood has counselled me, just in the wise and

friendly tone of your letter – I have endeavoured not only attentively to observe all the duties a woman ought to fulfil, but to feel deeply interested in them. I don't always succeed, for sometimes when I'm teaching or sewing I would rather be reading or writing; but I try to deny myself; and my father's approbation amply rewarded me for the privation.

Once more allow me to thank you with sincere gratitude. I trust I shall never more feel ambitious to see my name in print; if the wish should rise, I'll look at Southey's letter, and suppress it. . . . That letter is consecrated; no one shall ever see it but papa and my brother and sisters. This incident, I suppose, will be renewed no more; if I live to be an old woman, I shall remember it as a bright dream. The signature which you suspected of being fictitious is my real name. . . .

Since Charlotte was incapable of writing anything insincerely, this picture of her father advising her to turn away from literature to her womanly duties, and of his approbation amply rewarding her, is deeply interesting. Patrick seems to have been scrupulous in neither unrealistically encouraging nor cruelly stifling Charlotte's ambition. That she was not made to feel ashamed of her longings is proved by her showing him Southey's letter.

For many years after her receipt of this letter, Charlotte did make no attempt to see her name in print. Her ambition took a more prosaic, realizable turn: first the idea of the three sisters setting up a school of their own, on a loan from 'Aunt'; then, more excitingly, that of herself and Emily going abroad to study languages – to be financed from the same quarter, with the justification of attracting more pupils when they should return and establish the projected school.

Far from regarding this as a 'wild and ambitious scheme', as Charlotte had feared, Patrick appears to have welcomed the opportunity of further education for two of his daughters. In over twenty years he had not stirred from Yorkshire, but in February 1842 he roused himself to escort Charlotte and Emily across the Channel and to see them safely installed in a school in Brussels run by Madame Héger. Then he allowed himself the rare treat of a holiday and of a visit with deep personal significance. He had always been keenly interested in military matters; Charlotte thought that he would really have liked to be a soldier, and Ellen Nussey considered that his temperament would have been well suited to the privations and discomforts of camp life. At Cambridge he had joined the militia, drilling alongside the young Lord Palmerston, and he regarded himself as something of an expert on firearms. He had recently presented a paper advocating a new design of musket to a Select Committee of the General Ordnance; its rejection he had received only a few days before setting off for Belgium. Now he consoled himself by standing on the field of triumph of his and Charlotte's hero, the Duke of Wellington.

Meanwhile Charlotte was embarking on the single most important experience of her life. At first she was deeply contented, for not only did she thrill to find herself living within the stir of a great city, but the piquant status of pupil satisfied a deep craving in her nature. As she explained to Ellen in a letter that May, 'I was twenty-six years old a week or two since, and at this ripe time of life I am a schoolgirl, a complete schoolgirl, and, on the whole, very happy in that capacity. It felt very strange at first to submit to authority instead of exercising it – to obey orders instead of giving them; but I like that state of things. I returned to it with the same avidity that a cow, that has long been kept on dry hay, returns to fresh grass. Don't laugh at my simile. It is natural to me to submit and very unnatural to command.'

This Charlotte felt in a general way. But when the authority to which she had to submit was masculine, with an intelligence equal to or superior to her own, then she was in ecstasy. All her novels were to end with a proud, independent (but usually insignificant-looking) woman voluntarily bending to the will of a beloved 'master'. One of Charlotte's teachers in the Pensionnat Héger was Madame's husband. The fact that he was not conventionally handsome and that he could be fiercely demanding as well as most tenderly patient with his pupils, added to his charm for her. At last Charlotte had met a man as masterful and as worthy of her passionate though pure devotion as those of her adolescent narratives. By November, when she and Emily were called home by the sudden death of Aunt Branwell, she was in love.

She would not have called it by such a name. Monsieur Héger was a married man, and Charlotte a woman of the strictest integrity. She closed her eyes to the dangers, longed only for more of the sweets and single-mindedly arranged for her return to Brussels – this time alone, for Emily saw no point in being any longer away from home. Thanks to Aunt Branwell's legacy, they could think about opening their school. But Charlotte, as one in a trance, would go back.

Afterwards she admitted that she had been punished for doing what she knew to be wrong by the total withdrawal of peace of mind for more than two years. Loneliness and the tangible hostility of Madame embittered her second period in Brussels, but the pain was mostly of unrequited, stifled love and of the murmurings of conscience – one voice forever telling her that her passion was noble and innocent, another that it was unallowable and hopeless. After almost a year she found the energy to tear herself away. 'I think, however long I live, I shall not forget what the parting with M. Héger cost me.'

Work should have been her salvation – but her sense of duty to her father erected an unexpected obstacle on this route back to self-respect.

Every one asks me what I am going to do, now that I am returned home, and every one seems to expect that I should immediately commence a school [she told Ellen in January 1844]. In truth, it is what I should wish to do. I desire it above all things. I have sufficient money for the undertaking, and I hope now sufficient qualifications to give me a fair chance of success; yet I cannot permit myself to enter upon life – to touch the object which now seems within my reach, and which I have so long been straining to attain. You will ask me why. It is on Papa's account; he is now, as you know, getting old, and it grieves me to tell you that he is losing his sight. I have felt for some months that I ought not to be away from him; and I feel now that it would be too selfish to leave him (at least as long as Branwell and Anne are absent) in order to pursue selfish interests of my own. With the help of God I will try to deny myself in this matter, and to wait.

By the summer, however, a way round that obstacle had presented itself to her active imagination. She would establish the school at Haworth parsonage; the scheme met with her father's approval. As she wrote to M. Héger, 'There is nothing I fear so much as idleness, the want of occupation, inactivity, the lethargy of the faculties: when the body is idle the spirit suffers painfully.'

Despite all the sisters' efforts, however, no pupils could be secured, and soon the sorry state of Branwell, home once more in disgrace and drinking himself to death, put an end to Charlotte's scheme for a school at Haworth. The family had reached its lowest ebb. Greater tragedy was yet to befall them, but not greater hopelessness. Their aspirations for Branwell had turned to bitterest shame. The sisters' own plans, reduced to the most modest, most reasonable, most feminine proportions, had yet been thwarted. And to add to their worries and frustrations, Patrick's eyesight had almost failed him. He was suffering from cataract.

Nearly seventy years old and nearly blind, deprived of the prop of a strong-minded son, Patrick made the first movement towards that dependence on Charlotte which was to characterize their remaining years. With her hunger for proof of affection ('I can't help liking anybody who likes me,' she had once written) and her admiration for qualities of endurance, a new love sprang up between father and daughter in that season of affliction. She described the beginnings of it in the last letter she ever wrote to M. Héger, dated 18 November 1845:

My father is well but his sight is almost gone. He can neither read nor write. Yet the doctors advise waiting a few months before attempting an operation. The winter will be a long night for him. He rarely complains;

I admire his patience. If Providence wills the same calamity for me, may He at least vouchsafe me as much patience with which to bear it! It seems to me, Monsieur, that there is nothing more galling in great physical misfortunes than to be compelled to make all those about us share in our sufferings. The ills of the soul one can hide, but those which attack the body and destroy the faculties cannot be concealed. My father allows me now to read to him and write for him; he shows me, too, more confidence than he has ever shown before, and that is a great consolation. . . .

Indeed, this new close relationship was to prove more than present consolation; it was to be the chief source of comfort to both, in the trials to come; and it was to sustain them even through one terrible season of disagreement and estrangement. But those developments were unforeseen as they embarked on what threatened to be a long, harrowing winter but which in fact was an exciting and momentous one.

Shortly after writing her letter of 18 November to M. Héger, Charlotte made a discovery which broke through her debilitating obsession and reawakened all the old dreams of authorship. In December she lighted on some poems of Emily's, realized their worth and by January was plunging optimistically, and against genuine and bitter opposition from Emily, into publication. Charlotte's revived sense of destiny and her conviction that she was doing the right thing by her sisters as well as herself were unassailed by doubt and carried her through every difficulty. Businesslike and overbearing, Charlotte Brontë had masculine reserves to call on at the critical moment, timid and feminine though her demeanour habitually was.

Using some of their aunt's legacy, Charlotte arranged for the publication of a volume of poetry by herself, Emily and Anne, using semi-masculine pseudonyms. In fact, the poems went almost unnoticed, but meanwhile the sisters had confessed to one another that they had each been working on a work of prose. They began the habit of reading aloud to one another what they had written; under this stimulation their first novels were completed, fair copies made and a bundle comprising Emily's *Wuthering Heights*, Anne's *Agnes Grey* and Charlotte's *The Professor* was sent to a publisher in July 1846.

The first of half a dozen rejections was forwarded to Charlotte in Manchester, where she had gone to keep her father company while he was operated on for cataract, leaving Emily and Anne to cope with Branwell's drunken bouts at home. Patrick had been understandably 'most reluctant to try the experiment – could not believe that at his age and with his want of robust strength it would succeed', Charlotte later confessed. 'I was obliged to be very decided in the matter, to act entirely on my own responsibility.' As often happens when old age and infirmity strike, parent and child had reversed their roles.

During the operation and until the outcome was known, the fact that it had been performed on her initiative only added to Charlotte's share of the burden. Patrick had to endure his ordeal without any anaesthetic. 'Papa displayed extraordinary patience and firmness,' Charlotte wrote to Ellen the following day; 'the surgeons seemed surprised. I was in the room all the time, as it was his wish that I should be there; of course, I neither spoke nor moved till the thing was done, and then I felt that the less I said, either to Papa or to the surgeons, the better. Papa is now confined to his bed in a dark room, and is not to be stirred for four days; he is to speak and be spoken to as little as possible. . . .'

In these extraordinary circumstances, rejected by a publisher, deeply anxious about her father, troubled herself by raging toothache, worried about those left at home, and with endless hours of silence to occupy with thought, Charlotte did the best possible thing for her own sanity and her future reputation: she took up a pen and began to write *Jane Eyre*. Whether she had been pondering the theme before or whether it came to her now in sudden inspiration, the book soon had her spellbound. She wrote without stopping for three weeks, as the memories of Cowan Bridge and Maria came flooding back. *Jane Eyre* is that rare thing, a wish-fulfilment novel of the highest literary quality. It was certainly the book Charlotte found easiest to write, and its steady completion during the ensuing winter fortified her against the repeated rejections of the sisters' first manuscripts, as well as against the daily witnessing of Branwell's deterioration.

While Emily contented herself with the observation that Branwell was 'a hopeless being', both Charlotte and Anne spent many hours pondering the difference in education given to the two sexes: girls being over-protected, boys, with no innate superiority of moral fibre, being indulged and encouraged to take their pleasures freely in order 'to make men of them'. That both sisters expressed their conviction of the folly of this treatment – Charlotte in letters, Anne in her second novel, *The Tenant of Wildfell Hall* – indicates that both attributed Branwell's downfall at least partly to his faulty upbringing. In their eyes, it was the one grave mistake for which their father could be held accountable. He was certainly paying for his error in present suffering.

At least Patrick's operation had proved a total success and had fully vindicated Charlotte's decisiveness. Within three months, he was able to take three church services on a Sunday, his curate, Mr Nicholls, who had been so helpful during the crisis, being allowed a little holiday in his native Ireland. And six years later Charlotte was to encourage a friend whose own father was contemplating a similar operation, with the assurance that

Patrick 'has never since, during that time, regretted the step, or a day seldom passes that he does not express gratitude and pleasure at the restoration of that inestimable privilege of vision whose loss he once knew'.[8] Though Charlotte was too modest to say so, some of this gratitude must have been directed towards herself; the dreadful operation had proved yet another circumstance drawing father and eldest daughter together.

Events were quickening in the Brontë history. In June 1847 the publisher T. Newby accepted the novels of Emily and Anne, while rejecting *The Professor* (which was, in fact, never published in its author's lifetime). It must have been a curious sensation for all three sisters to find Charlotte, who had been their leader in every enterprise, thus passed over. In August, however, *Jane Eyre* was submitted to another firm, Smith Elder, was immediately accepted and in fact appeared that October, to overwhelming critical acclaim, before Newby had got round to publishing *Wuthering Heights* and *Agnes Grey*. By the end of 1847, therefore, all three sisters had published their first work of fiction.

They had told their father nothing of the volume of poetry, judging that the risk of some of their small capital to no avail would only have agitated him. With the success of *Jane Eyre*, however, the time for disclosure was ripe. The story of how Charlotte broke the news to him is deservedly famous. Mrs Gaskell recorded the scene twice, once in her biography of Charlotte, but this version, written six years earlier (and on which she based the other) was dashed off in a letter to a friend just the day after hearing it from Charlotte herself:

> She and her sisters . . . used to read to each other when they had written so much – their father never knew a word about it. He had never heard of *Jane Eyre* when, 3 months after its publication, she promised her sisters one day at dinner she would tell him before tea. So she marched into his study with a copy wrapped up and the reviews. She said (I think I can remember the exact words): 'Papa, I've been writing a book.' 'Have you my dear?' and he went on reading. 'But, Papa, I want you to look at it.' 'I can't be troubled to read MS.' 'But it is printed.' 'I hope you have not been involving yourself in any such silly expense.' 'I think I shall gain money by it. May I read you some reviews?' So she read them; and then she asked him if he would read the book. He said she might leave it, and he would see. But he sent them an invitation to tea that night, and towards the end of tea he said, 'Children, Charlotte has been writing a book – and I think it is a better one than I expected.'[9]

The fact that Southey's letter, all those years ago, had been shown to Patrick, proves that Charlotte's early ambitions had been no secret from him; but successive disappointments, and all the other tribulations that had afflicted the family, as well as his age, probably made her deem it wiser to keep their efforts from him unless success should crown them – as it now had. From this quiet beginning, Patrick's pride in his daughters' literary achievements, particularly in Charlotte's, grew to quite considerable proportions and became in time perhaps the chief interest and consolation of his declining years.

To Mrs Gaskell, after Charlotte's death, he gave his own account of how he had come to be in ignorance of his daughters' literary compositions because he had always 'judged it best to throw them on their own responsibility'. His approach was of a piece with that which had allowed his little children so much mental liberty and was certainly better for them than the censorship or censoriousness that some nineteenth-century clergymen would have shown. Few Victorian fathers, one would imagine, would have been content for *Jane Eyre* or *The Tenant of Wildfell Hall*, let alone *Wuthering Heights*, to appear under his daughters' names, unless very much toned down. But Patrick had always taken pride in his independent judgement. His modesty in recognizing that a clergyman of advanced age 'was likely to be too severe a critic for the efforts of buoyant and youthful genius!' was also remarkable in one of his sex.

It was as well that Patrick had the beginnings at least of solid pride in some of his family's achievements to help sustain him through the heartbreak which was about descend on the household. The nightmare of 1824 returned, as consumption claimed three more of his family in rapid succession. 'My son died first,' he told Mrs Gaskell, '– he was a young man of varied and brilliant talents – but these he marr'd by living too freely, which brought on a decline that shortened his days. Nearly in the same year, my daughters Emily Jane and Anne died, of consumption. . . .'

Branwell's death occurred in September 1848. It could not have been wholly unforeseen, but nothing had prepared the survivors for what happened next. Emily, who had always seemed the strongest of the family, took cold at his funeral and never left the house again, though refusing to acknowledge that there was anything wrong, to consult a doctor or even to stay in bed one single day. She died on 19 December, and on Christmas Day Charlotte wrote to her publisher (by then one of her most sympathetic correspondents), 'My father says to me almost hourly, "Charlotte, you must bear up, I shall sink if you fail me"; these words, you can conceive, are a stimulus to nature. The sight, too, of my sister Anne's very still but deep sorrow wakens in me such fear for her that I dare not falter. Somebody *must* cheer the rest.'

Did Patrick regret that he had not *insisted* on Emily's seeing a specialist, or did he put respect for her wishes above all else? The right of freedom of the individual in matters of conscience and religion had always been a principle he espoused. At any rate, he now hastened to call in the Leeds specialist for the ailing Anne; on 5 January, barely two weeks after the death of Emily, Anne was gently told that she had not long to live.

For the next few months, Patrick and Charlotte were united in the one idea of prolonging Anne's life. Unlike Emily, Anne co-operated with them. She had several times, in her capacity as governess, visited the resort of Scarborough, and she longed to see to sea once more. It was a race against time; the endless northern winter had to be endured before the weather was mild enough for such an invalid to travel. Then there was the question of who was to accompany her, Charlotte doubting whether she should leave her father alone in the parsonage. Patrick, however, was resolved to be valiant and unselfish. He knew, as he watched his two daughters and Ellen Nussey set off from Haworth on 24 May, that he would never see Anne again. She died just four days later, having been made happy 'to see both York and its Minster, and Scarborough and its bay once more'. Quiet, self-effacing Anne had perhaps more strength of character even than her sisters, and the circumstances of her death were characteristic. She looked beyond her own plight to the glories of the human spirit and of Nature; she sincerely wished to live, in order that she might do some good in the world, yet, accepting the inevitable, she approached death with dignity and resignation. Charlotte had always under-estimated this sister; had, perhaps, even been jealous of her closeness to Emily.

In the immediate aftermath of Anne's death, the first thoughts of both Patrick and Charlotte were for each other. 'I have buried her here at Scarboro', to save Papa the anguish of the return and a third funeral,' wrote Charlotte, taking all the sorrowful arrangements upon herself. Though longing to have his last remaining child back under his roof, Patrick urged her to remain at the sea and recuperate her health. Anxiety about Charlotte never left him from this period.

It did Charlotte good to try to exert herself for her father's sake, but otherwise he could offer her little to mitigate her loneliness. His very solicitude for her added to her burdens. She was not without alarm for her own health: she caught cold on the coast, and by her return home developed a sore throat, a sore chest, a slight cough and pain between her shoulders, but 'I dare communicate no ailment to Papa; his anxiety harasses me inexpressibly.'

The situation was equally worrying vice versa. 'Papa has not been well lately,' she wrote to Ellen that August. 'I felt very uneasy about him for some days, more wretched than I can tell you. . . . When anything ails Papa, I feel too keenly that he is the *last*, the *only* near and dear relation I have in the world.' As she wrote to her publisher, W. S. Williams,

'Branwell – Emily – Anne are gone like dreams – gone as Maria and Elizabeth went twenty years ago.'

The stimulating intellectual companionship she had enjoyed with her sisters all her life was not to be expected from an old man. Not that his vigorous intellect was failing: as late as 1854, Charlotte was able to write to a young friend, Laetitia Wheelwright, 'His mind is just as strong and active as ever and politics interest him as much as they do *your* papa. The Czar, the war, the alliance between France and England – into all these things he pours himself heart and soul.' But it was not the same as the give and take with her sisters. In politics, she had always taken her lead from her father, read his papers, adopted his heroes.

Besides, he was set in his ways. He did not change his habits now; his time was spent in the study, Charlotte's in the dining-room. In order 'to face the desolation at once', on her return home, 'I left Papa soon and went into the dining-room: I shut the door. . . . The agony that *was to be undergone* and *was not* to be avoided, came on. . . .' Each suffered, each existed, across the passageway from one another.

This physical separation was to strike Mrs Gaskell very much when, as a guest of Charlotte, she visited the parsonage five years later. In a letter to a friend, written shortly after the visit, she exclaimed, 'Mr Brontë lives almost entirely in the room opposite. . . . We dined – she and I together – Mr Brontë having his dinner sent to him in his sitting-room according to his invariable custom (fancy it! and only they two left).'[10]

Charlotte's best resource was writing. *Shirley* had been begun in a period of confidence but had been subjected to many long interruptions while Charlotte's heart and mind were occupied by her dying sisters. Now she took the manuscript up again and consciously attempted, in the character of Shirley, to give the world a portrait of Emily 'as she would have been, had she been placed in health and prosperity'. Few have found the likeness convincing; but Charlotte was strangely satisfied by it.

In *Shirley*, too, appears the only character with whom, even in part, it is possible to identify Patrick Brontë. It is reasonable to look for him somewhere in Charlotte's work. Few great writers have so transparently used real models for their characters as Charlotte Brontë. She herself is in all her books; she also made use of the Hégers, her publisher George Smith and his mother, the whole family of her friend Mary Taylor, little Maria and many others. Charlotte's gift was to be able imaginatively to enter into the life of people whose surface intrigued her, dissecting and analysing them 'like a curious surgeon', as her father was to say of his own habits.

Rarely (it would seem) did she combine two known people into one fictitious character, but in Ellen Nussey's view Mr Helstone is an amalgam of two Yorkshire parsons, one of whom is Mr Brontë. It is a harsh portrait of a father, if so, for Mr Helstone causes deep unhappiness to all the women who have to share his home. While he is invariably gallant and charming to the women he meets, in his heart he despises them, and his contempt eventually manifests itself in his conduct. Had Charlotte detected this paradox in her father? Certainly his 'tone of high-bred courtesy' and 'elaborate old-fashioned compliments' were remarked upon by all female visitors to the parsonage, from Ellen Nussey in the 1830s to Mrs Gaskell in the 1850s.

Patrick contributed something to the plot of *Shirley* also, for its location and period – Yorkshire, just before Charlotte was born – and its scenes of Luddite rioting were inspired by the tales told of that time to the little Brontës by their father, who had first-hand experience of these events. Without the memory of these stirring stories, entering her imagination at an impressionable age, it is doubtful if Charlotte would have found the subject sufficiently romantic to treat.

Dearer to her heart was 'the woman question' which is another theme of the novel. In addition to her twin heroines, Charlotte presents a spectrum of old maids and ill-used wives to illustrate the predicament of women. It was a subject which had always interested her but which in her present circumstances had assumed a prominent place in her thoughts. In a letter to W. S. Williams, who had asked advice about careers for his daughters, she wrote: 'Lonely as I am, how should I be if Providence had never given me courage to adopt a career – perseverance to plead through two long, weary years with publishers till they admitted me? . . . As it is, something like hope and motive sustains me still. I wish all your daughters – I wish every woman in England, had also a hope and a motive. Alas! there are many old maids who have neither.'

Charlotte's attitude to her earnings is interesting. She received an outright payment of £500 for *Shirley* – a sum to be compared with the £20 per annum paid her as a governess. Far from seeing this as a step towards moral independence from her father, as Beatrix Potter was in similar circumstances to do, Charlotte asserted that her greatest pleasure in the money was on her father's account. Thanking her publisher, George Smith, for the 'Bank-Bill', she wrote: 'I assure you I felt rather proud of its amount; I am pleased to be able to earn so much, for Papa will be pleased when I tell him. I should like to take care of this money: it is Papa's great wish that I should realise a small independency. If you could give me a word of advice respecting the wisest and safest manner of investing this £500, I should be very much obliged to you.' And when George Smith offered to invest the sum for her, if she would return the bill endorsed, she accepted gratefully, adding, perhaps under the persuasion that to care too much about money was unladylike, and must therefore be attributed to Patrick: 'The thought of laying a foundation for future independency gives me a certain pleasure, and to my father it gives very great pleasure, but you will understand me when I say that I hope never to allow it to become more than a very subordinate motive for writing: I will not permit it to hurry my pen: if I did both you and the Public would soon tire of me, and certainly I should cease to respect myself.'[11]

The completion of *Shirley* allowed Charlotte, always the slave to conscience, to take a holiday. She travelled to London and Edinburgh, as the guest of George Smith and his family, finishing her journey with a short visit to Ellen Nussey at her home, Brookroyd, where exhaustion caught up with her. Ellen wrote a 'cautiously worded' letter to Patrick, who replied in great alarm, instructing her to 'call in the ablest medical adviser, for the expenses of which I will be answerable'. He added, 'When, once more, she breathes the free exhilarating air of Haworth, it will blow the dust and smoke and impure malaria of London out of her *head and heart.*' In that last phrase lay an ominous hint of future conflict between father and daughter, for, as Charlotte told Ellen when she reached home: 'I found on my arrival that Papa had worked himself up to a sad pitch of excitement and alarm. . . . I have recently found that Papa's great discomposure had its origin in two sources – the vague fear of my being somehow about to be married to somebody – having "received some overtures" as he expressed himself – as well as in apprehension of illness.'

Patrick's pride in the acknowledged genius of his daughter, his delight in the company she was beginning to keep, and the homage that was paid her, though gladdening his old age, were sometimes at war with his fears for her health. Within a month of Charlotte's return to Haworth and despite his recent alarm, Patrick was sending her off on another holiday, his insistence inspired perhaps by snobbery.

Charlotte's submission illustrates the extent to which a Victorian daughter, even one who was famous and financially independent, allowed her movements to be dictated by her father. 'I am going on . . . a journey, whereof the prospect cheers me not at all, to Windermere in Westmorland, to spend a few days with Sir J. K. Shuttleworth. . . . I consented to go with reluctance, chiefly to please Papa, whom a refusal on my part would have much annoyed: but I dislike to leave him.' In fact, the visit was productive of much present and future benefit to Charlotte, for it was at the Shuttleworths' house that she met Mrs Gaskell, fellow-novelist, who was to become her sympathetic friend and biographer.

By the following February Patrick, anxious that his daughter keep her name before the public, was urging her to write another book. 'I think I can pacify such impatience as my dear Father naturally feels,' said Charlotte but she felt an obligation to her publishers. She began *Villette* that summer, but it was not until November 1852 that she 'finished my long task . . . packed and sent off the parcel to Cornhill'. Abandoning his former attitude of non-interference, Patrick took an eager interest in the progress of this book, to the extent of urging Charlotte to give it a happy ending. In deference to his wishes, she swathed the conclusion in ambiguity. She would not, however, compromise her artistic integrity so far as to allow Lucy Snowe her heart's desire. That would not have been truthful to the Brussels experience, of which *Villette* is a valediction.

With *Villette*, Charlotte's literary production was complete. In it she had exorcised not only her love for M. Héger, ten years after the event, but her more recent and calmer – though still powerful – attraction to George Smith (Graham Bretton). (There were to be many readers who objected to this twofold love-interest of Lucy's, as improbable.) Passion and romance washed out of her by the disappointments of real life, Charlotte was, however, not yet finished with the perplexities of courtship, perplexities in which her father's attitude played no small part.

Unlikely as it must have seemed to one who had since the age of fifteen been acutely conscious of her physical unattractiveness and who now had neither youth nor cheerful spirits to recommend her, she was to have two further chances to marry offered to her in her late thirties. In her twenties two young clergymen – one of them Ellen Nussey's brother – had proposed to her, but she had not been tempted for a moment by their unromantic offers. Undoubtedly at that time her father would have let her go willingly enough; the case was different now. She had his wishes to take into consideration as well as her own prospects of happiness, which were difficult enough to calculate as it was. With neither of her suitors did she delude herself that she was in love; but if one of them could offer her companionship, devotion even?

The first to court her was James Taylor, an employee of Smith, Elder. His suit was unpropitious; though they had literary tastes in common and she enjoyed corresponding with him, in his physical proximity her 'veins ran ice'. On the verge of leaving for India for several years on company business, he visited Haworth but was sufficiently sensitive to her reaction not to make the proposal he had undoubtedly come to make. The chief interest of the affair is the response it evoked in Patrick Brontë, especially in comparison with what followed. Charlotte told Ellen:

I discover with some surprise Papa has taken a decided liking to Mr Taylor. The marked kindness of his manner when he bid him good-bye, exorting him to be 'true to himself, his country and his God', and wishing him all good wishes, struck me with some astonishment. Whenever he has alluded to him since, it has been with significant eulogy. When I alluded that he was no gentleman, he seemed out of patience with me for the objection. You say Papa has penetration. On this subject I believe he has indeed. I have told him nothing, yet he seems to be 'au fait' with the whole business. I could think at some moments his guesses go further than mine. I believe he thinks a prospective union, deferred for five years, with such a decorous reliable personage, would be a very proper and advisable affair.

This long-sighted plan is open to two interpretations, one selfish, the other unselfish. Patrick might have calculated that his own need of Charlotte would be over in five years and that then it would be good for her to have a husband; one who would not take her away from him *now* was to be encouraged. Or his calculations might have been based on Charlotte's child-bearing capability. The later her marriage was, the less likelihood of her frail and tiny body having to endure this ordeal, which he was quite convinced she could not survive.

He was nervous that an unknown suitor, less safe than Taylor, was in the offing. Only a month after Taylor's departure, Charlotte went shopping in Leeds for clothes for another London visit. On mulling over the purchase of this finery, Patrick came to the conclusion that, 'I am somehow, by some mysterious process, to be married in London, or to engage myself in matrimony. How I smile internally! How groundless and impossible is the idea! Papa seriously told me yesterday, that if I married and left him, he should give up house-keeping and go into lodgings!'

The danger, when it came, was not from London but from Haworth itself. Patrick's curate, Arthur Bell Nicholls, had served the parish and the family faithfully since the period of Patrick's near-blindness. Until 1852 Charlotte had scarcely given him a second thought, so low was her opinion of curates generally and so stolid and dull did this particular one appear. Then a few 'dim misgivings' about his attitude to her had arisen, and she had observed the 'little sympathy and much indirect sarcasm' with which her father had begun to refer to him. Nicholls' long-pent-up and hardly suspected passion erupted one Monday evening in December that year, when he tapped on her sitting-room door and 'shaking from head to foot, looking deadly pale, speaking low, vehemently yet with difficulty – he made me feel for the first time what it costs a man to declare affection where he doubts response'.

Promising a reply the next day, Charlotte did not reserve for herself the right to consider this strange development in private overnight, as she surely might have done. Thirty-six years old though she was: 'I asked him if he had spoken to Papa. He said, he dared not. I think I half led, half put him out of the room. When he was gone, I immediately went to Papa, and told him what had taken place. Agitation and anger disproportionate to the occasion ensued; if I had *loved* Mr Nicholls and had heard such epithets applied to him as were used, it would have transported me past patience; as it was, my blood boiled with a sense of injustice, but Papa worked himself into a state not to be trifled with, the veins on his temples started up like whipcord, and his eyes became suddenly bloodshot. I made haste to promise that Mr Nicholls should on the morrow have a distinct refusal.'

Patrick's anger, she told Ellen three days later, arose from the idea that Mr Nicholls had been less than honest in so long concealing his intentions – though, judging by the flood of ill feeling they generated when they were announced, it is hard to know how else the poor man could have behaved. Not content with his daughter's obedient but pitying rejection of her suitor, Patrick sent Nicholls 'a most cruel note'. Although Charlotte had her own doubts and objections, she could not sympathize with her father's avowed ones: 'Papa thinks a little too much about his want of money; he says that the match would be a degradation, that I should be throwing myself away, that he expects me, if I marry at all, to do very differently.'

Presumably Victorian prudery prevented Patrick's naming his fear of childbirth to Charlotte; but fear alone could hardly account for the violence of his reaction, and he cannot be acquitted of snobbery. Of selfishness, though, perhaps he can. He seems genuinely to have believed that his curate possessed a dour and sulky temper; writing to Charlotte in London, where she stayed in the new year to see *Villette* through the press, he informed her that in church Nicholls had exhibited 'mortified pride and malevolent resentment' towards him, and that he wished 'every woman may avoid him for ever, unless she should be determined on her own misery – all the produce of the Australian *diggins* would not make him, and any wife he might have, happy'.

In the midst of such hard feeling, Patrick had sufficient sense of humour to attach to this letter a note purporting to come from the dog, Flossy, whom Nicholls had been in the habit of taking for walks:

My kind mistress, as having only paws, I cannot write, but I can dictate and my good master has undertaken to set down what I have to say – he will understand the dog's language, which is not very copious, but is nevertheless significant and quite sufficient for our purposes, and wants. Which are not many – I fear that my master will not do my simple language justice, but will write too much in his own style, which I consider quite out of character, and wrong – you have condescendingly sent your respects to me, for which I am very grateful, and in token of my gratitude, I struck the ground three times with my tail – but let me tell you my affairs, just as they stand at present, in my little world – little in your opinion, but great in mine. Being old now, my youthful amusements have lost their former relish – I can no longer enjoy, as formerly, following sheep, and cats, and birds, and I cannot gnaw bones, as I once did – yet, I am still merry and in good health and spirits

– so many things are done before me, which would not be done if I could speak (well for us dogs that we cannot speak) so, I see a good deal of human nature that is hid from those that have the gift of language. [Here Patrick gets to the point.] One thing I have lately seen, which I wish to mention – no one takes me out to walk now, the weather is too cold, or too wet for my master to walk in, and my former travelling companion [Nicholls] has lost all his apparent kindness, scolds me, and looks black upon me – I tell my master all this, by looking grave, and puzzled, holding up one side of my head, and one lip, showing my teeth then, looking full in his face and whining. Ah! my dear Mistress, trust dogs rather than men – they are very selfish, and when they have the power, (which no wise person will readily give them) very tyrannical – that you should act wisely in regard to men, women and dogs is the sincere wish of yours most sincerely, Old Flossy.

As soon as a replacement could be found for Nicholls, he left Haworth. He took his last service in May and almost broke down in front of Charlotte. When her father got to hear of it, he called Nicholls an 'unmanly driveller'. Patrick was still 'implacable on the matter'.

But Nicholls had perseverence. From his new parish he wrote to Charlotte six times, and at last she replied. Out of pity she was drawn into a correspondence; she began to value the steadfastness of his attachment. In refusing Nicholls, was she throwing away the 'purest gem' life could offer her, an honourable man's devotion? Or was she avoiding being shackled to a bad-tempered husband? She needed more time to judge, but the clandestine correspondence troubled her conscience. 'I grew very miserable in keeping it from Papa. At last, sheer pain made me gather courage to break it – I told all. It was very hard and rough work at the time, but the issue after a few days was that I obtained leave to continue the communication.'

It was at precisely this time of deepest division between father and daughter that Mrs Gaskell paid her visit to the parsonage and gathered those impressions of the relationship which were to colour her *Life of Charlotte Brontë* and consequently the public's view of Patrick. To a friend she wrote at the time: 'He was very polite and agreeable to me; paying rather elaborate old-fashioned compliments, but I was sadly afraid of him in my inmost soul; for I caught a glare of his stern eyes over his spectacles at Miss Brontë once or twice which made me know my man; and he talked at her sometimes. . . . He is very fearless. He won't let Miss Brontë accompany him in his walks; goes out in defiance of her gentle attempts to restrain him, speaking as if she thought him in his second childhood; and comes home moaning and tired, having lost his way. . . . There are little bits of picturesque affection about him – for his old dogs, for instance.'

In the biography, written while Patrick was still alive, she attempted to be both truthful and fair. 'He never seemed quite to have lost the feeling that Charlotte was a child to be guided and ruled, when she was present; and she herself submitted to this with a quiet docility that half amused, half astonished me. But when she had to leave the room, then all his pride in her genius and fame came out.' Elizabeth Gaskell herself had been brought up by aunts, her father abandoning her to their care; her extraordinarily serene personality might be partly owing to the fact that she was never obliged to play the dutiful Victorian daughter. She could hardly understand how difficult it was to throw off the habits of authority on one side, submission on the other, which were inherent in the relationship. Nor could she appreciate the years of undemonstrative affection and mutual support which the present disagreement was interrupting – but not, in the end, capable of destroying.

By the following April, 'What seemed at one time impossible is now arranged.' Charlotte summarized for Ellen: 'I had stipulated with Papa for opportunity to become better acquainted – I had it, and all I learnt inclined me to esteem, and, if not love, at least affection. Still, Papa was very, very hostile – bitterly unjust. I told Mr Nicholls the great obstacles that lay in his way. He has persevered. The result of this, his last visit, is, that Papa's consent is gained – that his respect, I believe, is won, for Mr Nicholls has in all things proved himself disinterested and forbearing. He has shown, too, that while his feelings are exquisitely keen, he can forgive. Certainly I must respect him, nor can I withold from him more than cool respect. In fact, dear Ellen, I am engaged.'

To Mrs Gaskell she confessed, 'I could almost cry sometimes that in this important action in my life I cannot better satisfy Papa's perhaps natural pride.' But to set against this, the ever-dutiful daughter could justify her decision: 'On one feature in the marriage I can dwell with unmingled satisfaction, with a *certainty* of being right. It takes nothing from the attention I owe to my father. I am not to leave him – my future husband consents to come here – thus Papa secures by the step a devoted and reliable assistant in his old age.'

One last, perhaps allowable, crotchet there was, when on the evening before the wedding Patrick announced he could not give Charlotte away. Whether the peevishness of an old man who had been defeated or a more symbolic refusal to hand his only remaining daughter to the man whose love he feared would kill her, the refusal could not prevent the ceremony, as on consulting the Prayer Book it was discovered that a woman could just as well perform the office. Miss Wooler, Charlotte's former teacher and employer, the only guest invited beside Ellen Nussey, diplomatically stepped in.

Charlotte was married in June 1854, eighteen months after Nicholls' first, seemingly hopeless proposal. It was an extraordinary instance of how a man could wear down indifference and opposition to get what he wanted – and even be admired for it. Charlotte may have reflected with some bitterness how unthinkable – nay, impossible – it would be for a woman to pursue her heart's desire thus.

She was not married long enough to outgrow the novelty of being cherished or to find anything irksome in her marriage. She seemed to take pleasure in not having an hour at her own disposal, and her husband's insistence that Ellen give a written pledge to burn all Charlotte's letters or he would forbid them corresponding merely amused her. Her honeymoon in Ireland passed happily, though by the end she found herself 'longing, longing *intensely* sometimes, to be at home' with her father, whose health was giving her concern. To Miss Wooler she wrote on reaching home: 'My dear father was not well when we returned from Ireland. I am, however, most thankful to say that he is better now. May God preserve him to us yet for some years! The wish for his continued life, together with a certain solicitude for his happiness and health, seems, I scarcely know why, even stronger in me now than before I was married.' Father and daughter had emerged from the period of estrangement with their value for one another even enhanced.

Charlotte died the following March, pregnant, having endured four months of suffering and 'sickness with scarce a reprieve'. Her father's fears had indeed been justified. 'I always told you, Martha,' he said to the servant, 'that there was no sense in Charlotte marrying at all, for she was not strong enough for marriage.' He opened his heart to Martha in order to forbear reproaching his son-in-law. The two men continued to live in uneasy truce until Patrick's death six years later; for the sake of Charlotte's memory, Nicholls would not abandon the old man.

Patrick had one more important service to render his beloved daughter. He it was who instigated the biography and chose Mrs Gaskell to write it. Nicholls intensely disliked the publicity, but in this Patrick had his way. His reward was to see no very flattering portrait of himself, but that mattered little to him in comparison with the glory of having for ever preserved and displayed the genius of the remarkable family he had fathered.

In the last year of his life, he was visited – after some hesitation – by Mrs Gaskell and one of her daughters, Meta. They found him confined to bed, spotlessly clean, mentally alert, kindly and mellow, not at all the dragon Meta had been led to expect. 'He said to Mama,' she wrote to a friend the next day, '"As I told you in my first letter, the Memoir is a book which will hand your name down to posterity." . . . He alluded to his own "eccentricity", with a certain pride; and his "independence" – his independence, too, of other people's opinion; not but that he valued the opinion of good people. Mama said "Yes – I was just telling my daughter, as we came up the hill, that I thought you had always done in everything what you thought right." "And so I have," he said, "and I appeal to God." '[12]

The mixture of fierce individuality and strict moral integrity which Patrick Brontë brought to the task of fatherhood, and passed on to his three famous daughters, helped to make them the artists of stature that they were. Charlotte alone had also to contend with interference in her private life, over-dependence and the trials of old age. Deprived perhaps of the tenderest kind of love in her childhood, she yet found, as they both grew older, that her father's love for and need of her became stronger and were supportive and restrictive in about equal measure. His direct influence on her liberty to write, or on what she wrote, was negligible; it was the system she had to fight, not one man. She won through, against all the odds, by her own efforts; he could not help, but he did not hinder, and his pride in her could not have been greater. He was perfectly right when he said that, if he had been more calm and conventional, 'I should in all probability never have had such children as mine have been.'

V

George Eliot
1819–80

*'Where shall I be without my Father? It will seem as if a part of my moral
nature were gone.'*

The person we think of as George Eliot is the novelist of genius,
the progressive intellectual, the respected sage, the woman who had the
bravado and the bravery to defy Victorian convention and to live with the
man she loved. But for a full half of her life she was none of those things,
nor knew that they were in store for her. For thirty years she was Mary
Ann Evans, her father's 'little wench', first shaped and then constrained
by his ideas, a provincial girl bred to practical country methods and the
narrow morality of a class anxious to preserve its respectability. The
contrast could not have been more extreme. As she wrote in her journal,
'Few women, I fear, have had such reasons as I have to think the long sad
years of youth were worth living for the sake of middle age.'[1] Her story is
of the chrysalis/butterfly variety; its especial fascination lies in tracing the
enduring influence of her father's dominant personality upon the
apparently liberated life and work of her maturity.

For Mary Ann Evans by no means wholly rejected his values when she
courageously remade her life after his death. She looked back with
affection and respect to the old ways as well as forward with confidence to
the gradual moral improvement of British society. This ambivalence is
what gives her novels their satisfying subtlety and tension. Like Thomas
Hardy's work, and from much the same causes, hers transcends being
either simply a lament for the past or a polemic for a radical revision of
values. But, as a woman, it took more than merely growing up: it took the
death of her father and keeper to allow her to celebrate what was good,
and to repudiate what was illiberal, in her birthright.

Indeed, if Robert Evans had survived well into his daughter's adulthood, she would probably never have found fulfilment either in work or in
love, let alone become a novelist (for it was her lover who persuaded her to
write fiction). Robert Evans' death not only freed her mentally – she had
already discovered how painful it was to oppose him on a point of
conscience – but freed her physically: from her duties as his housekeeper,
from the necessity of living in the Midlands. Again like Hardy and like

Shakespeare too, she needed the experience of London to put her provincial upbringing into perspective. As young men, they were off as soon as they chose, with no one to gainsay them (not even Shakespeare's wife); Mary Ann had to bide her time, but the delay, in allowing her character to develop all the strength required to support her through her pioneering lifestyle, yet not prolonged until she was too weary and disheartened to move decisively forward, was good for her. For if Robert Evans' death occurred at precisely the right time for Mary Ann's metamorphosis into George Eliot, the thirty years of their living relationship were equally indispensable to her development as a woman and a writer.

On Mary Ann Evans' baptism entry, her father's profession is given as 'farmer'. She herself, however, explained more fully: 'My father did not raise himself from being an artizan to be a farmer; he raised himself from being an artizan to be a man whose extensive knowledge in very varied practical departments made his services valued through several counties. He had large knowledge of building, of mines, of plantations, of various branches of valuation and measurement – of all that is essential to the management of large estates. He was held by those competent to judge as *unique* amongst land-agents for his manifold knowledge and experience, which enabled him to save the special fees usually paid by landowners for special opinions on the different questions incident to the proprietorship of land.'[2]

Besides this knowledge, he possessed great physical strength, a capacity for hard work and, most importantly to his employers, absolute integrity. This latter attribute was one of the few points of resemblance between himself and his youngest daughter, for he was the least introspective, the least contemplative of men. Simplicity and shrewdness were the cornerstones of his character, and of his success in life.

He was born in 1774, one of five sons of the village carpenter of Norbury in Derbyshire. He received a scanty education, and spelling remained a weak point all his life, a drawback when he had to correspond on business matters with members of the gentry. (Indeed, some of his spelling is truly comical – 'butefull' for 'beautiful', 'laphd' for 'laughed'.) He was brought up to his father's trade and, his abilities soon becoming apparent, he was employed first as forester, then as bailiff, by Francis Parker of Wootton Hall in neighbouring Staffordshire. In 1801 Robert married one of the servants from the Hall, Harriet Poynton, who bore him two children, Robert and Fanny, before dying in 1809 in giving birth to their third child, who did not survive.

Meanwhile Robert Evans had made two further steps up the social ladder. The year after his marriage his employer inherited property at Kirk Hallam, between Nottingham and Derby; Robert not only moved there to manage the new estate but bought a farm of his own at Kirk Hallam. Then, in 1804, Parker inherited yet another property (the inheritance requiring him to change his name to Newdegate), a splendid Gothick house at Arbury in Warwickshire. The estate of 7,000 acres included some of the richest coal seams in the county. Again, Robert moved with him, to Arbury Farm, later known as South Farm.

There were other neighbouring estates within the Newdegate family possession, and Robert's freelance services were in demand at them all. His prosperity was a reflection not only of his very considerable personal qualities but of the general prosperity of the land, at a period of expansion in agriculture, mining and road-making. If he had served his own self-interest, he could have made himself really rich, he later told his son proudly, 'but that he had always made it his first aim in life to do the best he could for all the clients who had employed him'.

So much worldly progress had Robert Evans nevertheless made in the dozen years between 1801 and 1813 that, when he chose a second wife, she was not another servant. Christiana Pearson was the daughter and sister of well-established farmers, and her three elder sisters, the originals of the ghastly aunts in *The Mill on the Floss*, were all married to local men of some standing. The second Mrs Evans bore three children at South Farm: Christiana, known as Chrissey, in 1814, Isaac Pearson Evans, named for his maternal grandfather and uncle, two years later, and, on 22 November 1819, Mary Ann, who was given the names of two of her Pearson aunts.

Her father was thus forty-six years old when Mary Ann was born, a man whose simple but strongly held convictions had been bred into him in the preceding century and never thereafter amended. Virtually two generations – generations of rapid change in British life and thought, moreover – separated the father and his youngest daughter, as was to become, in due course, painfully apparent.

Mary Ann hardly knew her birthplace, for the family moved into the much more substantial Griff House nearby in the spring of 1820. This roomy house was her home for all of her girlhood and suited her mixture of dreaminess and tomboyishness to perfection. With its attics, where a moody child could retreat to recover her equilibrium, its spacious outbuildings, where something interesting was always going on, and its free access to the countryside, it was an idyllic place in which to grow up.

Soon after the removal, Mary Ann's half-brother and sister left home, he to become sub-agent under his father at Kirk Hallam, she to keep house for him. Possibly the second Mrs Evans, who was noted for her sharp tongue, was not a congenial stepmother to the sixteen-year-old Fanny. Shortly after their departure, in March 1821, Mrs Evans gave birth to twin boys, who died at ten days old. Her own health never fully recovered, though she lived another fifteen years. There were no more pregnancies, whether by incapacity or refusal, though she was only thirty-three when the twins were born. Her delicate health perhaps militated against a bond of true affection between herself and her youngest, wildest, clumsiest daughter. Neat and ladylike Chrissey was no trouble to anyone, Isaac was his mother's pride and joy, and Mary Ann found herself the pet and favourite of her father. 'The one deep strong love I have ever known', she was to call her feeling for him (before she had experienced a reciprocal romantic love), her assessment implying a weaker and altogether less satisfactory relationship with her other parent.

To take her out of her mother's way, when the older children had gone to school, Robert would allow the infant Mary Ann to accompany him on his daily expeditions through the estates he managed, leaving her in the servants' halls while he was in conference with the master. On these travels she began to appreciate the value to a human life of being 'well rooted to some spot of a native land', as she wrote in *Daniel Deronda*; she acquired that invaluable 'love of tender kinship for the face of the earth, for the labours men go forth to, for the sounds and accents that haunt it'. Again, in *Middlemarch*, she was to expound on the gentle details of Warwickshire scenery: 'These are the things that make the gamut of joy in landscape to midland-bred souls – the things they toddled among, or perhaps learnt by heart, standing between their father's knees, while he drove leisurely.' Delight in the countryside was thus inextricably linked in her mind with her father's company and, more, with pride in the active part he took in keeping it well cultivated, orderly and prosperous.

From her father and her early experiences, she took her lifelong preference for a pastoral landscape, as opposed to the barren romantic scenery of mountain and moor that swelled the hearts of others with elation. The satisfaction to be found in gazing on scenes of good farming practice, and appreciation of the dedication and hard work involved, were among Robert Evans' most important bequests to his daughter.

Thenceforward Mary Ann's life was an inevitable progression away from his world. She was sent to three successive local boarding-schools between the ages of five and sixteen, losing her country speech and steadily acquiring not only intellectual accomplishment such as her father had not known but a propensity to intellectual enquiry wholly foreign to his nature. Such a man, practical, self-reliant, largely self-educated, doing very well from the world as he found it, was not one to question matters of religion, politics or morality. He took the attitude that what was good enough for his masters was good enough for him; he had better things with which to occupy his time than useless philosophical speculation.

Thus, as Mary Ann grew, she found that the only parent who had ever shown her fondness simply ceased to understand her. The other troubles of her childhood, the criticism of her narrow-minded Pearson aunts, and the failure of her beloved Isaac wholeheartedly to return her devotion, she transmuted to fiction in *The Mill on the Floss*; but her father was no Mr Tulliver (except in the matter of spelling). Robert Evans never failed in anything he undertook, he never troubled himself with doubts. In an essay called 'Looking Back', written towards the end of her life and under the shelter of a fictitious narrator (whom she called Theophrastus Such), George Eliot described with affection and respect the mind to which her own larger mind was incomprehensible:

> Nor can I be sorry, though myself given to meditative if not active innovation, that my father was a Tory who had not exactly a dislike to innovators and dissenters, but a slight opinion of them as persons of ill-founded self-confidence.... To my father's mind the noisy teachers of revolutionary doctrine were, to speak mildly, a variable mixture of the fool and the scoundrel; the welfare of the nation lay in a strong Government which could maintain order; and I was accustomed to hear him utter the word 'Government' in a tone that charged it with awe, and made it part of my effective religion, in contrast with the word 'rebel', which seemed to carry the stamp of evil in its syllables, and, lit by the fact that Satan was the first rebel, made an argument dispensing with more detailed inquiry.... Altogether, my father's England seemed to me lovable, laudable, full of good men, and having good rulers, from Mr Pitt on to the Duke of Wellington, until he was for emancipating the Catholics....

When a son begins to find his father's views outdated and stultifying, the ground is laid for a classic conflict; but a daughter in such a case can hardly even join battle. Strong-minded men who have made a success of their lives are not disposed to accord much weight to the opinions of inexperienced females, who are much easier to shout down or laugh off than their brothers. Victorian girls, besides, were brought up to think it wrong to dispute with their elders. Out of duty and out of affection, Mary Ann kept her burgeoning thoughts to herself as much as possible, as she embarked on what were to be 'the long, sad years of youth'.

At Christmas 1835 she left school for good, and almost immediately the household was convulsed by illness. On 31 December, as he drove about on his usual business, Robert Evans suffered a sudden attack of kidney stone and reached home in great pain and difficulty. The Nuneaton surgeon was called for and stayed with him through the night, his life being at one time despaired of. Mrs Evans was also rapidly sinking, and Mary Ann, just sixteen, seemed about to become an orphan. With his usual strength of character, Robert insisted on resuming his journal as soon as he possibly could, writing on 3 January, 'This was a terable day and night I thought I could not live this day and night – I was blooded several times in the arm and six or seven dozen of leeches set on about my kidneys.' As he recovered, the two doctors who had been attending him night and day had to switch their attentions to his wife, who was now in great pain. On 3 February Robert wrote, 'My dear Wife Christiana died this morning about 5 o'clock after a Dreadfull night of pain but I was happy to see her go off at last without a Struggle her Breath stopd.'

For a little over a year Chrissey and Mary Ann divided the household duties between them, Mary Ann attempting to prove her love for her father by mending his clothes and reading Walter Scott's novels, which he loved, aloud to him in the evenings. In May 1837 Chrissey married, and the running of the house devolved wholly upon Mary Ann, who was 17½. Although she had servants to perform all the drudgery, she was responsible for directing the work of the kitchen and the dairy, and she chose to do some of the baking, preserve-making and cheesemaking herself. Everything eaten by the family and servants had to be made at home; the laundry too was an immense undertaking. But, like Emily Brontë, Mary Ann Evans found a certain tranquillity of spirit to be compatible with these menial tasks. She had, besides, inherited from her father the notion of pride in a job well done, and belief in the character-building value of hard work. In due course she was to take the same professional attitude to her writing, always giving the best of herself in anything she undertook to perform.

In 1840 Robert Evans reached a decision which was ultimately to widen and expose the gulf between himself and his daughter. He was about to retire, to make way for Isaac and his bride, Sarah, who were taking over both Griff House and the work which Robert Evans was growing too old to perform. He was sixty-six, and his phenomenal strength had never returned after his serious illness. The choice was whether to retire to one of the properties he owned in the country or to purchase a new home for himself and Mary Ann in the nearby city of Coventry. After consultation with Isaac, he chose the latter course. Both men were anxious for Mary Ann to find a husband, and Coventry undoubtedly offered greater opportunities.

In the event, Coventry brought Mary Ann not the stability of marriage but the heady pleasure of friends with ideas more sophisticated and stimulating than any she would have encountered in the country.

Robert and Mary Ann moved to Bird Grove, Foleshill, in March 1841, after a considerable expenditure on new furniture. It was an imposing semi-detached villa set in large gardens and backed by fields, standing on the main road into Coventry, less than a mile away. Mary Ann had not only a bedroom but an inter-connecting study – a rare woman with a working room of her own. She must have felt that her father was doing everything in his power to make her happy (which included trying to find her a husband), at no small sacrifice to himself in terms both financial and personal. The man accustomed to striding about farms and giving directions on the management of the countryside cannot have found much that was congenial to his nature in petty suburban life. Social duties of the sillier variety could not compensate for the feeling of sudden uselessness which is the penalty paid on retirement of the man who has lived for his work.

Mary Ann too was at first dismayed by her new environment and felt out of place amid the smart clothes and superficial talk of her neighbours. Not only the 'thick wall of indifference' presented by those strangers but the lack of true companionship between herself and her father, increasingly apparent as they were thrown more together, caused her to write to her former schoolteacher, Maria Lewis: 'I have of late felt a depression that has made me alive to what is certainly a fact – that I am alone in the world. I do not mean to be so sinful as to say that I have not friends, most undeservedly kind and tender, and disposed to form a far too favourable estimate of me, but I mean that I have no one who enters into my pleasures or my griefs, no one with whom I can pour out my soul, no one with the same yearnings, the same temptations, the same delights as myself.'[3]

Her emotional and intellectual loneliness was, however, assuaged when towards the end of the first year in Coventry she made the acquaintance of Charles and Caroline Bray, and later of Caroline's sister, Sara Hennell. Those lively, intelligent, free-thinking people and their friends who visited them in Coventry, becoming Mary Ann's friends too, formed a sympathetic and supportive circle in which for the first time since her infancy she felt the balm of being understood. Moreover, the brother of Caroline and Sara, Charles Hennell, had recently published a book *An Inquiry into the Origins of Christianity*, reading which confirmed in Mary Ann the loss of religious faith that she had been silently grappling with for years. 'My whole soul has been engrossed in this most interesting of all enquiries for the last few days,' she wrote to Maria Lewis, 'and to what result my thoughts may lead I know not – possibly to one that will startle you.' Maria was indeed startled by what her former pupil, who had once been so pious, told her when she came to stay at Bird Grove on New Year's Day 1842. The following day, which was a Sunday, Mary Ann announced to her uncomprehending father that it would be hypocritical in her any longer to attend divine service. His journal entry for that day records none of the arguments, the probable tears, merely, 'Went to Trinity Church in the forenoon. Miss Lewis went with me. Mary Ann did not go.'

After one angry outburst which had no effect on her resolve, he went into a sulk and declined to discuss the matter further. Instead, he appealed to Chrissey and Isaac to intervene. Isaac, seeing his youngest sister's chances of marrying further endangered by this singularity, dutifully 'schooled Mary Ann', according to his father's journal, but again to no avail. For nine weeks Robert Evans refused to speak to his daughter, and she with equal stubbornness refused to go to church. Eventually she appealed to him by letter: 'As all my efforts in conversation have hitherto failed in making you aware of the real nature of my sentiments, I am induced to try if I can express myself more clearly on paper so that both I in writing and you in reading may have our judgements unobstructed by feeling, which they can hardly be when we are together.'

After giving an account of her beliefs, and her reasons for them, in terms that were probably meaningless to him, she added, 'Such being my very strong convictions, it cannot be a question with any mind of strict integrity, whatever judgement may be passed on their truth, that I could not without vile hypocrisy and a miserable truckling to the smile of the world for the sake of my supposed interests, profess to join in worship which I wholly disapprove. This and *this alone* I will not do even for your sake – anything else however painful I would cheerfully brave to give you a moment's joy.'

Among Isaac's arguments had been the accusation that their father was spending a great deal of money on the establishment at Foleshill purely in order to find a husband for Mary Ann, money that was slipping out of the family and which was totally wasted if she insisted on making herself unmarriageable. Such an accusation was intolerable, and the main thrust of her letter was not so much to explain herself, which she probably knew was useless, as to remove this charge (she was careful to keep to the accepted euphemisms for husband-hunting and marriage):

From what my brother more than insinuated and from what you yourself intimated I perceive that your establishment at Foleshill is regarded as an unnecessary expense having no other object than to give me a centre in society – that since you now consider me to have placed an insurmountable barrier to my prosperity in life this one object of an expenditure held by the rest of the family to be disadvantageous to them is frustrated – I am glad at any rate that this is made clear to me, for I could not be happy to remain as an incubus or an unjust absorber of your hardly earned gains which might be better applied among my Brothers and Sisters with their children.

I should be just as happy living with you at your cottage at Packington or any where else if I can thereby minister in the least to your comfort – of course unless that were the case I must prefer to rely on my own energies and resources feeble as they are – I fear nothing but voluntarily leaving you. I can cheerfully do it if you desire it and shall go with deep gratitude for all the tenderness and rich kindness you have never been tired of showing me. So far from complaining I shall joyfully submit if as a proper punishment for the pain I have most unintentionally given you, you determine to appropriate any provision you may have intended to make for my future support to your other children whom you may consider more deserving.

To this eloquent letter Robert Evans found himself unable to reply but, being a man of deeds rather than words, the crisis provoked him to action. Three days later he recorded in his journal that he had put Bird Grove up for sale and had written to Lord Aylsford to inform him 'I should leave Coventry and come to my cottage at Packington and I gave him the reasons for it.' Mary Ann was left wondering whether she would be invited to join her father at Packington or would be left homeless and provision-less. She began to formulate plans to take lodgings, perhaps in Leaming-ton, and to earn her living by teaching. She told Caroline Bray that only the idea of leaving her father distressed her: 'All else, doleful lodgings, scanty meals, and *gazing-stockism* [being stared at and pointed out] are quite indifferent to me.'

Isaac, however, was not so indifferent to scandal. He tried to smooth things over by inviting Mary Ann to Griff while their father's anger cooled. At Griff Mary Ann heard that alterations to the cottage at Packington had begun, but she could not discover his intentions regarding herself. 'I must have a *home*, not a visiting place,' she wrote in anguish to one Coventry friend who was attempting to find out the truth and who had presumably extracted the mumbled concession that Packington would not actually be denied to Mary Ann.

From this low point in their relationship, the only options were total breach or reconciliation. In fact, the bond between father and daughter proved too strong to be broken. While Mary Ann was away, Robert discovered that he did not like living without his 'little wench', and her own tender feelings were too deep-rooted to bear the estrangement. Both were ripe for reconciliation, which was effected through Isaac's wife, Sarah. Robert agreed that Mary Ann could come home on the condition that she attend church and observe all outward signs of conformity; but, he conceded, she could hold what views she liked privately.

She had not won much – the right to shut her ears to the sermon and gaze at the beauty of the architecture instead – but it had to do. On 15 May Robert Evans noted in his journal, without comment, 'Went to Trinity Church Mary Ann went with me today.' For the remaining seven years until his death, except when she was away on visits, he was always accompanied to church by Mary Ann. She had surrendered most, yet it was he who harboured feelings of resentment. Several years later, when he was seriously ill, Cara Bray noted how 'he takes opportunities now of saying kind things to Mary Ann, contrary to his wont. Poor girl, it shows how rare they are by the gratitude with which she repeats the commonest expressions of kindness.' It was the vanquished Mary Ann who showed the greater magnanimity. In the later part of her life she told Emily Davies, the campaigner for women's higher education, of 'having come into collision with her father and being on the brink of being turned out of his house. And she dwelt a little on how much fault there is on the side of the young in such cases, of their ignorance of life, and the narrowness of their intellectual superiority.'

Even after that compromise Isaac continued to fret about his sister's husband-catching potential. He deplored his father's decision to remain at Foleshill, and the degree of liberty he allowed Mary Ann, fearing that she would never get 'a husband and a settlement, unless she mixes more in society. . . . Mrs Bray, being only a leader of mobs, can only introduce her to Chartists and Radicals, and such only will ever fall in love with her if she does not belong to the Church.' But Robert, perhaps through weariness, remained at Bird Grove for the rest of his life. Mary Ann, moreover, was, however grudgingly, allowed to mix with whom she chose, to take long holidays away with her friends, to read and study whatever she liked and to complete her first full-length published work, a translation of Strauss's *Life of Jesus*. That arduous and scholarly undertaking occupied two years of her life. Although by the end of that period she confessed herself 'Strauss-sick', the work was congenial to her because of its sympathetic examination of Jesus the man, divested of any supernatural element.

In October 1845 Mary Ann had been planning to tour Scotland with the Brays; at the last minute her father made a fuss about her leaving, and Charles Bray had to persuade him to let her go for the good of her health. The very day the party set off, the old man broke his leg, but fortunately Isaac's letter recalling her home did not catch up with them until the holiday was almost over; as soon as she received it, she hurried back. She reached Coventry on 28 October to find the leg mending but her father more demanding of attention and amusement than ever. Translation work increasingly had to be fitted in with long bouts of reading to him and attending to his wants. Cara Bray told her sister that, 'as her work advances nearer its public appearance, she grows dreadfully nervous. Poor thing, I do pity her sometimes with her pale sickly face and dreadful headaches, and anxiety too about her father. This illness of his has tried her so much, for all the time she had for rest and fresh air, she had to read to him. Nevertheless she looks very happy and satisfied at times with her work.'[4]

For all its superior pleasures, Mary Ann was scrupulous never to neglect her father in favour of intellectual activity. 'I shall have less time than I have had at my own disposal,' she admitted to Sara Hennell as it became apparent that her father's health was in permanent decline, 'but I feel prepared to accept life, nay, lovingly to embrace it, in any form in which it shall present itself.' In that remark it is possible to detect Mary Ann, under force of circumstances, taking the current assumption by which unmarried daughters were conveniently shackled to the care of ageing parents, their own needs set at nought, and making a virtue of it. As all her novels attest, it became part of her deeply held philosophy that the individual, by cheerfully accepting whatever duties were laid on him by the chance circumstances of his life, enhanced the value of that life as well as of the lives around him. It was a view she was to disseminate through her fiction all her life, and it undoubtedly had its origins in the difficulties as well as the rewards of her relationship with her father during those last years of his life. *Not* to have cultivated acceptance would have rendered her existence intolerable at this period.

Often enough, despite her striving after unselfishness, her life did seem almost intolerable. Her youth was passing away, and she could not help chafing at the many restrictions which bound her. Sometimes dreams of freedom possessed her. 'Oh the bliss of having a very high attic in a romantic continental town, such as Geneva – far away from morning calls, dinners and decencies; and then to pause for a year and think,' she wrote to a friend in 1848. Looking back, ten years later, she recognized that she had been 'very unhappy, and in a state of discord and rebellion towards my own lot' for much of her youth.

Sea air was prescribed for Robert Evans, and she took him to Dover for a fortnight in 1846 and to the Isle of Wight in 1847. In April the following year he became so ill that he had to spend six weeks on a bed in the dining-room, with Mary Ann sleeping on a sofa to be near him. The strain made her look 'as thin as a poker', Cara said. As soon as he was well enough to travel, she took him to the sea again, to St Leonard's. By September he seemed to be failing rapidly, as Cara Bray wrote to Sara Hennell: 'The doctors expect his death to take place suddenly, by a suffusion of water on the chest; and poor Mary Ann, alone with him, has the whole care and fatigue of nursing him night and day with his constant nervous expectation. She keeps up wonderfully mentally, but looks like a ghost.'

He lingered for another eight wearying months. 'Father makes not the slightest attempt to amuse himself, so that I scarcely feel easy in following my own bent for an hour,' she complained to the Brays. 'But I look amiable in spite of a constant tendency to look black; and speak gently though with a strong propensity to be snappish.' Only to her closest friends could she make such a confession. To other correspondents she dwelt on the happier aspects of his dependency upon her: 'His mind is as clear and rational as ever, notwithstanding his feebleness now, and he gives me a thousand little proofs that he understands my affection and responds to it. These are very precious moments to me. My chair by my father's bedside is a very blessed seat to me.' There is no reason to doubt her sincerity; her lifelong yearning was to be loved and wanted, and to some extent it was fulfilled during these last years with her father, when, as so often happens in the frailty of old age, the balance of obligation between parent and child was transposed.

As his death drew near, she began to wonder what would happen to her when she was free to choose her own path in life. His was the only restraint on her free will which she allowed to be legitimate. The opinion of others, even of Isaac, was not to take precedence over the dictates of her own conscience; but where her father was concerned, filial respect and duty weighed in the balance. When he was gone, therefore, she would be reliant on herself. It was an awesome thought, for she recognized that her nature was subject to physical as well as intellectual cravings. Longing for love and for a strong man to lean on, yet acutely conscious of her want of personal beauty, she was too apt to behave recklessly when any man seemed attracted. She had already made a fool of herself over one pedantic old scholar, a married man, who took a fancy to her, Dr Brabant (original of Casaubon in *Middlemarch*). One of her later London friends, Bessie Parkes, told her daughter that she believed Mary Ann 'had a passionate, illicit love affair before she ever came to London, with that very attractive man, I think a Doctor Something, with whom and with whose wife she was intimate as a girl'. The description hardly fits Brabant; perhaps it is a confusion between him and Charles Bray. For Mary Ann had certainly leant over-much on Bray, a situation tolerated by Cara, who had a lover of her own. Mary Ann never hid the fact that she needed 'someone to look after me' and that she had passionate love to offer. As her father's life finally slipped away, and with it both emotional outlet and respectable anchor, that knowledge of her own desires was in her thoughts as she wrote, 'What shall I be without my Father? It will seem as if a part of my moral nature were gone. I had a horrid vision of myself last night becoming earthly sensual and devilish for want of that purifying restraining influence.'[5]

Mary Ann was to make many decisions of which her father would have disapproved in the next half dozen years, but by acting on her own judgement she slowly emerged from the enduring depression and frustration which the basic circumstances of her life had engendered and which the being indispensible to and appreciated by him at the very end had only masked. 'How wretched I was then – how peevish, how utterly morbid!' she remembered later of the period immediately following her father's death in May 1849, as she struggled to establish a new and more satisfactory way of life. Five days after the funeral the Brays took her to Europe, and she remained abroad, alone, until the following spring. Fulfilling her old dream, she settled in Geneva, finding lodgings with the family of a painter, François d'Albert Durade. With desperate symbolism, she remade her image, changing her name to the more sophisticated Marian, and her hairstyle from girlish ringlets to the more businesslike style shown in Durade's portrait of her.

Exile gave her time to recover her spirits and to ponder how she would live when she returned home. For the present, she was subsisting on the £100 realized by the sale of the Bird Grove furniture. By her father's will his Derbyshire property was left to Robert, the property in Warwickshire to Isaac. Fanny and Chrissey, who had received £1,000 apiece on their marriages, now gained £1,000 more. Marian had an equitable £2,000 but, as she had no husband to manage it for her, she could not touch the capital. The interest, slightly less than £100 a year, was hardly sufficient to live upon and certainly would not enable her to set up a home. (She found, too, that her father had one further unkindness in store for her beyond the grave: although his will had not been made until eight months before his death, when he had appeared to lose his resentment in appreciation of her care for him, he bequeathed the set of Sir Walter Scott's novels, which she had sacrificed so much time, over the years, to read to him, to Fanny.)

Marian was reluctant to engage in teaching, which was notoriously ill-paid and time-consuming. The other possibility was writing, but the *Life of Jesus*, which had cost her so much hard work, had brought in only £20 and had not even borne her name as translator. Her way was not clear, and she hesitated to go home until it was, for fear of coming into conflict with Isaac, who wanted her to live in respectable maiden-aunt dependence at Griff or with Chrissey. Such a plan was unthinkable, though almost any other unmarried young woman of the time would have submitted to it. 'My return to England is anything but joyous to me, for old associations are rather painful,' she wrote in anticipation. She was accompanied on her journey by Durade, on whom, following her usual pattern when anyone was kind to her, she had become emotionally dependent. Like his predecessors, Durade was a married man.

Back in England after a round of family visits and after staying several months with the Brays, whose home was always available to her, she gathered courage sufficient to answer the call to London. A country-lover who felt ill when confined to any city for too long, she yet knew that only in London could any talents she possessed find full scope.

It was not easy for a woman alone to settle in the capital, but Marian's opportunity came via the publisher John Chapman, for whom she had done some reviewing on the strength of her Strauss translation and who now invited her to edit his financially precarious magazine, the *Westminster*, without pay but with free board at his house in the Strand. To that *ménage à trois*, for Chapman openly kept a mistress as well as a wife in the house, Marian was now added, and after a little jockeying for position between the three women, she settled down to be no more than a colleague – an invaluable colleague – to Chapman.

For she had, hardly surprisingly, been taken in at first by his gallantry. Her yearning for someone to love and be loved by was becoming unbearable as she reached her early thirties without ever having formed a satisfactory relationship. Mildly disappointed in Chapman, she suffered more severely when an intimate year-long friendship with fellow journalist and intellectual Herbert Spencer, who was free to offer marriage, ended with his backing off from commitment; cold-hearted and self-absorbed, Spencer was unable to return her love (which in defiance of the conventions she declared, to his horror).

During her first three years in London, Marian established herself as reliable and proficient (though ill-paid) journalist, settled thoroughly to the male, professional working life, made a niche for herself among the literary figures of the capital and threw herself (no other expression will do) at three successive men. In work and in personal relationships she possessed a determination rare in a woman to get what she wanted by her own efforts, a quality she had certainly inherited or learnt from her father. Her confidence had been undermined by the long years of enforced dependence upon him, but once freed, she behaved much as he would have himself. Like him, she made a success of her life, on her own terms, but without compromising her integrity.

At the age of thirty-four Marian at last found emotional fulfiment with the writer George Henry Lewes, a man whose quick intelligence, wide knowledge, warmth of feeling and prepossessing vitality complemented her nature perfectly. Most acquaintances thought that, despite his many gifts and his charm, he was a little vulgar, but Marian did not mind that. Their mutual love endured for and enriched the remainder of their lives, some quarter of a century. Lewes was unable to divorce his wife, whose adultery he had once condoned, though they had ceased to live together some time before Marian came to London. Marian therefore had to choose between relinquishing her lover and flouting Victorian convention; she had no hesitation in choosing the latter, knowing that it would mean social ostracism – for her though not for Lewes, such was the double standard in operation then. She never had cause to regret her decision, but more deeply hurtful than the ill-will of all London was the silence of her brother Isaac, once so dear to her. As soon as he understood the terms of her relationship with Lewes, he ceased all communication with her, conducting any necessary business (such as that connected with the paying of her interest) through the family solicitor, Vincent Holbeche. Moreover, having puffed himself up to believe that he was head of the family, although he was not even the eldest son, Isaac prevailed on Fanny and Chrissey also to break with their shocking youngest sister.

Not that Marian was, even remotely, an advocate of free love. Neither in life nor in her fiction did she encourage others to follow her lead. To her family back in the Midlands, she had not announced her unconventional situation with pride or defiance; indeed, she had naïvely, almost deceit-fully, tried to mislead them into supposing her legally married. It was not principle but circumstances which kept her and Lewes from marrying. 'Assuredly if there be any one subject on which I feel no levity it is that of marriage and the relation of the sexes – if there is any one action or relation of my life which is and always has been profoundly serious, it is my relation to Mr Lewes,' she wrote in a letter of vindication to Cara Bray. 'Light and easily broken ties are what I neither desire theoretically nor could live for practically. Women who are satisfied with such ties do *not* act as I have done – they obtain what they desire and are still invited to dinner': a dig perhaps at Cara's own discreetly conducted affair.

Marian called herself Mrs Lewes, always referred to George as 'my husband', paid all her earnings into his account and, when their growing income, almost all earned by her, enabled them to become property-owners, the purchases were invariably made in his name. Marian was no feminist, no radical but, like her father (though with infinitely larger human sympathies), deeply conservative at heart. Rebellion was an expedient, a youthful phase with her; once she had got what she wanted from life, once her deepest nature had found its sources of satisfaction, she increasingly slipped back to something very near her father's beliefs. 'I wish there were some solid, philosophical Conservative to take the reins,' she wrote during a political crisis of her middle years, while women's suffrage she referred to as 'an extremely doubtful good'.[6] Like many women who achieve hard-won success in a male-dominated world, she was far from anxious to open doors to others of her sex. Nevertheless, in portraying the indefinable yearnings of Maggie Tulliver and Dorothea Brooke to do some good in the world, George Eliot advanced Charlotte Brontë's case for questioning the limitations imposed on women, to the detriment of society as well as themselves.

With his three sons to support and educate, Lewes and Marian were obliged to live extremely frugally. Financial considerations and the stigma of illegitimacy encouraged them to practise some form of birth control. In a perceptive move to displace Marian's maternal yearnings, to boost her self-esteem and to bring in more money, Lewes persuaded to to try her hand at fiction when they had been living together for two years. In all three objectives his initiative was crowned with success. For her first story, as an anonymous writer, she was paid £50; before long, such was the public appetite for her work, she was earning literally thousands of pounds for each novel. Lewes acted as her agent (first shielding her identity completely, even from her publisher) and could be downright avaricious on her behalf. His private name for her was Polly; few women have had more names in their time, each indicating of a different strand in her persona. When at last obliged to select a name to appear before the public, she chose to be male and to honour, in 'George', the man without whom she would never have become a novelist.

When she began to write fiction, tentatively enough, it was to her father's England, 'lovable, laudable', that she instinctively turned. It was not so much escapism or sentimental hankering after times past as a compulsion to examine the influences that had shaped her which drove her to look back. As she confessed to her friend Barbara Bodichon in 1859, between writing *Adam Bede* and *The Mill on the Floss*, 'at present my mind works with the most freedom and the keenest sense of poetry in my remotest past, and there are many strata to be worked through before I can begin to use *artistically* any material I can gather in the present.'

Her first three short stories, or novellas, published in 1856–7 in *Blackwood's Magazine* and subsequently in book form as *Scenes of Clerical Life*, were all based on identifiable characters, locations and incidents of her youth. These were tales which had been common knowledge in her parish, rather than personal or family histories. But as she gathered confidence she gradually homed in on what mattered, using her next novel to depict her father as a young man, and the one after that to portray her youthful self. *Adam Bede*, which was begun in October 1857 and completed in November the following year, is set at the turn of the century, when her father would have been twenty-five. The novel, she told Blackwood, would be 'full of the breath of cows and the scent of hay', and it is redolent of the world known to her and her father in their respective childhoods. The village names are based on those of the villages in Derbyshire where Robert had grown up; the schoolmaster, Bartle Massey, is given the exact name of Robert's own village teacher; and the hero, Adam Bede, is Marian's imaginative, affectionate reconstruction of her father as a young man. Adam shares Robert's original trade of carpentry, and his philosophy that, 'There's nothing but what's bearable as long as a man can work . . . the best o' working is, it gives you a grip hold o' things outside your own lot' and 'If it's only laying a floor down, somebody's the better for it being done well, besides the man as does it.'

In her summary of Adam Bede, George Eliot celebrated all that was admirable in her father:

He was not an average man. Yet such men as he are reared here and there in every generation of our peasant artisans – with an inheritance of affections nurtured by a simple family life of common need and common industry, and an inheritance of faculties trained in skilful courageous labour: they make their way upward, rarely as geniuses, most commonly as painstaking honest men, with the skill and con-science to do well the tasks that lie before them. Their lives have no discernible echo beyond the neighbourhood where they dwelt, but you are almost sure to find there some good piece of road, some building, some application of mineral produce, some improvement in farming practice, some reform of parish abuses, with which their names are associated by one or two generations after them. Their employers are the richer for them, the work of their hands has worn well, and the work of their brains has guided well the hands of other men.

For all her admiration of Adam's work ethic and strict sense of honour, however, George Eliot requires more of him: he has to learn toleration of other people's shortcomings and differences from himself. 'He had too little fellow-feeling.' That enlargement of human sympathy, that acquisition of 'patience and charity towards our stumbling, falling com-panions', is the hallmark of George Eliot's writing, and the direction she had often wished her own father's upright character to take.

With *The Mill on the Floss*, which immediately followed, Marian moved on from her father's growing-up to her own. In this second novel she replicated many of the circumstances of her girlhood but gave her heroine, Maggie, a totally different (and on the whole less admirable) father – though the bond of special early affection between father and daughter, followed by growing incomprehension, remained from real life.

After *Silas Marner*, another book which celebrates the therapeutic value, yet questions the all-sufficiency, of work, Marian published *Romola*, her one novel set in the far past and in a foreign country, Italy. Its lack of success, both artistically and financially, drove her back for her next two novels to the England of the 1830s, England before the coming of the railways, the England of her father's maturity and her own earliest consciousness. *Felix Holt, Radical* was published in 1866, and *Middlemarch* in 1871–2. In this panoramic view of English provincial society, an older Robert Evans appears as one of the many minor characters, Caleb Garth. He is Adam Bede mellowed: supremely confident of himself but not so harsh on others. Caleb is a successful land agent, like Robert Evans, and just as proud of his work, which he sees as giving significance to his life as well as being of service to other people. It's a fine thing, he declares, 'to have a chance of getting a bit of country into good fettle, as they say, and putting men into the right way with their farming, and getting a bit of good contriving and solid building done – that those who are living and those who come after will be the better for. I'd sooner have it than a fortune. I hold it the most honourable work that is.' To which his wife replies, 'It will be a blessing to your children to have had a father who did such work: a father whose good work remains though his name may be forgotten.'

This, surely, may be taken as Marian's valediction to her father – just as *Middlemarch* itself is her last exhaustive portrait of his world. In her next – and as it turned out, her final – novel, *Daniel Deronda*, she felt ready to tackle the issues of contemporary society, though with less mastery of her material and certainly with less of the sense of poetry she had spoken of to Barbara Bodichon. *Daniel Deronda* was published in 1876, and a collection of essays, *Impressions of Theophrastus Such*, in which she allowed herself some semi-autobiographical retrospection, three years later.

George Henry Lewes had died the year before. His wife, Agnes, survived him, so he and Marian were never able to regularize their union, as they had hoped. Her fame and honour had become such as to render ineffectual, gradually, the stigma of society; she was accepted and looked up to as a great moral teacher, and the circumstances of her private life were magnanimously overlooked. The discovery by the reading public that 'George Eliot' was a woman living with another woman's husband had caused only a temporary hiccough in her sales, despite her own and her publisher's apprehensions. *Middlemarch* alone brought her over £8,000 in its first five years. It is extremely doubtful whether any woman in Britain in the nineteenth century *earned*, by her own honest labour, more than Marian Evans. Nor was any woman more admired for the morality of her sentiments. It was a remarkable combination, and her father surely would have been proud of her, despite himself.

The last episode of her life was perhaps the most bizarre. After Lewes' death she was at first inclined to shut herself away, *à la* Queen Victoria, whose exact contemporary she was. But she was tempted out of her morbid seclusion by a young friend, John Cross, whom she addressed as 'Dear Nephew' in letters deep-edged in black. Within eighteen months they were married. Some commentators, then and now, suspected that she had found evidence, after Lewes' death, that he had been unfaithful to her, which had caused a revulsion of feeling; others merely felt that her lifelong need for a strong man to lean on overcame, yet again, adherence to convention and propriety. Cross was forty, Marian sixty. Their honeymoon was enlivened by his attempt to commit suicide (apparently) by jumping off the hotel balcony, though, as he landed in the Grand Canal, Venice, his life was saved.

At any rate, Marian was an 'honest' woman at last. She now strangely reverted to her given Christian name, as if no longer uneasy with her real identity, signing herself Mary Ann Cross. She had been Marian for thirty years. Isaac's delight in her status is even more amusing than her own. After twenty-three years of estrangement he wrote,

> My dear Sister,
> I have much pleasure in availing myself of the present opportunity to break the long silence which has existed between us, by offering our united and sincere congratulations to you and Mr Cross, upon the happy event of which Mr Holbeche has informed me. My wife joins me in sincerely hoping it will afford you much happiness and comfort. She and the younger branches unite with me in kind love and every good wish. Believe me,
> Your affectionate brother,
Isaac P. Evans.

To which Mary Ann replied: 'It was a great joy to me to have your kind words of sympathy, for our long silence has never broken the affection for you which began when we were little ones', and after eulogy of her husband and wishes for Isaac's family, she signed herself, 'Always your affectionate Sister, Mary Ann Cross'.

Mary Ann died quite suddenly in December 1880, of renal failure, only seven months after her wedding. Isaac attended the funeral, and his sister Fanny wrote to him, 'We may be thankful that she had found a good husband and a *Name*, it comforts me to know that she who for so many years was believed to be the wife of Lewes, had not Mary Ann Evans inscribed on her coffin.'

As a last word from the family on the genius they had nurtured and misunderstood, it is pitiful, yet poignant, with its echo of Mary Ann's own pre-occupation with her identity. If she had not possessed the strength to escape from their narrow-minded world, there would be one fewer women among the great English novelists; but if she had not also possessed the tenderness which made her still care for that world, the qualities of sympathetic observation and understanding for which she is admired would have been considerably diminished.

'Family has often a deep sadness in it,' she had written in *Adam Bede*. 'Nature, that great tragic dramatist, knits us together by bone and muscle, and divides us by the subtler webs of our brains; blends yearning and repulsion; and ties us by our heartstrings to the beings that jar us at every moment. . . . The father to whom we owe our best heritage – the mechanical instinct, the keen sensibility to harmony, the unconscious skill of the modelling hand – galls us, and puts us to shame by his daily errors.' Her words encapsulate the paradox of her relationship with Robert Evans, the father to whom she owed her 'moral nature', the father she had simultaneously loved and resented, admired and deplored.

VI

Emily Dickinson
1830–86

'Father's real life and mine sometimes come into collision.'

Like her Brontë namesake, Emily Dickinson was poet, visionary, spinster, recluse. Both women divided themselves into two distinct selves, only one of which was presented to the world. This one was the dutiful daughter, expending time and physical energy on household chores, on 'keeping the place comfortable for father', as Emily Dickinson described the work.[1] The other self, in both women's cases, was the snatcher of every solitary hour to devote to the real business of their lives: imagination, contemplation, self-discovery and self-expression. Both were intensely secretive about this inner existence, and wary of any trespass upon it. Emily Brontë published her poems only with the fiercest reluctance, when prevailed upon by her sister Charlotte; of more than 1,700 poems written and put away by Emily Dickinson, only seven were offered for publication, anonymously, in her lifetime. Nor were the remainder prepared for the press in confidence, or even hope, of posthumous recognition. Rather they were left in a chaotic state, with instructions to burn all her papers, and it was only by chance that another devoted (but this time unliterary) sister, Vinnie Dickinson, decided they should be kept.

The work, and more especially the poetry, of the Brontë sisters, of George Eliot and Elizabeth Barrett Browning was followed with intense interest and admiration by Emily Dickinson, isolated in the male-intensive culture of mid-nineteenth-century New England. The issues that were important to these women writers, the feminine perspectives they insisted on bringing to bear, excited and encouraged her, as her letters prove. It was not that she modelled herself on them in any way; she seems to have found her own voice as soon as she began to write, though no voice had spoken with quite the same rich brevity before. But these women who had surmounted obstacles, published their work and been accorded real respect, who had proved that authorship of the most elevated kind was not incompatible with womanhood, gave her the sense of a female tradition in literature, of her own right to be, and ability to be, a serious poet.

With Elizabeth Barrett Browning, especially, the resonances are manifold, and Emily Dickinson knew enough about the older woman's life to be fully aware of them. Both had fathers whose similarities did not end with their being called Edward: they were men preoccupied with money, property and social standing; they were intensely religious, yet saw nothing incongruous in supporting slavery; each struggled to retain or restore his inheritance and put great emphasis on the sacredness of home, were they were accustomed to laying down the law to their families.

Unlike the passionate Elizabeth Barrett Browning, Emily Dickinson largely avoided conflict with her father. She cultivated an exaggeratedly docile demeanour, which took her to the extreme of never leaving his house for twenty years. The echoes with Elizabeth Barrett Browning, shut up in her airless chamber, are powerful, all the more so since the motivation of both women is doubtful, their submission just as likely to be subversion.

Because her life was so outwardly uneventful, because she never had to adjust to fame or public exposure, because she neither openly challenged his authority nor apparently craved his affection, there is a static quality about Emily Dickinson's relationship with her father quite different from the tussles Elizabeth Barrett Browning had with hers, as first one and then the other seemed to gain the upper hand. Yet despite its calm surface the Dickinson relationship justifies a closer inspection, both because it seems to represent the plight of so many mid-Victorian unmarried daughters on both sides of the Atlantic and because this particular mouse of a daughter happened, after her death, to be discovered to have been one of the most original and controversial poets in the language.

From her father, and the whole New England ethos which he represented so uncompromisingly, Emily Dickinson drew the habit of introspection and soul-searching which is the hallmark of her poetry. The minds and natures of father and daughter were in some respects similar: both strove for spiritual perfection; both were self-contained, Edward isolating himself from his family, Emily from social networks and conventional young-lady activities. Yet, paradoxically, much of what Edward Dickinson stood for was anathema to his daughter. In matters of morality, religion and politics, his stance was essentially backward-looking. As a father, a citizen and a politician, he bent his efforts to repress and conserve, not to liberate, encourage or reform. Emily was no radical: current affairs did not interest her, appearing to her of fleeting importance compared with the big issues of life, death and immortality; but her mind was ever receptive to new thought and experience, while Edward's most decidedly was not. The complexity of life which Emily celebrated was unperceived by that simplistic, unimaginative man.

A lawyer and prominent citizen of Amherst, Massachusetts, Edward

Dickinson belonged to the seventh generation of a family who had established themselves in New England as part of the great Puritan migration. The virtues of these people had been ground into him: he was sober, honest and industrious, and so were most of his neighbours. Dancing, card-playing and novel-reading were frowned on in Amherst in the 1820s and 30s. Edward himself read only 'lonely and rigorous books', according to his daughter Emily, and those only on Sundays. For many years he wished his children to read no other book than the Bible; the Sabbath was his favourite day, and listening to his daughters play hymns on the piano his favourite relaxation. By the 1860s and 70s, greater contact with the outside world was bringing stimulating new ideas and a richer cultural life to the younger generation of Amherst, including Emily, but her father never changed his values or his views. Like many a stern parent from every era of history, one of his favourite grumbles was the ways of 'the present generation'.

'A Puritan out of time for kinship and appreciation, but exactly in time for example and warning', one of his friends, Samuel Bowles, said of him. Though offered as praise, it is not an attractive portrait, particularly if considered from a son or daughter's point of view. Not more promising of liberty in the home is this self-portrait, sketched by Edward as a young man when taking part in a character guessing-game: 'I am naturally quick and ardent in my feelings,' he wrote, 'easily excited, though not so easily provoked – decided in my opinions – determined in accomplishing whatever I undertake – hard to be persuaded that I am wrong when I have once formed an opinion upon reflection – sometimes unyielding and obstinate – rather peculiar – have a little personal irritability in my constitution.' It is not difficult to project that such a person, on assuming the responsibilities of a man and a father, would brook no opposition from his family and would seek to rule his household with despotism – benevolent or otherwise.

In this he was encouraged by the exceptionally masculine nature of the society which had obtained in New England from the time of the early homesteaders and which was barely beginning to be eroded during his life span. The harshness of the physical conditions encountered by the settlers, combined with the harshness of the brand of religion they had fled in order to practise, served to elevate the male to even more than his accustomary eminence. 'He for God only, she for God in Him' was never so fervently believed as here. In his own household, every man was, if not a god, an Old Testament prophet, while the local community was run by a collection of those beings. Although women in New England were commonly better educated than their contemporaries in the Old World, the purpose of their education, in so exaggeratedly patriarchal a society, was not to fit them to play a part in public affairs. Women were trained to be obedient wives, good housekeepers, and if there was any time over from those duties, to be active in works of church and charity. If they dabbled in the arts, it was only in order to make the home a more pleasant and cultured place for their husbands and children.

Edward grew up as the eldest son of one of the two leading citizens of Amherst. Samuel Fowler Dickinson was a lawyer and a philanthropist who seems to have been considerably less cautious and worldly than his son, though hardly less stubborn and intolerant. By 1814, when Edward was eleven, Samuel had become sufficiently prosperous to build the first brick house in the town. Of imposing, classical design, it stood (and indeed still stands) on a bank above Main Street, set in substantial grounds surrounded by a sheltering hedge. It both dominated the town and stood apart from it. The Homestead, so aptly named, so exclusive of the world outside, was, as the century progressed, to link Edward and Emily in the powerful hold it took over their minds, though to each it represented something different. For Emily it was at once refuge and prison, symbol both of her independent inner life and of self-effacing daughterly dutifulness. To Edward, less subtly, it was the visible proof of his respectability and importance in the community. The temporary loss of The Homestead was to be traumatic for him and to affect his relationship with all his children.

Seven years after the building of The Homestead, Samuel Dickinson became one of the principal founders of Amherst College, instituted to counter the liberal ideas which were being propagated elsewhere (though it soon became infected itself). The college brought the polish of erudition and literacy to what was otherwise a small farming community at Amherst. It was also to bring bankruptcy to Samuel, whose generosity outstripped his means.

But this disaster was wholly unforseen in Edward's youth, as he basked in the prestige of his family name and looked forward confidently to inheriting The Homestead. In 1826 he return from his law studies at Yale to assist in his father's practice. Two years later he married Emily Norcross, a twenty-three-year-old woman from a neighbouring town who had attended a finishing school for young ladies in New Haven. She seems to have been the conventional meek and pliant young woman well fitted to be the mate of a forceful man. Edward took her to live with his father and younger brothers and sisters in The Homestead, half of which was now made over to him.

During their engagement Edward warned his fiancée in a letter that cleverness in a woman did not make for harmony in the home. 'I should be sorry to see another Mme de Staël – especially if anyone wished to make a partner of her for life,' he wrote. 'Different qualities are more desirable in a female who enters into domestic relations – and you have already had my opinions on that subject.'[2] She did not argue but turned herself into an exemplary wife, winning prizes for her cookery, attending college and church functions at her husband's side and producing three children in quick succession. Austin was born in 1829, Emily Elizabeth on 10 December the following year, and Lavinia in 1833.

It was shortly after Vinnie's birth that public humiliation befell the family as a result of Samuel's excess of zeal and unworldliness. He was obliged to sell his half of The Homestead and to decamp to Ohio, where his younger children might begin life anew. Edward grimly clung on to his position in Amherst, determined to build up the legal practice and to repurchase the lost half of The Homestead. The West held no attraction for him; there was no spirit of adventure in his nature, just an iron conscience and a strong sense of civic and family pride.

The shock to him of that setback was extreme. For seven years he lived on at The Homestead, uncomfortably sharing with its new half-owner. It is notable that no more children were born to Edward and Emily Dickinson after that date. The effect on the children they already had was unfortunate. Not only did their father lose whatever youthful high spirits he had once possessed but he became too much preoccupied with work and making money to have time or attention for his young family. 'Father, too busy with his briefs to notice what we do,' Emily was later to write. (Of course, this also had its advantages.) As for her other parent, 'I never had a mother,' she rather cruelly claimed. 'I suppose a mother is one to whom you hurry when you are troubled.' It is hard to know why Mrs Dickinson was not more sympathetic to her children, unless her spirit had been utterly broken by her husband.

The children evidently lived in awe and fear of their father. 'I never knew how to tell time by the clock till I was fifteen,' Emily told a new acquaintance when she was forty. 'My father thought he had taught me but I did not understand and was afraid to say I did not and afraid to ask anyone else lest he should know.'[3] After his death she remembered how, '"I say unto you," Father would read at Prayers, with a militant Accent that would startle one.' And once she wrote to her absent brother Austin, 'I don't love to read your letters all out loud to father – it would be like opening the kitchen door when we get home from meeting Sunday, and are sitting down by the stove saying just what we've a mind to, and having father hear.'

Like most children, however, Emily only gradually became conscious of the deficiencies in her parents which she brooded on in later years. The letters written to girl friends during her childhood and adolescence give a happier and warmer picture of what it was like to grow up in that family and that community. Enjoying the companionship of her sensitive and intelligent brother and of her practical, downright, often amusing sister;

belonging to a congenial group of girl friends; attending school; visiting cousins; taking part in all the seasonal occupations of a country neighbourhood; tending her pets and the domestic livestock: all these filled her time and her heart and made the role of her parents in her early life less prominent. It was the kind of innocent, busy, full girlhood which only the American lifestyle of the nineteenth century seemed to promote. Reading Emily's youthful, enthusiastic letters, one is reminded of the world of *What Katy Did, Anne of Green Gables* and *Little Women*. It is something to do with a country life, well rooted in the turn of the seasons, yet cultured and educated too. School, college, occasional visits to the cultural metropolis of a Boston or a Philadelphia balanced the routine of small town gossip, bringing in the harvest, laying up provisions, which themselves offered no small degree of security and satisfaction. Though only girls from reasonably well-off homes could enjoy such pleasures, a much more class-free (though by no means less sexist) society operated than in Britain, where country-dwellers polarized between the under-educated daughters of labourers and girls from wealthy families isolated from work and weather in great houses.

When Emily was ten, she was enrolled at Amherst Academy, daughter-foundation of the college, which she attended for the next seven years, except (as frequently happened) when prevented by illness. There she studied an admirable range of subjects: Latin, French, German, history, philosophy, composition, biology and geology. The natural sciences were taught at Amherst with an almost religious fervour, as evidence of God's greatness and bounty. In her last year at the academy, Emily looked forward with a sense of privilege to higher education, and the chance to become a boarder at Mount Holyoke Seminary, some eight miles from home. Her father saw her off with admonitions 'that I shall not disgrace myself'. During her first term she suffered from acute homesickness and on her return after the Christmas vacation became physically ill. The state of her health was reported to her parents, and Austin was despatched to fetch her home, much against her will.

It was not, she told her friend Abiah Root, 'that I do not love home – far from it. But I could not bear to leave teachers and companions before the close of term and go home to be dosed and receive the physicians daily, and take warm drinks and be condoled with on the state of health in general by all the old ladies in town. . . . Father is quite a hand to give medicine,' she added, 'especially if it is not desirable to the patient, and I was dosed for about a month after my return home, without any mercy.' She returned to college but, 'Father has decided not to send me to Holyoke another year, so this is my last term. . . . It startles me when I really think of the advantages I have had, and I fear I have not improved them as I ought.' There was an intense evangelical atmosphere at Mount

Holyoke, to which Emily, on scrupulously examining her conscience, could not subscribe. All her family and friends were 'converted' at about that time; she stood 'alone in rebellion'. How large a part her crisis of faith played in her father's decision to remove her, whether there was any element of punishment in the withdrawal or whether he was motivated only by concern for her mental and physical welfare is unclear. Her own reaction seems to have been a blend of relief and disappointment – but chiefly the former.

Although Edward was an austere and undemonstrative man, feared and obeyed by wife and children, he was capable of occasional kindness and even occasional sensibility. It is recorded of him that once he rang the church bells to alert the townspeople to a particularly lovely sunset; on another occasion he was seen feeding the birds in his slippers in the snow. Such instances would hardly have been remembered, had they not been uncharacteristic of his usual stern, emotionally repressed behaviour. He gave Emily her beloved dog and many books but then spoiled the effect by warning her not to read them lest they 'joggle' her mind. Later, books which had been recommended to Emily by friends and 'preceptors' of her own generation had to be smuggled into the house without his knowledge.

In 1835 the citizens of Amherst had effectively given Edward a vote of confidence by choosing him to be treasurer of the college, a post he retained till his death and discharged with his customary diligence and integrity. That went some way towards retrieving the family honour, but nothing less than the repurchase of The Homestead would satisfy him. However, the half-owner was unprepared to sell, and in 1840, finding the sharing situation intolerable, Edward moved out and took his family to live in rented property in a nearby street.

During the 1840s politics assumed great importance in his life. (Both his professions, law and politics, reinforced his natural propensity to tell others what to do, a propensity already encouraged by the extreme submissiveness of his wife.) He was elected to the Massachusetts State Senate and later to the United States House of Representatives. In 1852 he attended the Whig National Convention, which supported the Missouri Compromise seeking to extend slavery into the new territories of the West, and the Fugitive State Law, which decreed that an escaped slave could be pursued and recaptured anywhere in the United States. It seems likely that Emily did not approve her father's politics, though not daring to say so at home. But she wrote to a friend, Sue Gilbert, 'Why can't I be a delegate to the great Whig Convention? – don't I know all about Daniel Webster, and the Tariff, and the Law? . . . I don't like this country at all. . . .'

Other people's rights meant little or nothing to the self-righteous Edward. Slaves and suffragists equally had short shrift from him. He termed the early suffragists 'a class of females . . . some sentimental, some belligerent, some fist-shakers, some scolds'. As the century progressed, the old values were increasingly being challenged, but Edward could neither countenance change nor empathize with those who were different from himself. In his failure to see and marvel at the paradoxes, riddles and enigmas of life, he was as unlike his elder daughter as it was possible to be. Yet, despite the omen of Emily's religious crisis, it is improbable that he had any comprehension of the ideas that were fermenting beneath her quiet exterior. As she grew older, she spoke less and less, scorning all unnecessary communication and reserving her deepest and most intriguing thoughts for poetic utterance.

Edward, in contrast, was the great orator, the law-giver and the public man. In February 1852 the decision was made to bring the railway to Amherst, and he was elected one of the directors of the board. 'Father is really *sober* from excessive satisfaction, and bears his honours with a most becoming air,' Emily reported. Then, in 1855, came the realization of his favourite ambition. After more than twenty years, he was able to repurchase the half of The Homestead which had passed out of Dickinson ownership and triumphantly to move his family back to their proper home. His children were all in their early twenties and might be expected at this time to begin to establish homes and lives of their own. It is hard to know how much coercion was put upon them to remain within his sphere of influence. Much later, Vinnie was to tell those curious about her sister's life that neither of the girls had married because they 'feared displeasing father'.

It is certain that Edward put pressure on Austin to remain in Amherst and to follow almost exactly in his own footsteps. Austin definitely bore the brunt of paternal expectations by virtue of his sex, while Emily, keeping a low profile as it were, quietly went her own way and thought her own thoughts. But she suffered and resented on her brother's account and was ultimately disappointed when Austin, with all the superior strength and liberty of his gender, was not more successful in standing up to their father.

After attending Amherst College, Austin taught for a year in Boston, enjoying the variety and freedom of life in a city. Law did not much appeal to him, but his father desperately wished him to join the family practice; the year in Boston was by way of a concession, while Austin tried to decide what to do. Edward invested all his hopes in his only son, yet when they were together there was friction. As Emily wrote to her brother in Boston, 'You and father do nothing but "fisticuff" all the while you're at home, and the minute you are separated, you become such devoted friends. . . . I believe at this moment, Austin, that there's nobody living for whom father has such respect as for you, and yet your conduct together is quite peculiar indeed.' Six months later she told her brother, 'For all you differ, Austin – he can't get along without you, and he's been just as bleak as a November day, since you've been gone.' In another letter to Boston she told him, 'We don't have many jokes now, it is pretty much all sobriety, and we do not have much poetry, Father having made up his mind that it's pretty much all real life.'

Emily kept up a regular correspondence with her beloved brother during the few years he was away from Amherst, first in Boston and then, capitulating so far as to study law, at Harvard Law School. Sometimes her father commanded her to read out loud Austin's replies, and then all her ingenuity was taxed to avoid betraying what they did not wish him to hear. 'I received what you wrote, at about 2½ o'clock yesterday,' she told Austin on one occasion. 'Father brought home the same, and waited himself in order to have me read it – I reviewed the contents hastily – striking out all suspicious places, and then very *artlessly* and unconsciously began. My heart went "pit a pat" till I got safely by a remark concerning Martha, and my stout heart was *not* till the manuscript was over.' At the end of his law studies, Austin spent a month in Chicago to assess whether he could establish a successful practice there. But his father prevailed upon him to return to Amherst and join his own law practice.

Edward's political duties kept him often in Washington, and in the spring of 1854 there was a scheme for the rest of the family to join him there for a month's visit. Already, however, Emily's reluctance to leave home was considerable – and it was respected by her father, to his credit. He told Austin, 'I have written home, to have Lavinia come with yr mother and you – & Emily too, if she will – but that I will not insist upon her coming.' Emily preferred to stay at home, with her school friend Sue Gilbert, who had recently become engaged to Austin, for company. The girls enjoyed their unwonted liberty. 'I am keeping house with Emily, while the family are in Washington,' Sue wrote to a friend. 'We frighten each other to death nearly every night – with that exception, we have very independent times.'

The following spring Emily was more adventurous, and accompanied Vinnie to Washington. Her father was completing his term as congress-man, and this would be her last opportunity to visit the capital. On the way back the sisters stayed briefly with friends in Philadelphia. It was there that Emily probably met and developed an unreciprocated romantic attachment to a forty-year-old married clergyman, Charles Wadsworth. Certainly there was some such unrequited emotion in her life, and Wadsworth has been judged to be the likeliest candidate. She initiated a correspondence with him, on subjects of spiritual concern, and they met once or twice thereafter.

1855 was indeed a momentous year, a turning-point in many ways, in

Emily's life. She made her longest journey from home, and perhaps fell in love. She moved into the house which was to be her home, at once her refuge and her prison, for the rest of her life. And her mother began to suffer from a long-drawn-out illness which made her dependent on her daughters, changing their relationship, so that they felt she was their child. Thenceforward they increasingly took over the housekeeping – and no slight task it was. The Homestead was a twelve-roomed house, and at times there was only one servant employed to run it, though at others it required the work of three. Unpaid labour of daughters must have been relied on to fill the gaps. All the food consumed was made on the premises, including the bread, whose baking was Emily's special province. Soon, her father would eat no one's bread but hers. This was both a compliment and a terrible tie. (The only time she saw her name in print was when she won a prize for her rye and Indian bread at an Amherst agricultural show.) The demands on her time frequently irked her: 'Vinnie away – and my two hands but *two* – not four, or five as they ought to be – and so *many* wants – and me so *very* handy – and my time of so *little* account,' ran one weary and resentful letter to a friend.

In July 1856 Austin married Sue Gilbert. To prevent any dream of independence, or perhaps to bolster his own dream of a Dickinson dynasty, Edward built another house for the young couple next door to The Homestead. Naturally it was pleasant for Emily to have them so close, and in due course to have their growing children to observe and enjoy, but she recognized that Austin had sacrificed a great deal to their father's selfish love of his only son.

By the age of twenty-five or twenty-six, therefore, the pattern of Emily's existence had crystallized into that which was to prevail for the remaining thirty years of her life. She preserved her self-respect by working hard for her keep, and in order to fit in the writing which meant everything to her, she gradually gave up all activity, either of a social or a charitable nature, outside the home. As early as 1853, she had written, 'I don't go from home, unless emergency leads me by the hand, and then I do it obstinately, and draw back if I can.' It was in that year too that she confessed to Austin, 'I've been in the habit myself of writing some few things.' With the single-mindedness of the committed artist, she began to make the limitations of her lifestyle work to her advantage. The heightened perception made possible only by rigorous self-denial became an intoxicant increasingly necessary to her. Cleverly, she converted a restrictive situation into one in which she won both ways: she satisfied her conscience by outward conformity to her father's will; she fulfilled the deepest needs of her nature by emphasizing her individuality. Indeed, her increasing refusal to participate in the life of the community could be seen as a bid for autonomy, a rebuff to her family, whose life revolved around local affairs, and to the community itself, which expected a woman, if she failed in her primary duty of attracting a husband, at least to make amends by occupying her time selflessly in performing good works. While Edward cared what his neighbours thought of him, Emily deliberately cultivated a persona to bewilder them – dressing in white, remaining upstairs when visitors called and indulging in the various other mild eccentricities recorded of her later years.

A personal perspective on the family was provided by the loyal Vinnie, when all but she had gone: 'Father was the only one to say "damn",' she wrote. 'Someone in every family ought to say damn, of course. As for Emily, she was not withdrawn or exclusive really. She was always watching for the rewarding person to come, but she was a very busy person herself. She had to think – she was the only one of us who had that to do. Father believed; and mother loved; and Austin had Amherst; and I had the family to keep track of.'[4]

The mutual isolation of each member of that curious household, where, Vinnie was to say, they lived 'like friendly and absolute monarchs, each in his own domain', is apparent from the description of her father which Emily sent to one old friend, Joseph Lyman. After unavailing struggles to like her father, it would seem that Emily had at last been able to arrive at a cool and detached appraisal of his personality.

'My father seems to me often the oldest and oddest sort of foreigner,' she wrote. 'Sometimes I say something and he stares in a curious sort of bewilderment, though I speak a thought quite as old as his daughter. . . . Father says in fugitive moments when he forgets the barrister and lapses into the man, that his life has been passed in a wilderness or on an island – of late he says on an island. And so it is for in the morning I hear his voice and methinks it comes from afar and has a sea tone. . . .'

Her rejection of his values, her contempt of all that 'the barrister' stood for, and her determination not to surrender herself to him are plain. It is perhaps more surprising to find no pity in her voice. Long years of subjection must have driven out pity. Doubtless she thought he had only himself to blame, if his children did not love him and he did not understand them. Yet it is piquant that the factor which made Edward so unlovable and remote to his family, and which set the tone of the household, is precisely the factor which gives his daughter's poetry its originality and essential New England flavour. In discussing the poems after her death, Samuel Bowles, friend of the family and editor of the local paper, said of the New England people, 'We conversed with our own souls until we lost the art of communicating with other people.'[5] That is what Edward and Emily each did in their own idiosyncratic ways.

Vinnie's word 'friendly' lends an (artificial?) note of warmth to what sounds otherwise like a soul-destroying degree of isolation amongst the entire household. Vinnie admired her sister's powers but was no intellectual equal. Though extremely fond of 'brave, faithful, punctual Vinnie', Emily recognized that her sister would never want more from life, or see more in life, than her 'pussies and posies'. The mental gulf between Emily and her mother was even wider. 'My mother does not care for thought,' she told a new correspondent. It was only when her mother grew frail and dependent that at last 'affection came'. Austin, who was mentally equipped to be a soul-mate to Emily, had disappointingly submitted to their father's will and was preoccupied with the public life of the town, in which he came to play as active a role as his father, and with his marriage to Sue, which became increasingly unhappy. Emily's greatest affection, in the latter part of her life, was for Austin's children. She also cultivated a wide circle of intellectual correspondents. Though resembling her father in her self-containment, she was not a comparable failure in sustaining rewarding personal relationships. Unlike him, she valued other people's differences from herself as part of the rich pattern of human life.

Vinnie knew that Emily wrote poetry but was incapable of appreciating it and was utterly astonished by the quantity she found after her sister's death. Emily showed several hundred of her poems to Sue but felt betrayed when Sue submitted a few of them for anonymous publication in the newspaper edited by Samuel Bowles. As the marriage of Austin and Sue deteriorated, Emily became estranged from her former friend. For real encouragement in her compulsion to devote her life to poetry, she looked to others who had trodden that path before. It was the example of Elizabeth Barrett Browning which first justified Emily in the 'divine insanity' of being a poet.

The death of Elizabeth in 1861 moved Emily to write three poems in praise of her and the inspirational quality of her life and work. The following year the *Atlantic Monthly* published an article by Thomas Higginson entitled 'Letter to a Young Contributor' which gave advice to would-be authors of both sexes. Emily was prompted to write to him and to enclose four of her poems. Her aim in approaching him was not to seek fame but to try to gain a truer perspective on her work. Her mind was too near itself to judge properly, she said. But stubbornly, if politely, she declined to make the amendments he suggested. 'If fame belonged to me, I could not escape her,' she wrote philosophically when he suggested that with the aid of his hints some of her poetry might even be publishable. She was no more prepared to compromise to gain the acceptance of the male world of letters than she was to compromise and accept her father's view of politics, ethics, religion.

The contemporary literary life of New England was dominated by male thinkers and writers, led by Emerson and Thoreau. There were local

Fanny Burney

Dr Charles Burney

Maria Edgeworth

Richard Lovell Edgeworth

Edward Moulton-Barrett

Elizabeth Barrett (Browning)

Charlotte Brontë

Reverend Patrick Brontë

Mary Ann Evans (George Eliot)

Robert Evans

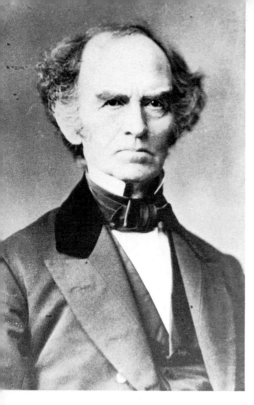

Edward Dickinson

Emily Dickinson

Beatrix and Rupert Potter

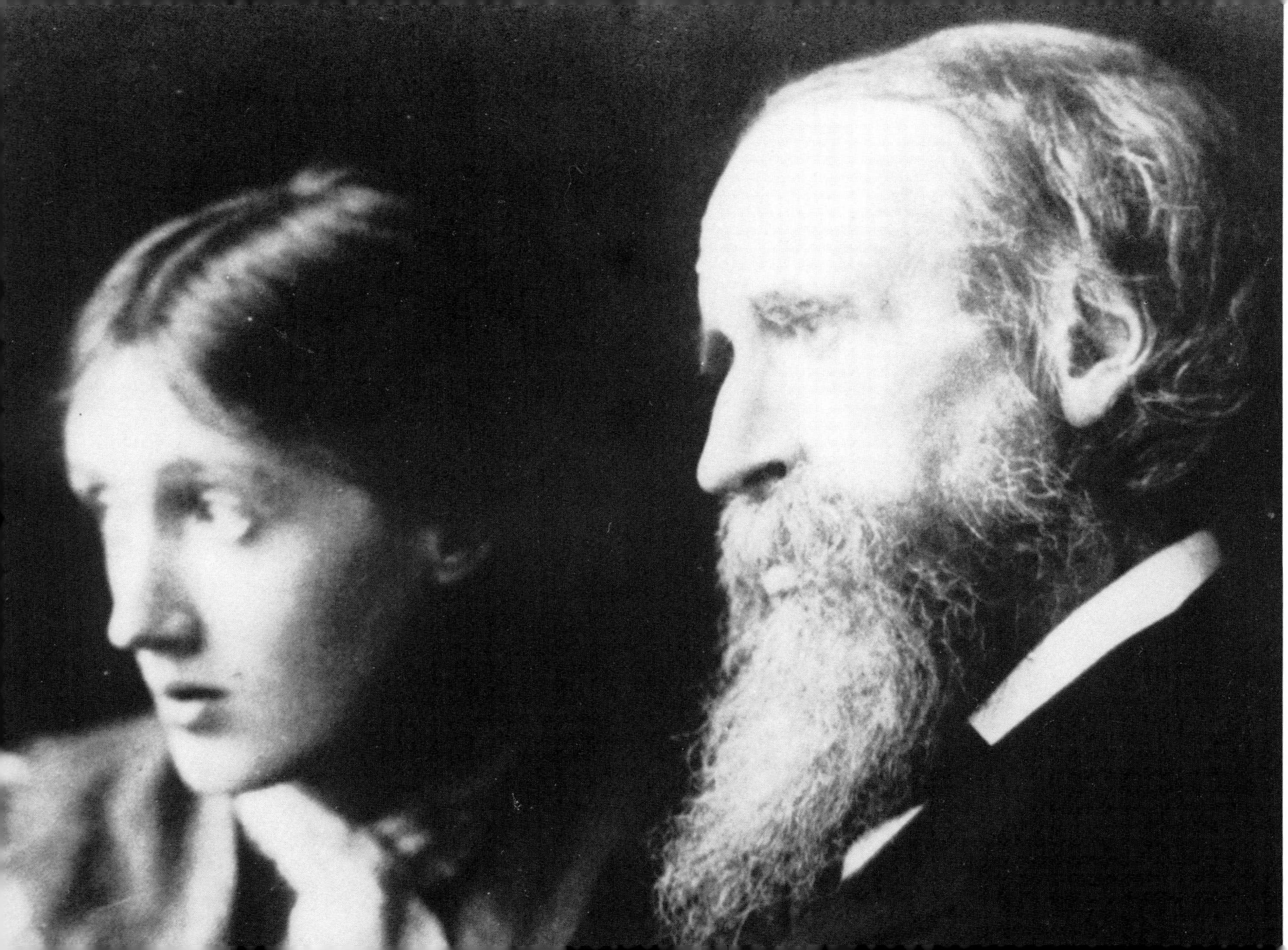

Virginia and
Leslie Stephen

published women poets, but they dealt in sentimental trash of a kind that Emily feared she would, as a woman, automatically be expected to produce. Her rejection of the goal of public acclaim may have been a rejection of all her father strove and stood for. He represented the male world of achievement; she was not prepared to subject her work to the critical examination of that world – not perhaps so much because she feared its censure as because she did not value its praise.

Two-thirds of Emily's poetry was written in the inspired, almost frenzied years between 1858 and 1865. Her output rose to a crescendo in 1862, with 366 poems, and after 1865 was never greater than twenty a year. But as her output dwindled, her habits became more and more unconventional, her seclusion ever deeper. Thomas Higginson, intrigued by her correspondence, made repeated efforts to entice her to visit him and his wife in Boston. She sent him a series of refusals, all evoking the name of her father. In the spring of 1866: 'I had promised to visit my Physician for a few days in May, but Father objects because he is in the habit of me.' In June of the same year: 'I must omit Boston. Father prefers so, he likes me to travel with him but objects that I visit.' It is impossible to know whether Edward's control over her was really as harsh, and his habits as selfish, as these replies make out or whether Emily was deliberately manipulating Higginson's impression of her father to incite his pity and mischievously throwing the blame on Edward for her own preferred behaviour in never leaving home.

Higginson raised the subject again three years later, and Emily turned the invitation on himself: 'Could it please your convenience to come so far as Amherst I should be very glad, but I do not cross my Father's ground to any house or town.' Again, her use of her father's name, and of the possessive case, is surely indicative of the connection (be it only an imaginary connection) she herself made between her father and her reclusion. 'I never leave home' would have been the obvious phrase to use otherwise.

In August 1870 Higginson at last paid his visit to Amherst, and he recorded his impressions for his wife. The Homestead, he told her, was 'a house where each member runs his or her own selves'. 'I asked if she never felt want of employment, never going off the place & never seeing any visitor. "I never thought of conceiving that I could ever have the slightest approach to such a want in all future time" (& added) "I feel that I have not expressed myself strongly enough."' Two other revealing things said by Emily were, 'How do most people live without any thoughts?' and 'I find ecstasy in living – the mere sense of living is joy enough.'[6]

From anecdotes she told him, Higginson decided that, 'Her father was not severe I should think but remote.' The remoteness was about to abate

– just a little. As he neared his allotted span, Edward's constitution began to fail him, to his fury and shame. In March 1871 Samuel Bowles told his son, 'The elder Dickinson has been quite feeble all winter, a sort of breaking-down with dyspepsia – & it shames him that he is hardly to be recognised in his old character.' Emily was surprised by the effect on herself, by the accession of tenderness which his unwonted helplessness induced. Just as with her mother's frailty 'affection came', so with the father who had always been so immeasurably the stronger. That spring Emily told a cousin, Louise Norcross, 'The terror of the winter has made a little creature of me, who thought myself so bold. Father was very sick. I presumed he would die, and the sight of his lonesome face all day was harder than personal trouble. He is growing better, though physically reluctantly. I hope I am mistaken, but I think his physical life don't want to live any longer. You know he never played, and the straightest engine has its leaning hour.'

Edward's iron will brought him a reprieve of more than three years. He had just travelled to Boston in June 1874 when death struck. The previous afternoon he and Emily had been unusually close. She told Thomas Higginson, 'The last Afternoon that my Father lived, though with no premonition – I preferred to be with him, and invented an absence for Mother, Vinnie being asleep. He seemed particularly pleased as I oftenest stayed with myself, and remarked as the Afternoon withdrew, he "would like it not to end". His pleasure almost embarrassed me, and my Brother coming – I suggested they walk. Next morning I woke him for the train – and saw him no more.'

The sequel was told in a letter to Louise and Frances Norcross: 'We were eating our supper the fifteenth of June, and Austin came in. He had a despatch in his hand, and I saw by his face we were all lost, though I didn't know how. He said that father was very sick, and he and Vinnie must go. The train had already gone. While horses were dressing, news came he was dead.' She added on a note of bewilderment: 'Though it is many nights, my mind never comes home.'

The mystery and finality of death was a subject which Emily treated frequently in her poems, and that of her father, who had always been the most powerful figure in her life, was calculated to inspire awe. 'Death enlarges everything,' she realized. It brought her relationship with her father into focus. That which had been blurred while he lived – out of self-preservation on Emily's part – now assumed its true significance in her mind. 'His heart was pure and terrible,' she told Higginson a month after his death, 'and I think no other like it exists.' Whatever their estrangement in life (and that *he* had regretted the isolation which his own forbidding presence made inevitable is obvious from his touching pleasure in Emily's voluntarily bestowing her company that last after-

noon), he was not easily forgotten in death. 'When I think of his firm light
– quenched so causelessly, it fritters the worth of much that shines,' she
wrote to a friend the following January.

'Home itself is far from home since my father died,' she claimed in
March, and used the same words to another correspondent in July. That
summer she referred to 'those amazing years when I had a father' and
more than two years after his death wrote, 'I dream about father every
night, always a different dream, and forget what I am doing daytimes,
wondering where he is.' In the summer of 1876 she wrote to Higginson,
whose own wife had recently been similarly bereaved, 'Loneliness for my
own Father made me think of her.'

Was it loneliness for her father which made her receptive to the love of
his lifelong friend, Judge Otis Lord? Lord and his wife had been regular
overnight guests at the Dickinson home for as long as Emily could
remember. When Lord's wife died, towards the end of 1877, he and
Emily found mutual consolation in one another for their respective losses,
and a sincere affection developed leading to discussion of marriage. He
was sixty-six, she forty-seven. That she was genuinely fond of Judge Lord,
a gentler man than her father, yet surely a substitute-figure in his
perceived strength and sagacity, her letters make clear. She seems to have
declined his proposal only because she prized her liberty more than the
status and duties belonging to the wife of a public man.

The woman whom wise Judge Lord, knowing her well, found 'normal'
and lovable enough to desire for a wife was to the residents of Amherst a
mystery and a myth. A newcomer to the town in 1881, a young married
woman named Mabel Loomis Todd, heard the stories and passed them
on in a letter to a friend:

> I must tell you about the *character* of Amherst. It is a lady whom the
> people call the *Myth*. . . . She has not been outside of her own house in
> fifteen years, except to see a new church, when she crept out at night, &
> viewed it by moonlight. No one who calls upon her mother and sister
> ever sees her, but she allows little children once in a great while, &
> one at a time, to come in. . . . She dresses wholly in white, & her mind is
> said to be perfectly wonderful. She writes finely, but nobody *ever* sees
> her. Her sister, who was at Mrs [Austin] Dickinson's party, invited me
> to come & sing to her mother sometime. . . . People tell me the *myth* will
> hear every note – she will hear, but unseen.[7]

As an example of how anyone who does not conform in the society of a
small town is liable to be misunderstood and vilified, this is fine, though it
must be said that Emily did everything to encourage such gossip. Doubtless it gave her some satisfaction, some sense of her individuality, in being

recognized, even if her genius was not. She acknowledged with relish that in previous ages she would have been burned for a witch. Mabel was to get to know her better, however. A year after her arrival in Amherst she began a long affair with the unhappy Austin, and she it was who after Emily's death helped the unsophisticated Vinnie to publish a selection of the poems.

'We dwell as when you saw us,' Emily updated Higginson in 1881. 'The mighty dying of my father made no external change. . . . When Father lived I remained with him because he would miss me – Now, Mother is helpless – a holier demand.'

Emily's mother died in 1882, seven years after a stroke had left her with complete paralysis and considerable mental confusion. ('She asks for my father constantly and thinks it rude he does not come – begging me not to retire at night, lest no-one receive him. I am pleased that what grieves ourself so much – can no more grieve him,' Emily had written in 1875.)

Judge Lord died in 1884. Shortly afterwards Emily suffered a nervous breakdown, and she was never wholly well again. On 15 May 1886 she died of the kidney disorder Bright's Disease. 'The day was awful,' Austin wrote. Four days later the funeral took place. Vinnie placed in her hands two flowers 'to take to Judge Lord', and Thomas Higginson read over her grave the 'Last Lines' of Emily Brontë – the 'gigantic' Emily Brontë, as her namesake had reverently termed her.

As befits a poet whose best work is enigmatic and yields up multiple readings from what is deceptively simple, Emily Dickinson's life too invites more than one interpretation. The central puzzles of her existence – why she withdrew so much from the world, why she made no attempt to gain recognition for her genius – certainly are not easily or flippantly explained. The explanations do not even have to take much account of her father: her own extraordinary character may contain all the answers. Yet, from the number of times she referred to him in her letters, the picture of him she deliberately presented to outsiders, the undying reverberations of his death, it would seem most sensible to acknowledge the importance of her father in almost every aspect of her life.

In evaluating what Emily Dickinson owed to her father, it is necessary to remember that the calm and ordered existence at The Homestead which enabled her to dwell so intensively in her thoughts, was made possible by his industry as well as by his autocratic rule. Moreover, the emotionally numbing effect of his stern personality, while sad for her as a daughter (and for him as a father), was good for her poetry in the sense that it drove her to communicate with herself.

Finally it may be said that, from the Puritan inheritance he passed on to her, she took what was conducive to her creativity and spiritual happiness and somehow, from within herself, found the strength to discard the rest.

For all the inherent weakness of her subservient situation in life, it was she, not her free and mighty father, who derived joy in daily living. It was *her* spirit, in her poetry, which triumphantly lived on. That is Emily Dickinson's achievement.

VII

Beatrix Potter
1866–1943

'Must confess to crying, my father being as usual deplorable.'

Beatrix Potter seldom complained, rarely confided her innermost feelings to paper – and she had no intimate friend in whom to confide them in speech. Her references to her father, other than the purely factual, are scanty. Nevertheless, her diary yields up a picture of suppressed conflict, of irritations and troubles bravely borne, of endless frustrating years characterized by a sense of life wasted, to no better purpose than to fulfil her parents' narrow expectations of her. Beatrix could not know, in the first half of her long life, how gloriously she would break free in the second. Fame ever meant little to her, was even a bore, but the accompanying financial independence, which enabled her gradually to assert her own preferences and values, to experience the lifestyle she longed for, was the greatest good which could have befallen her. Quietly determined, once she had the means in her power, she yet broke her chains gradually, with due consideration for her parents' feelings – perhaps with more consideration than they deserved. She had after all been reared as a dutiful daughter, and her brother's impudent assertion of independence was compatible with neither her female circumstances nor her feminine conscience.

Both Beatrix's parents exerted control over her unmercifully, well into her own middle age, but it was her relationship with her father that was by far the more important – rewarding and irritating by turns – while her mother she simply disliked and politely ignored as much as possible. Helen Potter was a cold, boring, snobbish woman, without an interesting idea in her head. Rupert Potter shared his wife's snobbery and in many ways was equally fussy and formal; but he was an entertaining talker, full of anecdotes and information that stimulated the eager mind of his daughter, who wrote down many of the things he said. His hobbies, which he pursued with the avidity of a man who had not his living to earn, were lifelines to Beatrix, who had likewise too little to occupy her. The few doors that were opened to her, before she had acquired the purposefulness to open some for herself, were all opened by her father. Sharing his interests, proving to be an intelligent and companionable daughter, she enjoyed an unusually close relationship with her father through much of her childhood.

Perhaps that made it all the more painful when differences arose in later years. There was not only a difference of outlook to contend with; it was not just that Beatrix despised the stuffy conventions by which her parents' lives – and perforce her own – were bound; it was not merely that she longed for a useful country existence and was kept idle and confined to London. No, there was also a fundamental difference in temperament between herself and her father. She was basically 'a cheerful person' (her own words); he was melancholy and pessimistic. The generation gap between them was thus exacerbated. Rupert's gloomy moods were felt throughout the household and caused much of Beatrix's despair. Her youthful optimism and capacity for joy in the richness of life were continually being repressed. It is perhaps a wonder that she did not have recourse to tears of frustration more often than she did. Happily, she had recourse to a healthier, more fulfilling outlet: the worlds she created for herself, from her mid-thirties onwards – worlds first imaginary and then real.

'My brother and I were born in London because my father was a lawyer there,' wrote Beatrix Potter when she was an old lady. 'But our descent – our interests and our joy was in the north country.'[1] Those two uncomplaining sentences encapsulate many of the problems of her early life. The living in an uncongenial place against her will – the spurious necessity for it, since her father did not actually accept briefs – the blissful escape of the annual holiday – the identification with her ancestors – and the comparative ease with which her brother, feeling exactly as she did herself, followed his own inclinations – all can be traced in those words.

Rupert Potter, born in 1832, was the first of his family to leave the north of England. His father, Edmund, was a factory-owner from Lancashire. In 1824, as a young man, Edmund had set up a calico printing works, from which all the family money was to be generated. Edmund belonged to the class of self-made, self-reliant industrialists who combined sound business sense with a strong religious faith (he was a Unitarian, numbering Mr and Mrs Gaskell amongst his friends), wide-ranging interests, including art and politics, and a reasonably enlightened attitude to his employees.

His eldest son, Crompton, followed him into the business, but the second, Rupert, whose tastes were academic and artistic, disliked the thought of a commercial life. At the age of twenty-two, after completing his education at the Unitarian Manchester New College, he was allowed to go to London to study law at Lincoln's Inn. In fact, his father was to follow him to the capital seven years later, when he was elected Liberal

Member of Parliament for Carlisle, leaving Crompton to run the print-works. Edmund packed a great deal of useful activity into his life, earning enough to support a large family, providing a livelihood for his workers, making technical advances in the textile-printing industry and playing his part in public affairs. (In Parliament his especial concern was to bring education within the reach of all.) His son Rupert was by comparison indolent, lacking his father's vigour and his concern for other people.

Rupert was called to the bar in 1857, and six years later he married the daughter of another cotton fortune, Helen Leech. Her father had been dead two years, so she was already in possession of her legacy, a fact, perhaps, which enabled Rupert virtually to retire from working for a living. An exceedingly comfortable lifestyle was possible on their joint unearned income: a house in a good district of London, their own carriage and a pair of horses, long holidays in large rented country houses, and two maids and three menservants to ensure that Rupert and Helen Potter never had to do anything disagreeable for themselves.

A sixth servant, a nursery maid, was added to the establishment three years after the marriage, when the first child was born to the Potters. Helen Beatrix, always known by the second of her two Christian names, was born on 28 July 1866. Some months before, her parents had moved from their first married home, in Harley Street, to the more private and sedate district of Kensington, where at 2 Bolton Gardens, 'my unlovely birthplace',[2] Beatrix was to live, for the most part unwillingly, for the next forty-seven years.

When she was six, she was joined in the third-storey nursery by the only other child born to the Potters, her brother Bertram. One cannot help wondering whether it was Helen's coldness as a wife or her exceptionally determined character which preserved her from the indignity and danger of frequent childbirth, the usual female lot of her times. Her photographs do *not* show an amiable expression, and there is not one affectionate reference to her in all of Beatrix's writings. It is impossible not to conclude that Beatrix straightforwardly if secretly disliked her, but the degree of esteem existing between husband and wife is harder to calculate. Both had inherited the iron wills of their forebears, and it would seem that neither was in the habit of submitting to the other. Nevertheless, there does not appear to have been any disagreement between them as to how they should live or how bring up their children. They always presented a united and implacable front.

Beatrix Potter was a contemporary of *Alice in Wonderland*, and she was dressed just like Alice, with her hair in a band which hurt, a pinafore to keep her clothes clean, and stockings striped like a zebra's legs. Her petticoats were voluminous, her boots tight-laced, and she could never venture outdoors without a hat. The discomfort and restrictiveness of her clothing were symptomatic of the lack of understanding of childhood displayed by middle-class parents of the time. To the Potters, and to many like them, over-sensitive perhaps about their near connections with 'trade', appearances, conformity, respectability were all.

Though Rupert had sketched and Helen produced some passable water-colours in their respective youths, there was nothing of the Bohemian about them. Helen gave up art, as she gave up almost every activity, on marriage. Rupert retained his interest, which manifested itself in a variety of ways. Principally, he took up photography, then a new art form. He also collected pictures, visited galleries and attended every new exhibition – perhaps the best justification for continuing to live in London. (The hours and hours he spent at his two clubs, the Reform and the Atheneum, reading the newspapers and exchanging male gossip, are less easy to regard with any leniency.)

Beatrix was a sensible, well-behaved little girl, and from an early age she was allowed to accompany her father to his favourite exhibitions and galleries, and to the Natural History Museum, all of which fed her eager appetite for mental and visual stimulation. She was even taken to the studio of a real artist, John Millais, with whom her father was friendly and for whom he provided photographic references, either of backgrounds or of the sitters themselves.

It was photography, indeed, that drew father and daughter closest together. The combination of art and science fascinated them both (just as it had Edmund Potter in the calico-printing industry). From her father Beatrix learned to look at her surroundings with the idea of making pictures; she also learned how to manage the cumbersome equipment and to master the delicate decisions essential in the days before photography was at all automated. In pursuing that mutual interest, father and daughter enjoyed a warm companionship – and it had the further advantage to Beatrix of enabling her to 'forget' to be excessively ladylike, since she was sometimes required to scramble about in the country, in search of the best vantage-points.

For most of their photography was done on holiday, the high spots of Beatrix's existence. Every Easter the Potters took lodgings somewhere on the south coast for a month; every summer and early autumn they went north for full three months. All the summers of Beatrix's childhood – from 1871 to 1881 – were spent at Dalguise, a large house and estate in Scotland. There Rupert sported a deer-stalker – though he does not seem to have hunted; but he fished, photographed and acted the part of a country gentleman. Helen Potter seems to have made no concessions to the change of surroundings; her life went on as uneventfully as if she were still in London, with all the usual rituals of formal mealtimes, carriage drives and servants. But at Dalguise both Beatrix and Bertram felt themselves come alive. The scenery, the plants and animals, the homely interiors of the farms and cottages, the simple country people, intent on making a living from the land, not on putting on a show, and full of interesting tales from the past, captivated the imagination of both children.

Beatrix and Bertram shared a love of animals and natural history as well as the interest in art inherited from their parents. Until he went away to school at the age of eleven – by which time most of Beatrix's own childhood was over, he was her only companion of her own generation and, when they returned to London, and her father to his clubs, the only companion of any age during most hours of the day. Except for a few cousins, who visited only occasionally and who found it difficult to penetrate her shyness, she was not allowed to mix with other children, and her lessons were provided by a succession of private governesses.

Beatrix did not envy her brother's schooling. Looking back from adulthood, she felt that she could have been taught anything, if she had been caught early enough, so avid was her mind for knowledge, so wide-ranging her interest in life, but that being at school would have squashed the individuality out of her. Her mental liberty was always the asset most prized by Beatrix, though physical liberty was entirely out of the question.

Her mind was exceptionally alert, and she was rarely bored, for she had the invaluable gift of being able to amuse herself with her own thoughts; she also exercised her brain by such self-imposed tasks as learning many of the plays of Shakespeare until she was word-perfect. But she *was* frustrated, and she was, inevitably, lonely. It was perhaps to alleviate her loneliness that, at about the time of Bertram's departure, she took to keeping a diary, taking the idea from one of her 'heroines', Fanny Burney, and even occasionally addressing her words to 'Esther', the name of Fanny's eldest sister.

The diary was, however, seldom used as the repository of her most intimate thoughts. She did not turn to it in order to analyse herself, her parents or her relationship with them; she did not agonize over her lot. Most of what she wrote was a straightforward record of interesting information she had picked up (often from her father's conversation), long accounts of visits to galleries (invariably accompanying her father), with her opinions of the pictures seen, and details of what they did on holiday. There was scarcely a sentence unfit for her parents themselves to read. And yet it pleased this extraordinarily self-contained girl to devise a secret code for these writings, which she kept up for sixteen years. It was as if, from adolescence, she felt that life was passing her by without anything to show for it, and that a record, even one that no one else would ever read (as she thought), would prevent its seeming quite so futile.

Her parents did not appear to realize that she was growing up. There was, of course, no question of a career, but even marriage was hardly contemplated in the Potter scheme of things. Beatrix was given no opportunity to meet potential husbands. Rupert had his circle of male friends, some of them quite influential, but the Potters did not mix in 'society' as such. Beatrix was not among that class of Victorian females who 'came out', who were invited to balls and parties. Of course, she would have utterly loathed all that, but she did have normal womanly longings for a home of her own, a husband and children to be the objects of her affection – as later comments were to reveal. Not for another twenty years was she to meet people in the best possible way, through a shared interest in work. Her parents kept her so closely confined that all through her twenties and early thirties no hint of romance drifted near her. They seemed to have assumed that she could want nothing better than to live with them and to minister to them in their old age. They really do not seem to have regarded Beatrix as an individual with her own personality to fulfil, her own life to live out. She was their appendage.

Her sense of duty was so strong that she consistently struggled to subdue the inevitable feelings of resentment and frustration. She attempted to be a good daughter, obedient and unselfish, trusting that with 'patience and waiting' her life would 'come right' in the end. But, docile though her demeanour deceptively was, Beatrix had a quietly stubborn and resisting spirit. Though her fury was mostly banked down, inevitably there were occasional storms, hints of which appear occasionally in the journal. In November 1883, after mentioning 'a violent domestic explosion' between her mother and a servant in 'the lower quarters' of the house, she added that there had also been 'several small eruptions up here. I have a cold, my temper has been boiling like a kettle, so that things are as usual.' (The last two words are revealing.) In January 1884, 'I am not, not in high spirits tonight, something unpleasant having happened.' On the last day of 1885, reviewing the passing year, she attributed to it 'Much bitterness and a few peaceful summer days. Oh life, wearisome, disappointing, and yet in many shades so sweet, I wonder why one is unwilling to let go this old year? not because it has been joyful, but because I fear its successors – I am terribly afraid of the future.'[3] She was 19½ when she wrote that, the very age for confident looking forward and reaching out to embrace life's possibilities.

When Bertram reached a similar age, his passage was made much smoother. First he wanted to paint, and then he wanted to farm; his parents indulged (or surrendered to – it is impossible to know) both wishes, and he was eventually installed on a farm in Scotland, well out of the way of their interference and of any expectations of his dancing attendance on them as his sister was forced to do. So far from his parents' sphere of influence, indeed, did Bertram live, that when he married a country girl, he managed to conceal the fact from them for seven years! There are suggestions that he had a drink problem and that his parents were glad enough to get him out of the way. Certainly he was of little support to Beatrix in their adult lives, leaving her to cope with their parents while he painted and farmed in blissful independence in Scotland. But quite apart from the differences inherent in merely being female, it would have been quite impossible to one of Beatrix's stern conscience to emulate him and so entirely abandon them and what she had been made to feel was her duty.

There are many echoes from the Brontë family here. Bertram, perhaps born with gifts equal to his sister's, did nothing with his life. Beatrix, schooled in adversity and self-denial, eventually, after years of despair and suffering and without once violating her principles, fulfilled her potential triumphantly, both in creative and in personal terms.

As Rupert Potter reached his fifties, the gloom in his character became more pronounced, to the discomfort of those who had to live with him. His pessimism was greatest on the subjects of politics and money. He shared the common fear of those who live on unearned income, that the value of his investments would diminish through factors beyond his control. 'Papa says it's Mr Gladstone's fault,' was an early refrain in Beatrix's diaries. 'My father thinks the country is going to the dogs, and his spirits get worse and worse,' she wrote in 1885, and 'Father says we shall have the taxes half a crown in the pound and conscription.' The following February , when there was some fear of rioting in London, 'My father is becoming very yellow, and lower than ever. Had a faintness on Wednesday. Has heard something about Gladstone which he cannot mention to ladies, at the Reform Club. Talks about going to the Colonies, Edinburgh, quiet provincial towns, but he has done that occasionally for the last ten years.'

In more indulgent mood she wrote, 'Now if my papa has a fault, he is rather voluble in conversation and . . . oppressively well-informed.' He became one of those peppery old gentlemen who can never forbear putting people right if they hear a mistake uttered. This could have its amusing consequences, as when 'One day at Sir John Millais', my father being photographing, overheard Lord Rosebery and another gentleman, whom he afterwards learnt to be Mr Buckle, Editor of *The Times*, in the course of conversation make some glaring mis-statement, not of a controversial nature, but of fact. My father could not stand it and set them right. . . . Lord Rosebery, supposing my father to be an ordinary working photographer, received the correction as a positive insult, and there was a scrimmage.'

Rupert was just as ready to give others the benefit of his opinions as of his information. A visit to the Bodleian together, where he found much to criticize in a collection of portraits, provoked this response in Beatrix: 'I am sure he has not the least idea of the difficulty of painting a picture. He can draw very well, but he has hardly attempted water-colour, and never oil. A person in this state, with a correct eye, and good taste, and great experience of different painters, sees all the failures and not the difficulties. He has never stared at a model till he did not know whether it was standing on its feet or its head. Then, seeing Mr Millais paint so often and easily, would make a man hard on other painters.' She added, significantly, 'It prevents me showing much of my attempts to him, and I lose much by it.'

Plainly Beatrix respected her father's intellect and his taste, and there were still moments of the old childhood companionship between them. At Torquay, in the spring of 1893, a drive with her mother and two other ladies 'through a most dreary suburb . . . disgusted' her so much 'that I privately incited papa to going into Kent's Hole [a cavern] next morning by way of a reviver. We slunk out after breakfast' and 'got away through the bushes'. And in Tweedmouth the following September the two of them spent the day together, photographing amongst the boats, 'and by dawdling about with plenty of time we had a very enjoyable expedition'.

On the whole, however, the annual summer holiday became less and less of a joy to Beatrix as her parents became more and more exacting. 'It is somewhat trying to pass a season of enjoyment in the company of persons who are constantly on the outlook for matters of complaint,' she wrote at the end of the same holiday. 'I and Elizabeth the housemaid were the only persons who were thoroughly pleased, whereof I take to be the moral that Elizabeh and I had better go there some day for a holiday, to lodgings.' Ten years later she was still accompanying her parents on their regular yet apparently unenjoyed sojourns away from the comforts of home; she confessed 'Our summer "holiday" is always a weary business.'

Much more pleasurable, a rare treat indeed, was a visit in June 1894 to a cousin, Caroline Hutton, in Gloucestershire (where she first heard the story that was to inspire *The Tailor of Gloucester*). Much difficulty was made about her going, though she was now twenty-eight. 'I used to go to my grandmother's, and once I went for a week to Manchester, but I had not been away independently for five years. It was an event. It was so much an event in the eyes of my relations that they made it appear an undertaking to me, and I began to think I would rather not go.' Happily, Caroline arrived and 'carried me off' and she did thoroughly enjoy her visit, and the company of her relatively liberated cousin. The visit had its unpleasant consequences, however; nothing in Beatrix's life went as she wished. She had hoped to be permitted to invite Caroline to join her family on their summer holiday but was denied, the deficiencies of the spare bedroom being made 'a convenient excuse'. She was disappointed and vexed for her own sake and because she thought it hurtful to one who had been kind to her and deserved better treatment.

The following summer, 1895, the Potters took their holiday in the Lake District. Rupert found new sources of displeasure. Motor launches on Lake Windermere enraged him. 'I shall never forget his expression, sitting in the stern of a very small boat waiting to outride the swell,' wrote Beatrix. They broke the journey home at Manchester, where Rupert in a sentimental mood went to call on the Misses Gaskell, only to find them so 'gushing' and so unbecomingly stout that he 'kept referring to it all evening'.

In October of that year, back in London, Helen Potter was sick for rather less than twenty-four hours and made it an excuse to keep to her bed for a fortnight. Beatrix received an intimation of what her life would surely be in future, as her parents' ailments (real or imaginary) increased and they became more dependent upon her. She had 'a weary time, bother with servants as well. There is supposed to be some angelic sentiment in tending the sick, but personally I should not associate angels with castor oil and emptying slops.' Her father too was unwell, 'troubled with gravel again', and Beatrix concluded this entry with: 'every prospect of a hard winter, I have become lower than is the habit with me, a cheerful person'.

That winter she did perhaps sink to her lowest depths of despair. On Sunday 3 November she went out for a brief, refreshing and surely well-earned visit to neighbours at number 28, but such was the power of her father over this normally cheerful young woman that she was reduced to tears on her return: 'Must confess to crying after I got home, father being as usual deplorable.'

With both her parents in poor health, there began to be talk of their regularly wintering abroad. The prospect of managing her never-satisfied parents in foreign hotels was horrifying. 'I fretted so wearily,' wrote Beatrix, 'that I went privately to see Dr Aiken Dec. 11th, and had it out with him. He was very kind. I told him plainly I thought it was very startling to be told to go abroad for five months of the year. If my father cannot stand the English winter it is a matter to consider, but seriously we could not stand living five months in an hotel. . . . I am anxious to do my best,' she added nobly, 'but really I cannot face going abroad with him.'

The previous May her father had to her surprise presented her with some bonds of the North Pacific Railway which had paid no interest for the previous two years. 'Income tax and other complications', she thought had prompted the gift. Acting entirely on her own judgement and thoroughly enjoying doing so, she sold and reinvested the £5,000 she obtained. Now, during her lowest winter, she derived her best consolation from 'the comfort of having money. One must make out some way. It is something to have a little money to spend on books and to look forward to being independent, though forlorn.' Her father was again feeling gloomy about his investments. On 20 December he 'got rid of £9,000 of my mother's Canadian securities' at a profit, but still Christmas that year was spoiled by the 'interminable rule of the sums and stock-broking calculations which would never come right'. (Not that Christmas was ever very joyful in the Potter household; as Unitarians they kept observance of its customs to a minimum, and there was no warmth of family feeling to supply the place of religious celebration. Year after year Beatrix remarked on what a dismal Christmas they had in comparison with other families she knew of.) Her father fretted all the following week, and by 5 January, when the news broke of the Jameson Raid, she wrote that he was again 'deplorable', having worked himself into a state of nervous exhaustion over the likely effects on his South African investments.

The following summer Beatrix attained her thirtieth birthday. On that day she wrote: 'I feel much younger at thirty than at twenty; firmer and stronger both in mind and body.' She had come through perhaps the worst winter of her life, and her character had matured and begun to show some of the determination, tempered always by her wish to do her duty, which was to carry her triumphantly through the next fifty years. Work was the only palliative to her unsatisfactory life, and work, of some kind or another, she must and would do. For many years she made a serious study of fungi, collecting and painting each specimen with loving accuracy and making discoveries about the mode of reproduction. In this field her work received an accolade when her paper on the subject was read (by a man: women were not allowed to be present) to the Linnean Society in April 1897.

She made her first tentative steps in another direction, one that would prove ultimately more rewarding, when she sold some drawings of rabbits as Christmas card designs. The £6 cheque which this brought in was at least as delightful to her as the £5,000 investment which had not had the satisfaction of being earned. By 1900 she was seriously considering attempting to publish an illustrated story for children which had started life some five years before as a picture letter to the eldest son of her former governess, now Mrs Moore. Six publishers turned down the idea, but by then Beatrix expected nothing to come easily to her, and she persevered. She had a small edition of her little book about Peter Rabbit printed privately and, proud of the look of him in print and pleased with the reactions of those who bought copies, she sent one to the publisher who had qualified his original rejection by admiring the designs. The firm, Frederick Warne, was won over and agreed to publish *The Tale of Peter Rabbit* provided Beatrix would redraw the pictures in colour. She agreed.

Her life had changed for ever. Quite apart from the delight of creating her stories and pictures, the whole business of publishing was intensely interesting to her. She had all her grandfather's financial astuteness, married to a perfect integrity, and all – or more than – her father's taste and knowledge on the artistic and literary aspects. But before calling for the first time at her publisher's office, she felt constrained to issue the following warning: 'If my father happens to insist on going with me to see the agreement,' she wrote in a postscript to a letter dated 22 May 1902, 'would you please not mind him very much, if he is fidgetty about things. I am afraid it is not a very respectful way of talking & I don't wish to refer to it again, but I think it is better to mention before hand he is sometimes a little difficult. I can of course do what I like about the book, being 36. I suppose it is a habit of old gentlemen; but sometimes rather trying.'[4] Only fear of having this darling project, this precious lifeline, spoilt by mis-understanding could have led her to the extremity of writing thus, violating, perhaps for the first time in her life, her code of honour as a daughter.

The immediate popularity of the book and its successors, the new purpose and business of her days, and the steady accumulation of more royalties than she had ever dreamed of made her parents as uneasy as Beatrix was content. She was too absorbed in the work for their liking, and becoming too friendly with the family of Warne, who were by Potter reckoning socially inferior. It was not only by coldness and silence that her parents signified their disapproval but by constant verbal assault. About to set off with her parents on their Easter holiday in 1904, Beatrix confessed, 'I have had such painful unpleasantnesses at home this winter about the work that I should like a rest from scolding while I am away.'

A year or so later, it was suggested that she visit a niece of the Warne family in Surbiton, to draw her doll's house for *Two Bad Mice*. 'I was very much perplexed about the doll's house,' she was obliged to write. 'I would have gone gladly to draw it, and I should be so very sorry if Mrs Warne or you thought me uncivil. I did not think I could manage to go to Surbiton without staying to lunch; I hardly ever go out, and my mother is so exacting I had not enough spirit to say anything about it. I have felt vexed with myself since, but I did not know what to do. It does wear a person out.' The reply was a kind invitation for her mother to accompany her to Surbiton. Worse and worse! Beatrix had to explain, 'I don't think that my mother would be very likely to want to go to Surbiton. You did not understand what I meant by "exacting". People who only see her casually do not know how disagreeable she can be when she takes dislikes.'

Those rather confidential letters were addressed to Norman Warne, one of the three sons of the original founder of the publishing house, and the only one unmarried. Between him and Beatrix a gentle attraction, founded on shared interests and similar tastes and temperaments, developed over the course of two or three years into a real sense of friendship such as Beatrix had rarely enjoyed before in her life. They were never alone together, meeting only in the office or in company with Norman's mother and unmarried sister, Millie, but in July 1905, a month after Beatrix's thirty-ninth birthday, the shy Norman sent her a letter (she was holidaying in Wales) declaring his love and offering marriage.

She accepted without hesitation – despite the ordeal of having to defy her parents. They were first of all shocked – they had not imagined that anything of *that sort* had been going on, with Beatrix so closely supervised – and then horrified on their own account. Beatrix's prospects of happiness did not, of course, figure in their reactions. The idea of losing the prop of their old age, and to a man in trade, was unthinkable. Beatrix, however, was quietly determined. She had every reason to believe Norman a good, kind man, affectionate to his nephews and nieces and sharing her own literary and artistic interests. And was not publishing, she indignantly asked herself, as clean and honourable a trade as cotton? She had never had much time for her parents' snobbery, but she was certainly not going to let it stand in the way of this chance of happiness or allow it to hurt a decent man who had the perception to love her. She insisted on wearing Norman's engagement ring.

Almost immediately, however, he fell ill. Just a month after the proposal, on 25 August 1905, he died, of pernicious anaemia.

Of course, Beatrix received no sympathy from her parents. Their glee was not expressed – or, at least, not in any form which has survived, but presumably they felt it as a reprieve, and trusted that their erring daughter had been restored to them and to her duty for ever. In contrast to her own parents' silence on the subject, Norman's family, who had been prepared to welcome her warmly to their number, were a great support. Beatrix also had a strong sense of resignation to unavoidable evils, and much practice in the habit of self-control, to see her through the crisis. 'I must try to make a fresh beginning next year,' she wrote to Millie Warne, who was to become a lifelong correspondent.

But when 'next year' came, she was still grieving. In February an aunt and uncle invited her to join them in Bath. From there she wrote to Millie a letter of unbearable poignancy: 'I find the names of the streets rather melancholy here; do you remember Miss Austen's *Persuasion* with all the scenes and streets in Bath? It was always my favourite and I read the end part of it again last July, on the 26th the day after I got Norman's letter. I thought my story had come right with patience and waiting like Anne Elliot's did.'

But, disappointed in one dear hope, Beatrix still had not only the preoccupations and satisfactions of creative work but another source of profound and fruitful enjoyment in her life. Her little books were bringing in an amazing amount of money, and shortly before Norman's proposal she had used some of it to buy a farm in the Lake District. To her parents this was represented as an investment; there was no question of her making her permanent home there, and a manager was installed to run the farm. Nevertheless, she had a toehold in a part of the country she loved, and she escaped as often as she could to Hill Top – where she occupied the oldest part of the farmhouse, an extension being provided for the farmer and his family. Making decisions about Hill Top, acquiring old bits of furniture and agricultural knowledge apace and becoming more and more involved with the community of Far Sawrey, Beatrix was in her element. This, as much or even more than writing and drawing, was what she had been born for. And the satisfaction of having provided it for herself, from her own talents and labour, was immense.

Her parents, inevitably, still made many demands on her. Though she was in her early forties, her time was by no means at her own disposal. She wrote to Millie, for example, from Hill Top on 9 October 1910: 'I have been very undecided in my movements, & finally came off here at very short notice. My brother came home, and thought I had better take a holiday (?) while I could get away. My father has been very complaining again, but I really do not believe there is anything the matter with him except muscular pain on the outside. He is going about again as usual, so unless I am sent for I shall stay a little longer, there is a very great deal to do. . . . I was much wanting a change, it has been rather a trying season.'

There was still no possibility of Beatrix's asserting her right to live at Hill Top permanently, farming and writing and drawing just as she pleased. Her duty was to remain at Bolton Gardens, unless she could cite the higher duty of having a husband to care for. By 1913 she had a prospective husband in view. William Heelis was a solicitor from Hawkshead whom had she got to know as she gradually added to her land holdings around Sawrey. His offer of marriage, which was in effect an offer of escape from Bolton Gardens, was accepted in a different spirit, though no less joyfully, than Norman Warne's. Beatrix was careful not to go from one set of restrictions to another. She was to be without question the dominant partner in the marriage.

The same objections met this engagement as its predecessor (country solicitors were not to be addressing daughters of barristers), but she was even more capable of withstanding them. Eight years of largely managing her own affairs had intervened, and by imperceptible degrees there had emerged in Beatrix the sturdiness and independence of character that were her northern inheritance and which living in the north country had nurtured.

'William has actually been invited up for a weekend soon,' she wrote to a friend in September 1913. 'They never say much but they cannot dislike him.' Her parents knew when they were beaten.

Not that it was easy to fix the dreadful day when she would leave them. In the same letter, reporting that her father had been unwell but that a nurse, just dismissed for getting in her mother's way, 'had done more for him than any doctor, & got him under her thumb', she continued: 'He is so well I am in fear they may not get anybody. If we were not coming to a difficult change amongst the home servants – I might be tempted to bolt at once, while he is feeling well and cheerful!'

Perhaps that is just what she did, since the wedding took place barely three weeks later, on 14 October 1913. It was as well that she took the step then, since a few months delay would have trapped her in her mother's widowhood. Rupert Potter's health continued to decline, an operation was attempted and cancer discovered. Beatrix shuttled between Sawrey and London, helping to nurse her father and ease the burden on her mother, just as they had always relied on her to do when the time came. She made eight journeys to London in the first four months of 1914, before reporting to the Warne family on 9 May: 'He died very peacefully last evening. I do not think he ever had acute pain but it has been rather a ghastly illness. We are very thankful it is over, as we feared he might drag on for weeks longer – he went suddenly at the end. . . . I suppose he was just worn out.'

Helen Potter, who had looked to her daughter to comfort her through her widowhood, now had to be established somewhere. She was installed with a paid companion and a retinue of lesser servants in a house in the Lake District, where she never ceased to moan or to keep Beatrix 'on the trot' until her death in 1932, at the age of ninety-three. ('There was no love lost between mother and daughter,' Helen Potter's cook later affirmed.)

After her marriage, Beatrix gradually ceased to produce new books or to think of herself as an author – she became a full-time farmer and thorough-going countrywoman, no longer Beatrix Potter but Mrs Heelis. Her eyesight was not up to the fine art work she had once done, and her fund of imaginative ideas had depleted itself in ten or twelve extraordinarily prolific years. Farming, especially sheep-breeding, and conservation of the Lake District became the abiding interests of the remainder of her life, which closed peacefully in 1943, full thirty hard-working years after the final escape from London and the Potter home.

It would be wrong, however, to infer that the books were just a stepping-stone from her parents' clutches to the kind of life she preferred. At the time they were created, her whole genius flowed into them, a genius that had long been waiting release. Genius is not too strong a word. As the merits and felicities, both verbal and visual, of the Beatrix Potter books become every year more justly appreciated and deeply studied, the original and exquisite nature of her genius becomes ever more solidly established. It was the result of the various strands of her upbringing, influenced by her father more than by any other person, acting on a mind that was both highly individual and steeped in a rich inheritance. Her gift of seeing with the freshness of a child's eyes yet from the vantage-point of perfect maturity and balance was a rare one. In helping to form her mind, and subsequently strengthening her character through endurance and trial, Rupert Potter, fussy, selfish and 'deplorable' though he was, played a part in the magic.

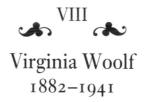

VIII

Virginia Woolf
1882–1941

'He obsessed me for years.'

When his daughter Virginia was born, the third child of his second marriage, Leslie Stephen was old enough to be her grandfather. Unlike most of the fathers in this study, therefore, he did not survive into his daughter's middle age, and his influence on the outward course of her adult life was not unduly great. His effect on her first twenty-two years, however – on the crucial period of her emotional and intellectual development – was profound, and his memory continued to trouble her for many more years, even after she had attempted to exorcise it by thoroughly exploring his character in *To The Lighthouse*.

Virginia's youth may be divided into two quite distinct periods. Until the age of thirteen, while her mother was still alive, she enjoyed a near-idyllic childhood. Her teens, the years dominated by her father only, were years of family tragedy and personal anguish. On Leslie's death she escaped, together with her sister and brothers, with almost indecent haste from the Victorian values which he had seemed to represent. (The fact that he had come to maturity in effect *two* generations before theirs aggravated the gulf in ideas of which many young people were aware at around the turn of the century.) But while the other Stephens made their escape wholeheartedly, Virginia, more sympathetic to his suffering and deeply conscious of the special bond between herself and him, was attacked by guilt and by regrets for his passing.

Twenty-four years later, as a mature woman and committed writer, she mused in her journal on 28 November 1928: 'Father's birthday. He would have been 1928–1832 = 96, 96, yes, today; & could have been 96, like other people one has known; but mercifully was not. What would have happened? No writing, no books; – inconceivable.'[1] Why would his existence have prevented her writing, when he was a writer himself and had always been proud of her developing talents? The answer must lie in the terrible effect which his overpowering personality had upon her fragile one. His fundamental tenderness for her and for all his children, of which he himself was quite happily convinced, was inadequate to counteract the selfishness – the brutality even – of his behaviour.

The key to Leslie Stephen's threat to his daughter's serenity lay in his egocentric attitude to women. Much as he respected, even venerated the women in his life, he nevertheless regarded them as unquestionably his 'slaves' (the word is Virginia's), whose highest calling was to tend his wants, soothe his ruffled spirits and minister to his vanity. His emotional demands grew heavier the older and more disappointed he became, and as one after another of the women in his life dropped dead from sheer exhaustion – or that was how it appeared to Virginia – the threat to herself, as his youngest daughter, drew ever closer. The monster's demands were of a nature to consume every other aspect of his victim's existence. Without stopping to consider whether it was just or appropriate to do so, he seemed bent on fashioning her into yet another 'angel in the house', a character which she knew from bitter observation was incompatible with leading any sort of life of one's own.

This grotesque aspect of Leslie Stephen's personality took some time to manifest itself in all its enormity. For the first thirty-three years of his life he managed to exist as a happy bachelor, with only a doting mother and a pious unmarried sister to fuss over him on his periodic returns home. A Cambridge don, he lived the typical academic life of non-involvement, mixing only with men who were his intellectual equals, regarding women as almost alien beings and working off his spare energy (and his sexuality?) in holidays of Alpine mountaineering.

Then some late-developing spark of ambition or originality impelled him to give up his comfortable career and endeavour to make a living as a man of letters in London. He had good connections in the literary world and was soon contributing serious pieces to the most respected journals of the day, as well as working on a book of philosophy. At Cambridge he had been ordained but, like many of his generation, lost his faith – though in his case without too much inner conflict. It was not matters of religion or philosophy that were to torture Leslie Stephen's soul – he had a cool, firm grasp of abstract argument – but matters of love. That emotion, which one part of him would have denigrated as 'women's business', had an extraordinary power to rack this 'skinless' man. (The adjective is his own and indicates the tone of self-pity that was to creep in.)

At thirty-five he fell in love for the first time and, like a typical Victorian, for all the wrong reasons. Minny, younger daughter of the novelist William Makepeace Thackeray, who had died a couple of years before, was docile and demure, adoring and admiring Leslie without qualification but quite incapable of meeting him on an intellectual level. He gushed about her 'purity' and married her in 1867. Their first child was born 3½ years later.

Minny had hero-worshipped not only her brilliant father but her elder sister Anny, who was brilliant too in her own scatty, ill-educated way – a way that drove Leslie to fury on occasion, because his sister-in-law was so little like what a woman should be, yet so palpably inferior to a man. 'I had a perhaps rather pedantic mania for correcting her flights of imagination and checking her exuberant impulses,' Leslie admitted.[2] Sparks frequently flew between them, and Minny of course was required to adminster the balm. She was so dependent upon her sister that she begged they all live together after the marriage and, as Leslie was not very well off, it suited him to move into the house which Anny and Minny had shared since their father's death. Fundamentally Leslie had a high opinion of Anny, her generosity of spirit and cheerfulness of temper, but in daily life at close quarters he found her trying. Among her faults in his eyes was carelessness about money – when she earned any from writing her high-spirited but sentimental novels, she was just as likely to give it away, and Leslie nursed a few lifelong grudges about her failure to contribute to the household expenses, while at the same time priding himself on refraining from reminding her of her debts.

If Leslie had married the sister with character and loved her despite her faults, he might have been forced to reconsider his ideas, or rather his assumptions, about subservience being natural and desirable in the female sex. On the terms upon which he lived with them, however, the Thackeray sisters merely reinforced his prejudices and his complacency. In eight years of marriage Minny never made him feel anything but godlike and protective, while conflict with Anny convinced him he had made the right choice.

In 1875, when their daughter Laura was five, Minny became pregnant for the second time. On the evening of 27 November, as Leslie was to recall in the reminiscences he set down for his children (characteristically called *The Mausoleum Book*), 'I was sitting at home with her in perfect happiness and security. . . . Mrs Herbert Duckworth looked in to see us. She found us – so she afterwards told me – so happy together that she thought the presence of a desolate widow incongruous, and left us to return to her own solitary hearth. . . . [Minny] went to bed in some discomfort, and thought it best to sleep in a room where one Mary Anne, a maid of Anny's, could keep an eye upon her. Anny was at Eton. During the night Mary Anne called me; I got up and found my darling in a convulsion. I fetched the doctor. I remember only too clearly the details of what followed; but I will not set them down. My darling never regained consciousness. She died about the middle of the day, 28 November, my forty-third birthday. You know why I have never celebrated that day! I was left alone.'

Since he had discovered, somewhat late in life, the pleasures of having his own female 'slave', 'alone' was what Leslie could not endure once more to be. The Stephens' visitor that fateful evening, Julia Duckworth, was an exceptionally beautiful woman of twenty-nine, who had been widowed five years previously. She had enjoyed just three years of happy marriage and had been left with two small children and another on the way. A constitutional melancholy, which suited her lovely face, had been naturally deepened by her loss; she was gentle, grave, wise, reserved but profoundly sympathetic to suffering of all kinds. On her visit of condolence, her manner was thought too 'restrained' by Anny, who would have preferred 'greater "outpouring"', but Leslie found her very soothing. Soon afterwards, trying to get on in the house with Anny alone, he snapped and made a scene about some unexpected bills. Anny persuaded Julia, who was a little frightened of him, to speak diplomatically to Leslie about his 'want of temper'. Delighted by the attention, he 'had the sense to confess his shortcomings and make promises of amendment'. He realized he had found not merely a replacement to fill Minny's role in his life but a partner who satisfied every need of his nature in a way poor Minny, much as he had loved her, had never done. He began his courtship by moving his household to be next door to Julia and her three children, George, Stella and Gerald.

Leslie's need to find someone was acute. In the summer after Minny's death, he opened the parlour door to find Anny in the embrace of a cousin seventeen years her junior (Anny was by now forty). Leslie insisted that young Richmond Ritchie do the honourable thing and marry her, despite his own (that is, Leslie's) revulsion at the thought of such a marriage. But they had been kissing, after all! Leslie congratulated himself on acting most selflessly in the affair, especially as his home was now deprived of its housekeeper, however unsatisfactorily she had performed her duties. (It is pleasant to record that Anny's marriage was evidently a happy one, according to the many people who left their observations of it.)

Leslie's unmarried sister, Milly, was now conscripted to run his house, but the experiment lasted only a month. He found her an affectionate but depressing companion, wholly perplexed when he expressed doubts on anything, falling to weeping if he were sad. She could neither stand up to him nor soothe and pacify him. Under her brother's demands her health broke down almost immediately, and marriage to Julia became more than ever essential, or Leslie would have to make do with a hired housekeeper, and where would be the comfort in that? So he applied the emotional blackmail that was increasingly to characterize the marriage and to be so acutely analysed by a daughter in her portrait of Mr and Mrs Ramsay.

There was considerable reluctance on Julia's side to overcome. Leslie's moodiness and intellectuality were daunting. Moreover, she had vowed after Herbert Duckworth's death to renounce all pleasure in the world, all hopes of personal happiness. But with great skill Leslie persuaded her that it was a matter of humanity, almost of duty, to marry him. His self-confessed great need of her must have had an irresistible appeal to the strong sacrificial streak in her nature. He possessed, besides, a quality rare in a man, a quality that both men and women found attractive in him: unashamed gentleness and tenderness. As befitted a man who valued the friendship of women, 'He did by instinct all the little things that women like', as one elderly female acquaintance was later to tell Virginia. In a letter to his prospective mother-in-law, he propounded his belief that men should cultivate the 'feminine' side of their nature, though not the 'effeminate'. So Julia married him in March 1878; their daughter Vanessa was born the following May, and son Thoby the September after that.

The threefold family now consisted of six children, which seemed quite enough, especially as one of them – Laura – had tragically turned out to be mentally defective; especially as Leslie was perpetually in a fret about money and expenses; especially as he needed a quiet house in which to work, for the only money that came in was what was earned by his pen. Leslie and Julia agreed to limit their family, and to practise birth control.[3] But whatever they relied on did not work – fortunately for the English novel (and for the feminist cause) in the twentieth century. Virginia was born on 25 January 1882; Adrian followed twenty-one months later.

Virginia wrote that she was 'born into a large connection, born not of rich parents, but of well-to-do parents, born into a very communicative, literate, letter-writing, visiting, articulate, late nineteenth century world'.[4] It was a propitious world for a boy of ability to open his eyes upon; altogether more problematic for a girl. Moreover, membership of the intelligentsia could not obscure the fact that late-Victorian society was deeply imbued with stifling respectability, rigid class-consciousness, gender-differential and repressed male sexuality, all of which were to leave their mark on Virginia.

The Stephens' home was a narrow, seven-storey house in a sedate Kensington backwater. The ten amalgamated Stephens and Duckworths and the seven maids required to service them lived out their various lives and pursued their various interests on the various levels of the house. Leslie's study was at the top; then there were the nursery and the schoolroom; bedrooms; reception rooms; the servants' quarters in the basement (seven of them sleeping as well as cooking there!). The sole water-closet was on one half-landing, and the sole tin bath on another.

It was Julia's function to ensure that all the elements meshed smoothly, that the 'panoply of life – that which we all lived in common' was kept in being. Most fundamentally, she protected Leslie from disturbance. But often Julia would be away – not refreshing herself with a solitary break, as Leslie frequently did, but devotedly nursing whichever of her large circle of family and friends had happened to fall ill, for she could resist no demand that was made on her. The one stipulation she had brought to the marriage was that she be allowed to visit sick-beds as before. Her only published work was a manual on nursing.

Mealtimes at 22 Hyde Park Gate were strictly punctual: 'At five father must be given his tea.' In the evenings, Leslie and Julia would often go out together, though he usually grumbled about it. The four younger children, so close in age, naturally made a unit that was more or less oblivious to what was going on in the rest of the house. Only when Thoby was old enough to go away to school, and to learn things Virginia was not expected to learn, did unity founder and she receive the cultural shock that was administered to so many girls in the nineteenth century. (In conformity with the inevitable pattern, from the beginning it was Thoby who bore the weight of his father's expectations.)

The young Stephens' sibling closeness alleviated the fact that both parents, in their different ways, were inevitably somewhat remote to their young children. Leslie's tendency to irritability and the pressure of his work combined to obscure too often the very real interest he felt in their development. Julia perforce made her husband's emotional demands her priority, while her reserves of sympathy and practical help were also drained by outsiders; her children rarely enjoyed the luxury of having her attention long to themselves. 'Can I remember ever being alone with her for more than a few minutes?' Virginia was later to ask herself, and Julia once let slip the sigh, 'Oh the torture of never being alone!' But as parents both Leslie and Julia were unquestionably caring: affectionate, if not demonstrative. Most importantly, emanating from their own mutual love (for it was clear that they worshipped each other) was a glow which bathed their children. 'Our life was ordered with great simplicity and regularity,' wrote Virginia. In all this there was security and serenity, enough to give the foundation of a happy childhood at least; the exquisite, the idyllic, was provided by Cornwall.

As it was Virginia to whom Cornwall meant the most and who was to seek to recapture its importance in her fiction, it is appropriate that the house at St Ives to which the family returned for two months every summer of her childhood was first discovered by Leslie within a few weeks of her birth. He was on a solitary walking holiday and reported the find to his wife in a letter from which his real delight in his young family, and concern for their well-being, shine out. The house, the garden sloping down to the shore, the view of the sea and the lighthouse made 'a pocket paradise'; from the upper windows the parents would be able to keep an eye on the children on the beach, and 'the babies will be able to go quite comfortably' down the path alone.[5] St Ives was the perfect antidote to London: 'perennial, invaluable' in Virginia's words. She loved it not only because it provided refreshment to the soul and stimulus to the imagination but because in that setting informal family life supremely flourished.

From an early age Virginia modelled herself on her father. Once she was reproved by her mother for twisting a lock of her hair while she was sitting reading. 'Father does it,' Virginia protested, only to be told that Father was an exalted being who could do what he liked. A recurring memory was of her father sitting reading, with one leg curled round the other, twisting his lock of hair; 'Go and take the crumb out of his beard,' her mother would whisper to her; and off she would trot obediently, delighting to perform that service for her father.

The perception of our parents as individuals, with unique, flawed but more or less fascinating characters, interacting with and influential on ourselves, normally arrives in adolescence, but to a novelist in the making may come earlier. During one nursery bathtime, Vanessa remembered, 'Virginia suddenly asked me which I liked best, my father or mother.' Vanessa unhesitatingly chose 'Mother', and Virginia countered with 'Father'. Vanessa received the impression that, unlike herself, her sister even in early childhood had considered both their parents 'critically and had more or less analysed her feelings for them'.[6] It was an early example of the fascination which her parents' characters were to exert over Virginia's mind till the very end of her life.

Perhaps her preference reflected her father's own special delight in her. It could be said that, if Thoby was his pride, 'Ginia' or 'Jinny' was his joy (while baby Adrian was always their mother's favourite, and Vanessa had to obtain her satisfaction from being the undisputed leader of the nursery quartet). From various letters which Leslie wrote while Virginia was small, her infant charm for him emerges clearly. When she was nearly two, he reported, she sat upon his knee looking at a book and every so often putting up her cheek and demanding 'kiss'. One day in 1884, when he told her he must go up to his room to work, she 'squeezed her little self up against me & then gazed up with her bright eyes through her shock of hair & said "Don't go, Papa!" She looked full of mischief all the time. I never knew such a little rogue.' Two years later, trying to get on with his work, 'I see her eyes flash and her sweet little teeth gleam.' 'Kiss my darling little bright eyes,' he ends another letter to Julia.[7]

For it was not only the good management and comforting presence of Julia which made the period before her death so infinitely more happy for Virginia than the years afterwards. Her father, too, during her early childhood, made her feel cherished and valued for what she was, so that his later assumptions about her role seemed almost a betrayal. At the age of five, in place of being read to, she told her father a story every night. At this age too she could write 'a most lovely hand', Leslie thought. 'She is certainly very like me,' he noted on her ninth birthday. The following month she began to produce a magazine, *The Hyde Park Gate News*, which came out at intervals over four years and which was read proudly by Leslie. The family was at this stage a mutual admiration society. Virginia's own child's pride in her father, and the extent to which she had absorbed the family legend that he was a great man, found expression in this piece of reporting, from issue number 45, dated 21 November 1892, when she was nearly eleven:

> Mr Leslie Stephen whose immense literary powers are well known is now the President of the London Library which as Lord Tennyson was before him and Carlyle was before Tennyson is justly esteemed a great honour. Mrs Ritchie the daughter of Thackeray who came to luncheon the next day expressed her delight by jumping from her chair and clapping her hands in a childish manner but none the less sincerely. The greater part of Mrs Stephen's joy lies in the fact that Mr Gladstone is only vice-president. . . . We think that the London Library has made a very good choice in putting Mr Stephen before Mr Gladstone as although Mr Gladstone may be a first-rate politician he cannot beat Mr Stephen in writing. But as Mr Stephen with that delicacy and modesty which with many other good qualities is always eminent in the great man's manner went out of the room when the final debate was taking place we cannot oblige our readers with more of the interesting details.

Leslie's major ambition had been to write a book which would profoundly influence the thought of his time, giving a new direction to men's understanding of themselves. From about the time of Virginia's birth, when he was fifty, he began if not to accept then to resign himself to the fact that he would never achieve this. In that year, he accepted the commission to compile *The Dictionary of National Biography*, the work for which he is best known. It occupied many years of his life – all of Virginia's childhood, in fact – and often made him cross and unwell. Accepting that enormous undertaking was tantamount to acknowledging that he had no further original contribution to make. His achievements were indeed considerable. He had published works of literary criticism, biography and philosophy, including the scholarly *History of English Thought in the Eighteenth Century*. He had been editor of the literary journal *Cornhill* for eleven years, and in that capacity had 'discovered' Thomas Hardy. Leslie had many friends and admirers and was highly respected in the literary world; he even came to be knighted; but his failure to realize all his ambitions depressed him and made his wife's gentle assurances absolutely essential to him. 'I have given up one thing after another & tried different lines & become jack of all trades & only done well enough to show that I might have done better,' one typical letter to Julia ran. 'You, poor thing, get nearly all my grumblings.' To the growing children, their father's groans and lamentations, their mother's ego-bolstering refrains, were familiar background noises which were, after the lapse of many years, to be perfectly reproduced in *To the Lighthouse*.

It was only after Julia's death that in her place Leslie took up his daughters' education, giving them lessons every morning for two years. His influence on Virginia's mind was, however, much more deep-seated and long-standing. The richness of English literature was inextricably linked to him in her memory. 'As he lay back in his chair and spoke the words with closed eyes,' she afterwards recalled, 'we felt that he was speaking not merely the words of Tennyson or Wordsworth but what he himself felt and knew. Thus many of the great English poems now seem to me inseparable from my father; I hear in them not only his voice, but in some sort his teaching and belief.'[8] He taught her, by example, how to read sensitively and how to respond to great literature; how to engage with the text and how to appreciate the rhythms of good prose. Above all, she absorbed from her father the conviction that words and ideas are endlessly fascinating and of supreme importance to civilized life. This shared conviction and delight made the bond between the father and this daughter stronger than that between him and any of his other children. 'She takes in a great deal & will really be an author in time,' Leslie assured Julia when Virginia was just eleven years old. He rather liked the idea of her being a historian, 'as I could give her a few hints'.

'Yes, certainly I felt his presence,' Virginia wrote, looking back at the end of her life; 'and had many a shock of acute pleasure when he fixed his very small, very blue eyes upon me and somehow made me feel that we two were in league together. There was something we had in common. "What have you got hold of?" he would say, looking over my shoulder at the book I was reading; and how proud, priggishly, I was, if he gave his little amused surprised snort, when he found me reading some book that no child of my age could understand. I was a snob no doubt, and read partly to make him think me a clever little brat. And I remember his pleasure, how he stopped writing and got up and was very gentle and pleased, when I came into the study with a book I had done; and asked him for another.'[9]

Nothing, then, in her charmed and cherished childhood hardened her or prepared her for the change that befell every aspect of her world when, after a short illness which no one at first took seriously, her mother died.

Virginia was 13¼ when, in her own words, 'the greatest disaster that could happen' occurred. It was not simply that the children lost a mother whose wise guidance through their teens must be missed. Far worse than the death itself was the effect which it had on their father, turning him into an ogre in their eyes and at a stroke destroying the peace and cheerfulness of their home. Just when Virginia most needed a strong, supportive father, she found herself doubly, and bewilderingly, bereft. She was never fully to recover her equilibrium; thereafter she trembled on the edge of mental breakdown. There is something immensely sad, as well as unforgivable, in Leslie's failure at this critical juncture to do his best for the sensitive little daughter he loved so well.

It was as an omen to the emotional estrangement to come that, stumbling from Julia's death chamber, he brushed unseeing past the bewildered Virginia approaching him with outstretched arms. Beyond mere grief, on the death of his wife Leslie was tortured by two emotions, which in their intensity blinded him to the needs and sufferings of his children. One was outrage. How could fate be so cruel to him? He had already lost one beloved wife; was it fair that he should have to endure sure suffering twice? Fifteen years older than Julia, he had always supposed she would be the survivor, nursing him with her exquisite tenderness to the end. The other unbearable emotion was guilt. Had he made her unhappy with his grumblings and his gloom? While she lived, had he told her enough how much he truly loved her? On these points he needed endless assurances, from his own children but chiefly from Stella Duckworth, his step-daughter, who at twenty-seven was suddenly expected, despite her own grief, to devote herself to running Leslie's household and alleviating Leslie's woes.

Twelve years later, looking back on her father's reaction, Virginia did not scruple to accuse him of self-dramatization. The death of Julia, she wrote in *Reminiscences*,

> . . . began a period of Oriental gloom, for surely there was something in the darkened rooms, the groans, the passionate lamentations that passed the normal limits of sorrow, and hung about the genuine tragedy with folds of Eastern drapery. . . . One room it seemed was always shut, was always disturbed now and then, by some groan or outburst. He had constant interviews with sympathetic women, who went in to see him nervously enough, and came out flushed and tear-stained, confused as people are who have been swept away on the tide of someone else's emotion, to give their report to Stella. Indeed all her diplomacy was needed to keep him occupied in some way, when his morning's work was over; and there were dreadful mealtimes when, unable to hear what we said, or disdaining its comfort, he gave himself up to the passion which seemed to burn within him, and groaned aloud or protested again and again his wish to die. . . . [Stella] spent a long time alone in his study with him, hearing again and again the bitter story of his loneli-ness, his love and his remorse. . . . Because it was his nature and habit to find ease in the expression of his feelings, he did not scruple to lay

before her his sufferings and to demand perpetual attention, and whatever comfort she had to give. . . . Suddenly she was placed in the utmost intimacy with a man who as her stepfather and an elderly man of letters she had hitherto regarded only with respect and a formal affection.[10]

Stella was not clever – she hardly ever read a book, and though inheriting her mother's loveliness, she had always laboured under a deep sense of inferiority in that intellectual household. Now, a pale and dutiful shadow of Julia, from 'sheer pure beauty of character' she did her best for Leslie and the young Stephens. Among her duties was going through the weekly housekeeping accounts with Leslie. What she suffered during these sessions was to be revealed only later, but she did have courage to extract from a man paranoid about expenditure much-needed clothes allowances for Vanessa and Virginia: £40 and £25 a year respectively.

Leslie had taken over their lessons from Julia, but formal teaching, as opposed to the gentle dissemination of his wisdom, at which he was superlatively good, made him bad-tempered. The 'sacrifice' of half of every morning 'did not make his mood the easier', Virginia recalled in her 1907 *Reminiscences*. And yet, just occasionally, he was capable of offering them a glimpse of normality. He took the family to the Isle of Wight that summer, and 'on a walk perhaps he would suddenly brush aside all our curiously conventional relationships, and show us for a minute an inspiriting vision of free life, bathed in an impersonal light. There were numbers of things to be learnt, books to be read, success and happiness were to be attained there without disloyalty. Indeed it seemed possible at these moments, to continue the old life but in a more significant way, using as he told us, our sorrow to quicken the feeling that remained. . . . Beautiful was he at such moments; simple and eager as a child; and exquisitely alive to all affection; exquisitely tender. We would have helped him then if we could, given him all we had, and felt it little beside his need – but the moment passed.'[11]

The pity is that Leslie could not sustain this support, so inspiring, so exquisitely adapted to the yearnings of the young people in his care. Had he been capable of it, not only would stability and optimism have been re-established in their lives but they would have been bound to their father in love, not in resentment. But his own needs and his own emotions were too insistent. The worst and most selfish behaviour took possession of him when, a year after her mother's death, Stella became engaged.

Stella's romance was the only bright, hopeful, normal episode of Virginia's fifteenth and sixteenth years. Leslie, however, was incensed that Stella should think of abandoning him and at first gave his very grudging consent only on condition that she and her fiancé, Jack Hills,

agree to live at 22 Hyde Park Gate after their marriage. The engagement
was dragged out from July 1896 to April the following year, as one obstacle
after another was put in their way. Gradually Stella began to realize that
she must assert Jack's right and her own to privacy and independence after
their marriage. To continue to live with Leslie would be intolerable. She
had done her duty all her life but never had she acted so courageously as
on the evening when she accosted Leslie in his study and told him it could
not be. The result was 'an explosion', as Virginia wrote in 1940 in *A Sketch
of the Past*, adding: 'As the engagement went on, father became increasingly tyrannical. He didn't like the name "Jack", I remember his
saying; it sounded like the smack of a whip. He was jealous clearly. But in
those days nothing was clear. He had his traditional pose; he was the
lonely; the deserted; the unhappy old man. In fact he was possessive; hurt;
a man jealous of the young man.'[12]

The Hills compromised and took a house in the same street, and the
wedding took place in April 1897. Leslie insisted on giving the bride away,
though her two grown-up brothers were offended. 'He ignored the fact
that they had any claim,' wrote Virginia. 'It was somehow typical – his
assumption; and his enjoyment of the attitude.' Immediately on return
from her honeymoon, Stella was taken ill; for a few months she lingered,
but in July that year, incredibly and devastatingly, she died.

The cause was a bungled appendicitis complicated by pregnancy;
Julia's death had been from rheumatic fever; but now the young Stephens
became convinced that it was the excessive demands of their father which
had fatally broken the health of both women. Virginia was even more
shocked and anguished by the death of Stella than she had been by that of
her mother. Two years older, she seemed to feel it more; the two years
groundwork in sorrow had sensitized her mind. She had the first of the
mental breakdowns which were to dog her at crucial periods of her life.
'Ginia I hope is improving, though still nervous,' her father noted
anxiously that September. Acutely impressionable, she had picked up his
own habit of remorse and turmoil after the death of a loved one. In her
case she did not vent her emotions on those around her but, by driving
them inwards, became more disturbed, more 'mad' than her father, whose
sufferings were always only too comprehensible to other people. It was a
pattern she was to repeat on the death of Leslie himself.

'Even if I were not fully conscious of what my mother's death meant,'
she herself later analysed, 'I had been been for two years unconsciously
absorbing it through Stella's silent grief; through my father's demonstrative grief; again through all the things that changed and stopped; the
ending of society; of gaiety; the giving up of St Ives; the black clothes; the
suppressions; the locked door of her bedroom. All this had toned my mind
and made it apprehensive; made it I suppose unnaturally responsive to

Stella's happiness, and the promise it held for her and for us of escape from that gloom.' She felt as though she had been not only cheated of that promise but brutally told not to be such a fool as to hope for anything good. Moreover, now no one stood between her father and Vanessa and herself.

'I shrink,' wrote Virginia in 1940, 'from the years 1897–1904, the seven unhappy years. Not many lives were tortured and fretted and made numb with non-being as ours were then. That, in shorthand, was the legacy of those two great unnecessary blunders. . . . I am not thinking of the deaths of mother and Stella; I am thinking of the damage that their deaths inflicted.' During those seven years, 'Nessa and I were exposed without protection to the full blast of [Leslie's] character.'[13]

At eighteen, Vanessa was now expected to take over the running of the house and the humouring of her father's whims. He turned to her in the unquestioning assumption that she would be the replacement for Julia and Stella. Reporting Stella's death to a friend in the United States, Leslie had added complacently, 'My Vanessa is taking her place as mistress of the house very calmly and will be invaluable.' But Vanessa was made of different stuff from Julia and Stella. Her physical resemblance to them was deceptive; she had the divine looks to become another ministering angel, but within was a healthy ruthlessness of character. 'Strong of brain, agile and determined,' Virginia described her sister at eighteen. She was as little susceptible as it is possible for a woman to be to emotional blackmail, which she despised. Her passionate commitment to the life of the artist gave her an integrity which refused to be compromised in saying or doing what she did not feel or think. She was not exactly unafraid of her father's tantrums, but she could steel herself to be unmoved by them.

It was fortunate that Vanessa was the elder of the two Stephen sisters, since Virginia was never capable of cultivating her detachment. Even at the height of her rage with Leslie, Virginia was conscious of her fundamental love for him, 'a passionate fumbling fellowship' grounded in vanished times and shared tastes. She was not so well able to shrug off the past as her sister, was not such a determinedly modern woman. Virginia would surely have been destroyed by Leslie – her health, her sanity and her individuality would all have been in jeopardy – had she inherited the mantle from Stella. It was bad enough observing what her sister had to suffer and standing next in line.

More than forty years after it had all happened, Virginia described that period in a passage worth quoting at length:

Nessa and I formed a close conspiracy. In that world of many men, coming and going, in that big house of innumerable rooms, we formed our private nucleus. . . . Very soon after Stella's death we realised that we must make some standing place for ourselves in this baffling, frustrating whirlpool. Every day we did battle for that which was always being snatched from us, or distorted. The most imminent obstacle, the most oppressive stone laid upon our vitality and its struggle to live was of course father. I suppose hardly a day of the week passed without our planning together: was he by any chance to be out, when Kitty Maxse or Katie Thynne came? Must I spend the afternoon walking round Kensington Gardens? Was old Mr Bryce coming to tea? Could we possibly take our friends up to the studio – that is, the day nursery? Could we avoid Brighton at Easter? And so on – day after day we tried to remove the pressure of his tremendous obstacle. And over the whole week brooded the horror, the recurring terror, of Wednesday. On that day the weekly books [household accounts] were given him. Early that morning we knew whether they were under or over the danger mark – eleven pounds if I remember right. On a bad Wednesday we ate our lunch in the anticipation of torture. The books were presented directly after lunch. He put on his glasses. Then he read the figures. Then down came his fist on the account book. His veins filled; his face flushed. Then there was an inarticulate roar. Then he shouted 'I am ruined'. Then he beat his breast. Then he went through an extraordinary dramatisation of self pity, horror, anger. Vanessa stood by his side silent. He belaboured her with reproaches, abuses. 'Have you no pity for me? There you stand like a block of stone . . .' and so on. She stood absolutely silent. He flung at her all the phrases about shooting Niagara, about his misery, her extravagance, that came handy. She still remained static. Then another attitude was adopted. With a deep groan he picked up his pen and with ostentatiously trembling hands he wrote out the cheque. Slowly with many groans the pen and the account book were put away. Then he sank into his chair; and sat spectacularly with his head on his breast. And then, tired of this, he would take up a book; read for a time; and then say half plaintively, appealingly (for he did not like me to witness these outbursts): 'What are you doing this afternoon, Jinny?' I was speechless. Never have I felt such rage and such frustration. For not a word of what I felt – that unbounded contempt for him and of pity for Nessa – could be expressed.

That, as far as I can describe it, is an unexaggerated account of a bad Wednesday. And bad Wednesdays always hung over us. Even now I can find nothing to say of his behaviour save that it was brutal. If instead of words he had used a whip, the brutality could have been no greater.

'When Nessa and I inherited the rule of the house,' she wrote elsewhere in the same fragment, '. . . it was the tyrant father – the exacting, the violent, the histrionic, the demonstrative, the self-centred, the self-pitying, the deaf, the appealing, the alternately loved and hated father – that dominated me then. It was like being shut up in a cage with a wild beast.' She likened herself at fifteen to 'a nervous, gibbering, little monkey', and her father to a 'pacing, dangerous, morose lion; a lion who was sulky and angry and injured; and suddenly ferocious, and then very humble, and then majestic; and then lying dusty and fly pestered in a corner of the cage' that was 22 Hyde Park Gate.[14]

Life in the cage, for the next seven years, was irksome in its every aspect and routine. The demands of Victorian society now bore down on the grown-up Virginia, and though the prime movers in forcing her to conform were her aunts, chiefly her aunt Mary Fisher, and her conventional step-brother George, she found her father totally unprepared to extricate her from its absurdities. 'Coming out' and all its ramifications were hateful to Virginia. Having no small talk, at parties she tried to hide in a corner with a book. She had little interest in clothes, and insufficient money to make a creditable appearance; though her allowance was raised to £50 per annum, this contrasted with the £1,000 per annum income of her half-brother George, still living at home. She began to equate money with power, especially in the relations between the sexes. George not only scrutinized and criticized her dress before escorting her in the evenings but he would come home and expect her to allow him liberties in her bedroom. She had already, at the age of six, been interfered with by her other half-brother, Gerald. Virginia had not much reason to think well of the male sex. Furtiveness, hypocrisy, abuse of power masquerading as protection: all threatened the happiness, or at least the normality, that should have been hers at that stage of her life.

The girls won some concessions. Vanessa left the house every morning for art school; while she was away, Virginia, by her own desire, studied Greek with a visiting tutor. For them both, these were the sanest hours of the day. From late afternoon onwards, their time, their very thoughts, were not their own. It was imperative that one, but preferably both sisters, preside over afternoon tea and make polite conversation with their father's visitors. (Virginia later wondered whether this ingrained politeness damaged her writing style, since she found it hard to be openly rude even in a review.) Even if no visitor had been invited that day, it was impossible for their father to pour out his own tea. He absolutely must have a female to fuss over him at this hour. Then the girls had to wash and change, in their often ice-cold bedrooms, into low-necked, short-sleeved frocks before enduring another evening pretending to be merely insipid, well-bred, if slightly shabby girls in quest of husbands. For all the 'drudgery and tyranny and rebellion' of these years, Virginia blamed her relations quite as much as the system. Many, many years later, on a visit to her mother-in-law, she suddenly 'felt the horror of family life & the terrible threat to one's liberty that I used to feel with father, aunt Mary or George. It is an emotion one never gets from any other relationship.'[15]

It seemed she had grown up for no other purpose but to look as decorative as possible and to minister to men's wants of one kind or another. If George was displeased by her looks or her conduct, he reproved her in 'the voice of the enraged male'. Virginia discovered that society was arranged to allow the maximum showing-off on the part of the male sex. She and Vanessa 'must sit passive and applaud the Victorian males when they went through their intellectual hoops'. Yet in fairness she acknowledged that her father, in theory if not always when his own comfort was directly concerned, was less maddeningly conformist than men like George. Certainly Leslie Stephen believed that 'women must be pure and men manly', but, she allowed, 'he smoothed out the petty details of the Victorian code with his admirable intellect, with his respect for reason – no one was less snobbish than he, no one cared less for rank and luxury.'[16]

Leslie's attitude was, indeed, confused and contradictory. 'I hate to see women's lives wasted simply because they have not been trained well enough to take an independent interest in any study,' he had written to Julia back in the days of their courtship. Vanessa was allowed her art, Virginia her Greek. But what did that amount to? Little more than token indulgence, for time thus spent was never allowed to conflict with their social or filial duties. Too often Virginia had heard him speak scathingly of female authors or would-be intellectuals; his own niece, Katherine Stephen, who actually rose to be Principal of Newnham College, was snubbed at lunch for giving her opinion with male forthrightness.

No, Leslie wanted his daughters to be clever, certainly not to be scatty like Anny Ritchie, with her wild exaggerations and hopeless grasp of facts (it is significant that he saw Virginia as a historian or biographer, never as a novelist), but their learning must be cloaked in female graces and certainly must never intrude on the world of 'school reports, scholarships, triposes and fellowships' upon which he 'laid immense stress'. This was 'the great patriarchal machine' with which daughters could have nothing to do, while 'every one of our male relations was shot into that machine at the age of ten and emerged at sixty a Head Master, an Admiral, a Cabinet Minister, or the Warden of a college.' Virginia was left with 'the outsider's feeling' which was to fuel those masterpieces of indignation *A Room of One's Own* and *Three Guineas*.

And yet, in 1900 Leslie could write with satisfaction to a friend of Virginia's 'becoming as literary as her papa'. Despite many fundamental differences between them, aggravated by 'the gulf between us that was cut by our difference in age ... we were his grandchildren', their early rapport was to some extent re-established. They would read together and discuss books and ideas. Only in her father could Virginia find her intellectual equal, soul-mate even. And she found it impossible not to give him credit for good intentions, however much his behaviour might be faulty. She knew that fundamentally he cared deeply for his family. And so they were drawn again to one another. It is not hard to imagine that in these last years of his life he derived his greatest enjoyment from her company. Vanessa was icy; his sons, though promising much satisfaction, were neither of them literary. In preparation for 'the real world of men', they were quite properly away at school or university; and in any case, at his own fireside, it was chiefly female company he craved. Female companionship of the calibre of his youngest daughter's was a rich possession that he fully valued only when time was running out for him. One passage in the diary Virginia kept when she was twenty reveals the peace and harmony they reached during their habit of sitting together in his study: 'For some time we would talk and then, feeling soothed, stimulated, full of love for this unworldly, very distinguished, lonely man, I would go down to the drawing room again.'

So when it was apparent that Leslie was dying, Virginia did not share her sister's straightforward emotion of relief. 'In me, though not in her, rage alternated with love,' remembered Virginia in *A Sketch of the Past*. 'It was only the other day when I read Freud for the first time, that I discovered that this violently disturbing conflict of love and hate is a common feeling; and is called ambivalence.' During the two years it took Leslie Stephen to die of abdominal cancer, 1902–4, Virginia was so racked by this conflict, this ambivalence, that following his death she immediately and seriously broke down.

From the autumn of 1903 to 22 February 1904, when he died, Leslie suffered much pain and weakness; only his tremendous vitality kept him going long after the doctors expected him to fail. The strain on the family, and on Virginia especially, was terrific, as these excerpts from her letters over those months show. (They were written to a sympathizing older female friend, Violet Dickinson, to whom Virginia turned in the absence of any fellow-feeling on the subject from Vanessa.) 'It feels rather grim, sitting here and waiting, and no escape.' 'It is very slow, but comes nearer every day, I see.' 'He said he didn't mind dying for himself, but he should like to see a little more of the children. He feels, I think, that we are just grown up, and able to talk to him – and he wants to see what becomes of us. In that way it is hard – for him.' 'Father is just the same – but it is very hard work. He does want to have done with it all, so, and can hardly read or amuse himself, and yet must go on, day after day. . . . If only it could be quicker!' 'It is so hard to wait and see him get slowly weaker day by day. But these are the things one has to go through in this Brute of a world apparently.' 'I don't think there is any good in going through these things –

and it is all pure loss. . . . But we have all been so happy together and there never was anybody so lovable.' 'Father died very peacefully, as we sat by him. I know it was what he wanted most. Nothing can hurt him now, and that was what one has dreaded. But how to go on without him, I don't know. All these years we have hardly been apart, and I want him every moment of the day. But we still have each other – Nessa and Thoby and Adrian and I, and when we are together he and Mother do not seem far off.'[17]

The third phase of Virginia's existence was as an orphan, coming to terms with the legacy of her parents' personalities. It was to be more than twenty years before she ceased to think of them every day. She wrote out her memories of them fully twice and touched on them in various other fragments, besides making them the subject of a novel.

During Leslie's illness, prompted chiefly by the wishes of Vanessa, the Stephens had already been hunting for a smaller house in a less stulti-fyingly respectable district of London, and after his death they set up the unconventional, unchaperoned household in Bloomsbury about which so much has been written. When Virginia recovered from her breakdown (her most serious yet), she slipped into this new and agreeable life, under her sister's leadership, and began to publish reviews and articles. It is interesting, however, that the first writing of hers to appear in print was the description of her father reading aloud to his family which she contributed to Frederick Maitland's official biography of him, published in 1906. Of course, it was in terms of the admiring and dutiful daughter that she put together her impressions. However, to Maitland, who had been one of Leslie's close friends, it was privately intimated by Leslie's sister, and perhaps by Vanessa, 'that Leslie's tempers were more than what he called (in his biography) coloured showers of sparks'. Maitland 'resolutely refused to believe' it. So Virginia wrote in 1940, still tussling with the character of her father. She was demonstrating that scenes such as those endured on Wednesdays over the account books 'were never indulged in before men. . . . If Thoby had given him the weekly books, or George, the explosion would have been minimised. Why then had he no shame in thus indulging his rage before women?' She attempted to analyse objectively:

Partly of course because woman was then (though gilt with an angelic surface) the slave. But that does not explain the histrionic element in these displays; the breast-beating, the groaning, the self-dramatisation. His dependence on women helps to explain that. He needed always some woman to act before; to sympathise with him, to console him. . . . Why did he need them? Because he was conscious of his failure as a philosopher. That failure knawed at him. But his creed, the attitude, that is to say, adopted by him in his public relations, made him hide the need he had for praise; thus to Fred Maitland and to Herbert Fisher he appeared entirely self-deprecating, modest and ridiculously humble in his opinion of himself. To us he was exacting, greedy, unabashed in his demand for praise. If then, these suppressions and needs are combined, it seems possible that the reason for this brutality to Vanessa was that he had an illicit need for sympathy, released by the woman, stimulated; and her refusal to accept her role, part slave, part angel, exacerbated him; checked the flow that had become necessary of self-pity, and stirred in him instincts of which he was unconscious. . . .

The fact remains that at the age of sixty-five he was a man in prison, isolated. He had so ignored, or disguised his own feelings that he had no idea of what he was; and no idea of what other people were. Hence the horror and the terror of those violent displays of rage. There was something blind, animal, savage in them. Roger Fry says that civilisation means awareness; he was uncivilised in his extreme unawareness. He did not realise what he did. No one could enlighten him. Yet he suffered. Through the walls of his prison he had moments of realisation.[18]

In 1906 the four Stephens travelled to Greece, a daring holiday which was to have tragic repercussions, for on his return Thoby died of typhoid fever contracted there. He was twenty-six; again the incredible had happened. Two days after his death Vanessa agreed to marry one of her admirers, Clive Bell, and Virginia was left with just Adrian, the least congenial of her siblings. Her first considered study of the family relationships and tragedies, *Reminiscences*, was written the following year, ostensibly for the Bells' first child, Julian, but obviously mainly for her own therapy.

In 1909 Virginia accepted a proposal of marriage from Lytton Strachey but almost immediately backed out of it, to his relief as much as her own. They remained friends. Writing to Virginia in 1912, he spoke of the Victorians as 'a set of mouthing bungling hypocrites' (feeling that was later to come to splendid fruition in *Eminent Victorians*). Strachey asked Virginia, 'Did I enrage you, by my rather curt remarks on *ton père*? Of course I think *qua* man he was divine.' To which Virginia replied, 'I don't suppose I altogether agree about the 19th century. . . . But you didn't shock my feelings as a daughter. The difference probably is that I attach more importance to his divinity '*qua* man' even in his books than you do. It always seems to me to count considerably.'[19] Her rejection of the Victorian era was never as wholehearted or simplistic as that of Vanessa and the majority of their Bloomsbury friends. With its passing, she saw, had been lost qualities of courtesy and civilization as well as hypocrisy and repression. Like so many creative artists of the highest order, she had a regard for the past as well as for the future. And, of course, the past for her was closely associated with her parents and their values.

In 1912 Virginia married Leonard Woolf. If it was a marriage which required more adjustments than most during its first two or three years – if Virginia could not overcome the frigidity created by her step-brothers' abuse, if Leonard refused her much-desired children because of her history of mental instability and if his response to another breakdown was so to stuff her with food that she swelled from eight to twelve stone and detested her body all the more – eventually it settled into a union which gave her quiet happiness, security and the best possible background in which to work.[20] In 1915 she published a novel she had long been working on, *The Voyage Out*, and thereafter had always a novel on hand as well as writing essays and reviews. The great thing about Leonard was that there were no explosions, no emotional blackmail, no draining demands. He was not a charming man – but, as Virginia knew from experience of her father, charming men are often the worst to live with. Leonard respected his wife's artistic integrity and her perfect right to the free use of her time. Putting her work first, she had the same need as her father to be cosseted in marriage, though her needs were by no means so voracious, nor did she employ such self-regarding techniques to satisfy them. If Leonard was to Virginia what Julia was to Leslie, then the Woolfs' relationship was better balanced, simply by virtue of the more giving partner being male. No husband ever subordinates himself the way a wife may.

From the retrospect of maturity and happy marriage, Virginia found herself dwelling on and resenting more and more the terrible impositions her father had laid upon her mother. Leslie had left his *Mausoleum Book* with its portrait of their mother and her marriage to his children. There, only softened, Virginia could read of the faults which so infuriated her and from which she and Vanessa were convinced that Julia had suffered far more than Leslie, in his self-centredness, had ever suspected.

'I used sometimes I must confess (as indeed I confessed to her),' Leslie had written, 'to express a rather exaggerated self-depreciation in order to extort some of her delicious compliments. They were delicious, for even if I could not accept her critical judgement as correct, I could feel that it was distorted mainly by her tender love. Although she could perceive that I was "fishing for a compliment" she could not find it in her heart to refuse me.'[21] This unashamed onslaught on her mother's integrity, together with the old conviction that Julia had worn herself out in his service, would not leave Virginia any peace until she had explored their relationship in a novel.

According to her diary, it was in October 1924 that she first envisaged her father as the subject of a story. On 14 May 1925 she recorded: 'I'm now all on the strain with desire to stop journalism & get on with *To The Lighthouse*. This is going to be fairly short: to have father's character done complete in it; & mother's; & St Ives; & childhood; & all the usual things I try to put in – life, death etc. But the centre is father's character, sitting in a boat, reciting We perished, each alone, while he crushes a dying mackerel.'

To the Lighthouse was written with great intensity and at speed; having mulled over the subject matter for most of her life, Virginia found the writing of it flowed inspirationally. The central concern is the quality of the marriage of the Ramsays, and the effect of their characters on their children. Its tightness and insight derive from its innovatory form, for it offers glimpses of just two days of Ramsay family life, with an interval of ten years during which Mrs Ramsay dies. Mr Ramsay is seen chiefly through two observers, roughly corresponding to herself and Vanessa. Lily Briscoe, like Vanessa, is an artist, cool and detached. Observing Mr Ramsay's treatment of his wife, she decides he is 'petty, selfish, vain, egotistical; he is spoilt; he is a tyrant; he wears Mrs Ramsay to death'. After Mrs Ramsay has died, Lily indignantly finds herself, simply because she is an available woman, expected to minister to his wants: she likens him to 'a lion seeking whom he could devour'. Cam, one of his daughters, shares Virginia's more complex attitude to her father. She is both more resentful and more sympathetic than Lily. Exasperated by his vanity and his despotism, she yet feels the pull of his strange charm and the greatness of his character which makes him tower morally over all the commonplace people who cluster about him, and which binds his children to him despite the injustices they suffer at his hands.

Vanessa found the portrait very truthful. After praising the portrayal of their mother, she wrote: 'You have given father too I think as clearly but perhaps, I may be wrong, that isn't quite so difficult. There is more to catch hold of. Still it seems to me to be the only thing about him which ever gave a true idea.'[22] On balance it does in fact approximate more to her view than to Virginia's own; there is more tenderness and understanding of her father in Virginia's autobiographical writings than in the novel, which leaves an overall impression in most readers' minds of a monster; though it is likewise true that it lacks some of the harshest notes found elsewhere. Perhaps they were too improbable for fiction.

In the year following the publication of *To the Lighthouse*, on the day which would have been Leslie's ninety-sixth birthday, Virginia confided in her diary her conviction that she would never have become a writer had he survived, adding, 'I used to think of him and mother daily; but writing The Lighthouse, laid them in my mind. And now he comes back sometimes, but differently. (I believe this to be true – that I was obsessed with them both, unhealthily; & writing of them was a necessary act.) He comes back more as a contemporary. I must read him some day. I wonder if I can feel again, I hear his voice, I know this by heart?' After *To the Lighthouse*, too, she noticed that she was referring to him as 'my father' not 'father' any more: another sign of distancing from him.

It was not true, as she hoped, however, that she had rid herself of her obsession. Until her death, Leslie was never far from her thoughts. This manifested itself sometimes in simple ways, as when eighteen volumes of Boswell's diary were published and her first feeling was sorrow that her father would never read them. At social gatherings, nothing interested her more than to hear other people's opinions of Leslie, which were nearly always favourable: Hardy's gratitude for his broadmindedness in publishing *Far From the Madding Crowd*, Francis Macaulay's view that he was 'a remarkable man; for though he could not believe in God, he was stricter than those who did', and Rose Macaulay's memory of her parents, calling him 'gentle & charming'.[23]

Fury with 'fathers in general' suffused much of Virginia's non-fiction writing: her essays about individual writers, and her two great feminist polemics. In *A Room of One's Own* she examined why and how women had been denied education and a chance to contribute to public life, the life of ideas and the arts and politics. She lamented all the individual frustration as well as the waste to the world of female talent. The events of the late thirties, the threat to civilization posed by the great dictators, prompted her to take the argument a stage further. In *Three Guineas* she derided the masculine values which she held accountable for the build-up to the Second World War. Women's qualities of empathy, imagination and humanity were in her opinion essential to save the world, qualities which had not been ground out of them by a rigid and highly competitive educational system, which she saw as so damaging to those 'feminine' aspects of their personalities which Leslie had in theory wanted to promote in men. With their emphasis on status and money, with their silly preoccupation with uniforms, medals, gowns and wigs, Virginia saw where reliance on male intelligence only had brought the world. Just as the father in his family, so the dictator in his territory. 'Society, it seems, was a father.' Unsurprisingly, in 'the real world of men' *Three Guineas* was not well received.

Then, in the early months of the war that so distressed all her sensibilities, she once again sought to capture the enigma of her own father in words. Her diary of April 1940 mentions the schism in her approach to him: 'As a child condemning; as a woman of 58 understanding – I should say tolerating. Both views true?'

To answer her own question, she began, in spare moments, to commit to paper an autobiographical fragment which she named *A Sketch of the Past*.

I am much nearer his age now than my own then [she mused on 19 June]. But do I therefore 'understand' him better than I did? Or have I only queered the angle of that immensely important relationship, so that I shall fail to describe it, either from his point of view or my own? I see him now from round the corner; not directly in front of me. Further, just as I rubbed out a good deal of the force of my mother's memory by writing about her in *To The Lighthouse*, so I rubbed out much of his memory there too. Yet he too obsessed me for years. Until I wrote it out, I would find my lips moving; I would be arguing with him; raging against him; saying to myself all that I never said to him. How deep they drove themselves into me, the things it was impossible to say aloud. They are still some of them sayable; when Nessa for instance revives the memory of Wednesday and its weekly books, I still feel come over me that old frustrated fury.[24]

She attempted to account for the defects in her father's character. 'The crippling effect of Cambridge and its one-sided education' had made him insensitive to the rights and feelings of others and had skewed his vision of women, so that, even while being idolized, they were never to be clever in their own right but always to derive their satisfaction from being help-meets to men. His mother, sister and first wife had indulged him, encouraging him to act the genius, for whom every allowance must be made. 'This is a sign of my genius,' he would say to justify an outburst of temper. But he was not a genius, and he knew it. 'This frustrated desire to be a man of genius, and the knowledge that he was in truth not in the first flight', which had been perfectly captured in the portrait of Mr Ramsay, led in her father 'to a great deal of despondency, and to that self-centredness which in later life made him so childishly greedy for compliments, made him brood so disproportionately over his failure and the extent of it and the reasons for it'. And finally her own mother had spoilt him. In the part of *A Sketch of the Past* which deals with the pleasures of St Ives, Virginia catches herself out getting side-tracked:

Every afternoon we 'went for a walk'. Later these walks became a penance. Father must have one of us go out with him, Mother insisted. Too much obsessed with his health, with his pleasures, she was too willing, as I think now, to sacrifice us to him. It was thus that she left us the legacy of his dependence, which after her death became so harsh a disposition. It would have [been] better for our relationship if she had left him to fend for himself. But for many years she made a fetish of his health; and so – leaving the effect on us out of the reckoning – she wore herself out and died at forty-nine; while he lived on, and found it very difficult, so healthy was he, to die of cancer at the age of seventy-two.

But, though I slip in, still venting an old grievance, that parenthesis, St Ives gave us all the same that 'pure delight' which is before my eyes at this very moment.

Even writing these memoirs did not lay the ghost of the past for Virginia. She had been free of mental instability for twenty-five years but began to fear that she was heading for another breakdown. A sympathetic woman doctor, Octavia Wilberforce, was invited by Leonard 'for tea' on several occasions during the winter of 1940–41. Virginia confided in her, confidences that Octavia reported directly to a friend. Virginia 'had been sorting papers. Love letters from her father to her mother. Had been swept away by them.' Virginia told her, 'Poor Leonard is tired out by my interest in my family and all it brings back.' Her father, she said, 'had made too great emotional claims upon us and that I think has accounted for many of the wrong things in my life'. Octavia commented, 'She so actively both loved and hated at the same time her father. Thought it a contribution that psychologists had explained that this was possible.'[25]

On 12 March Virginia told Octavia she was 'feeling desperate – depressed to the lowest depths'. The horrors of the war, the memory that it was during the previous war that she had before broken down, and the dread of going through that experience again, the emptiness that always followed on finishing a book, and her ineradicable preoccupation with her family, together made a burden too great to bear. On 28 March she left a loving note for Leonard on the mantelpiece, walked across the Sussex watermeadows which led from their country home to the river, put a heavy stone in her coat pocket and drowned herself.

During the previous quarter-century, Virginia Woolf had proved to be the genius, albeit of a different colour, that her father had once hoped to be. She possessed naturally the true genius temperament which he had cultivated deliberately, to the discomfort of those who had had to live with him. Like Leslie, she needed a supportive marriage and constant assurances that her work fulfilled her aspirations, but she was far less monstrous, less self-centred in her demands, having never been brought up to believe that the opposite sex was put on earth to serve her. Her upbringing, both its privileges and its pains, had fitted her to write perceptive literary criticism, innovative, intelligent, delicately crafted novels and pioneering works of feminist argument.

Her dying father had derived his worst anguish from the thought of not knowing how this brilliantly gifted daughter, this child most like himself, would turn out. In her own original way, during the thirty-seven years by which she survived him, she did in fact make the highest use of every emotional insight and every intellectual quality which were his legacy to her. Despite the unfavourable picture of him which she left to the world and which with modern scholarship increases in interest while his own works are known and admired by a dwindling number, he would surely have been large-minded enough to be proud of his daughter Virginia.

References

INTRODUCTION

1   Virginia Woolf, 'George Eliot', *The Times Literary Supplement*, 20 November 1919, reprinted in *The Common Reader*, first series (The Hogarth Press, 1925)
2   See Maggie Lane, *Jane Austen's Family* (Hale, 1984)
3   See Winifred Gerin, *Elizabeth Gaskell* (Oxford University Press, 1976)
4   See Claire Tomalin, *The Life and Death of Mary Wollstonecraft* (Weidenfeld & Nicolson, 1974)
5   See Jane Dunn, *Moon In Eclipse, A Life of Mary Shelley* (Weidenfeld & Nicolson, 1978)
6   See Martha Saxton, *Louisa Alcott* (André Deutsch, 1978)
7   See Victoria Glendinning, *Rebecca West, A Life* (Weidenfeld & Nicolson, 1987)
8   Rebecca West, *Family Memories* (Virago, 1987)
9   Virginia Woolf, *Three Guineas* (The Hogarth Press, 1938)
10   28 November 1928, *The Diary of Virginia Woolf* (The Hogarth Press, 1977–84)
11   *The George Eliot Letters*, edited by Gordon S. Haight (Yale University Press, 9 volumes, 1954–78)
12   Virginia Woolf, 'The Edgeworths and the Taylors', *The Common Reader*, First Series (The Hogarth Press, 1925)

I FANNY BURNEY

1   Maria Allen Rishton to Dr Charles Burney, Barrett Collection Burney Papers, British Museum; quoted Joyce Hemlow, *The History of Fanny Burney* (Oxford University Press, 1958)
2   *Memoirs of Doctor Burney, arranged from his own manuscripts, from Family Papers and from Personal Recollection by his daughter, Madame d'Arblay* (1832)
3   *Thraliana, the Diary of Mrs Hester Lynch Thrale (later Mrs Piozzi) 1776–1809*, edited by Katharine C. Balderston (Oxford University Press, 1942)
4   *Memoirs of Doctor Burney*
5   MS Berg collection New York Public Library; quoted Hemlow, *The History of Fanny Burney*

6   MS fragments of Dr Charles Burney's memoirs; quoted Hemlow, *The History of Fanny Burney*

7   The singer Paccierotti; recorded in *The Early Diary of Frances Burney, 1768–1778*, edited by Anne Raine Ellis (1889)

8   Recorded in the *Early Diary*

9   *Memoirs of Doctor Burney*

10 The recent feminist Ellen Moërs found *The Witlings* 'very funny and quite stageworthy. I shattered the calm of the splendid chamber in the New York Public library which houses the Berg collection by laughing aloud when I read the manuscript of the play, which is among the Berg treasures.' *Literary Women* (W. H. Allen, 1977)

11 *Autobiography and Correspondence of Mary Granville, Mrs Delany* edited by Lady Llanoven (1861); quoted Roger Lonsdale, *Dr Charles Burney* (Oxford University Press, 1965)

12 *Memoirs of Doctor Burney*

13 *The Diary and Letters of Madame d'Arblay, 1778–1840*, edited by Charlotte Frances Barrett (1842–6)

14 *Edinburgh Review*, 1843

15 *Memoirs of Doctor Burney*

16 *The Journals and Letters of Fanny Burney*, edited by Joyce Hemlow (Oxford University Press, 1972–81)

17 Marianne Francis to Mrs Piozzi, MS in John Rylands Library, Manchester University; quoted Lonsdale

18 *Memoirs of Doctor Burney*

19 *The Journals and Letters of Fanny Burney*

II MARIA EDGEWORTH

1   All quotations from letters to or from Maria Edgeworth are from Marilyn Butler, *Maria Edgeworth, A Literary Biography* (Oxford University Press, 1972)

2   *Memoirs of Richard Lovell Edgeworth, begun by himself and concluded by his daughter*, two volumes (1820)

3   Harriet Butler to Michael Pakenham Edgeworth, 3 June 1838; quoted Butler

4   Ibid

5   *A Memoir of Maria Edgeworth*, Frances Edgeworth (Joseph Masters, 1867)

6   Ibid.

7   Humphry Davy to his mother; T. E. Thorpe, *Humphry Davy* (1896)

8   Coleridge to his wife, *Letters of Samuel Taylor Coleridge*, edited by E. H. Coleridge (1895)

9   Mrs O'Connell to Sarah Ponsonby; Mrs G. H. Bell, *The Hamwood Papers* (1930)

10 Letter from Frances Beaufort to William Beaufort, MS copy in Harriet Butler's hand, quoted Butler

11 E. Somerville & Martin Ross, *Irish Memories* (1925)

12 *Letters and Journals of Lord Byron*, edited by Thomas Moore (1833)

13 *Sir Walter's Postbag*, edited by W. Partington (1932)

14 *Letters to 'Ivy' from the first Earl of Dudley*, edited by S. H. Romilly (1905)
15 *Letters and Journals of Lord Byron*, edited by R. E. Prothero (1898–1904)
16 Lady Holland, *Memoirs of Sydney Smith* (1855)
17 *Life, Letters and Journals of George Ticknor*, edited by G. S. Hillard (1876)

III ELIZABETH BARRETT BROWNING

1 Joseph Arnold to Alfred Domett; F. G. Kenyon, *Robert Browning and Alfred Domett* (Smith, Elder, 1906)
2 All quotations from letters pertaining to the early life of the Barrett family are from *The Brownings' Correspondence*, edited by Philip Kelley and Ronald Hudson (Wedgestone Press, 1984)
3 Ibid.
4 Ibid.
5 Ibid.
6 All quotations from the letters of EBB to RB and his to her are from *The Letters of Robert Browning and Elizabeth Barrett Barrett, 1845–1846*, edited by Elvan Kintner (The Belknap Press of Harvard University Press, 1969)
7 *The Unpublished Letters of Elizabeth Barrett to Miss Mitford*, edited by Betty Miller (John Murray, 1954)
8 *Glimpses into My Own Life and Literary Character, written by Elizabeth Barrett in the Year 1820 when Fourteen Years Old* (Boston, 1914); quoted Irvine
9 Kelley
10 Ibid.
11 Ibid.
12 *Glimpses*
13 *Letters of RB and EBB*
14 Dr William Coker to Edward Barrett, June 24 1821; quoted Kelley
15 Kelley
16 *The Early Diary of Elizabeth Barrett Browning*, edited by Elizabeth Berridge (John Murray, 1974)
17 Ibid.
18 *Letters of RB and EBB*
19 EBB to Miss Mitford
20 *Letters of the Brownings to George Barrett*, edited by Paul Landis and Ronald E. Freeman (University of Illinois Press, 1958)

IV CHARLOTTE BRONTË

1 All quotations from Charlotte Brontë's letters are from *The Brontës: Their Lives, Friendships and Correspondence*, edited by T. J. Wise and J. A. Symington (Shakespeare Head, Blackwell, 1932)
2 All quotations from Patrick Brontë's letters are from John Lock and W. T. Dixon, *A Man of Sorrow: The Life, Letters and Times of the Reverend Patrick Brontë* (Nelson, 1965)
3 Quoted in Lock
4 Letter dated 30 July 1855, quoted in Lock
5 Quoted in Lock
6 Ellen Nussey, 'Reminiscences of Charlotte Brontë', *Scribner's Magazine* (1871)

7 Letter to Mrs Gaskell, quoted in Lock
8 Letter to Laetitia Wheelwright, quoted in Wise and Symington
9 *The Letters of Mrs Gaskell*, edited by J. A. V. Chapple and A. Pollard (Manchester University Press, 1966)
10 Ibid.
11 *Brontë Society Transactions*, 1982
12 Quoted in Lock

V GEORGE ELIOT

1 J. W. Cross, *George Eliot's Life as Related in her Letters and Journals* (Blackwood, 1885)
2 *The George Eliot Letters*, edited by Gordon S. Haight, nine volumes (Yale University Press, 1954–78)
3 Ibid.
4 Ibid.
5 Ibid.
6 Ibid.

VI EMILY DICKINSON

1 All quotations from Emily Dickinson's letters are from *The Letters of Emily Dickinson*, edited by Thomas H. Johnson, four volumes (Harvard University Press, 1958)
2 Millicent T. Bingham, *Emily Dickinson's Home: the letters of Edward Dickinson and his family, with documentation and comments* (Harper & Bros, 1955)
3 Letter to Thomas Higginson; *Letters*
4 Bingham
5 George S. Merriam, *The Life and Times of Samuel Bowles* (1885)
6 *Letters*
7 Jay Leyda, *The Years and Hours of Emily Dickinson* (Yale University Press, 1960)

VII BEATRIX POTTER

1 Jane Crowell Morse, *Beatrix Potter's Americans – Selected Letters* (The Horn Book Inc., 1982)
2 Ibid.
3 *The Journal of Beatrix Potter from 1881 to 1897*, transcribed by Leslie Linder (Frederick Warne, 1966)
4 Unpublished letters of Beatrix Potter to Frederick Warne Ltd

VIII VIRGINIA WOOLF

1 *The Diaries of Virginia Woolf*, edited by Anne Olivier Bell (Hogarth Press, 1977–84)
2 Leslie Stephen, *The Mausoleum Book* (Oxford University Press, 1977)
3 According to Quentin Bell, *Virginia Woolf* (Hogarth Press, 1972)
4 Virginia Woolf, *Moments of Being*, edited by Jeanne Schulkind (Hogarth Press, 1985)
5 MS letters of Leslie Stephen to Julia Stephen, Berg collection, New York

Public Library; quoted Lyndall Gordon, *Virginia Woolf: A Writer's Life* (Oxford University Press, 1984)

6   Vanessa Bell, *Notes on Virginia's Childhood*, edited by Richard F. Schaubeck Jr (Frank Hallman, 1974)

7   Leslie Stephen to Julia Stephen

8   Personal reminiscences of her father by Virginia Woolf contributed to F. W. Maitland's official biography, *The Life and Letters of Leslie Stephen* (Duckworth, 1906)

9   *Moments of Being*

10   Ibid.

11   Ibid.

12   Ibid.

13   Ibid.

14   Ibid.

15   *The Diaries of Virginia Woolf*

16   *Moments of Being*

17   *The Letters of Virginia Woolf*, edited by Nigel Nicolson (Hogarth Press, 1975–80)

18   *Moments of Being*

19   *The Letters of Virginia Woolf*

20   For two contrasting but persuasive portraits of the marriage see Roger Poole, *The Unknown Virginia Woolf* (Cambridge University Press, 1978) and George Spater and Ian Parsons, *A Marriage of True Minds* (The Hogarth Press, 1977)

21   *The Mausoleum Book*

22   Dated 11 May 1927, Vanessa's letter is given in the appendix to *The Letters of Virginia Woolf*, Volume III

23   *The Diaries of Virginia Woolf*

24   *Moments of Being*

25   Octavia Wilberforce to Elizabeth Robins in New York, Monks House Papers, University of Sussex; quoted Spater

Principal works by authors mentioned in the text

(*p* denotes posthumous publication)

FANNY BURNEY
Evelina (1778)
Cecilia (1782)
Camilla (1796)
The Wanderer (1814)
Memoirs of Doctor Burney (1832)
Diary and Letters, 1778–1840 (1842–46, *p*)
Early Diary, 1768–1778 (1889, *p*)

MARIA EDGEWORTH
Letters to Literary Ladies (1795)
The Parent's Assistant (1796, 1800)
Practical Education (1798)
Castle Rackrent (1800)
Moral Tales (1801)
Early Lessons (1801, 1814)
Belinda (1801)
Popular Tales (1804)
Leonora (1806)
Professional Education (1809)
The Absentee (1812)
Patronage (1814)
Harrington (1817)
Ormond (1817)
Memoirs of Richard Lovell Edgeworth (1820)
Harry and Lucy Concluded (1825)
Helen (1834)

ELIZABETH BARRETT BROWNING
The Battle of Marathon (1820)
An Essay on Mind with Other Poems (1826)
Prometheus Bound and Miscellaneous Poems (1833)

The Seraphim, and Other Poems (1838)
Poems (1844)
Sonnets from the Portuguese (1850)
Casa Guidi Windows (1851)
Aurora Leigh (1857)
Poems Before Congress (1860)
Last Poems (1862, *p*)

CHARLOTTE BRONTË
Poems by Currer, Ellis and Acton Bell (1846)
Jane Eyre (1847)
Shirley (1849)
Villette (1853)
The Professor (1857, *p*)

GEORGE ELIOT
Scenes of Clerical Life (1857)
Adam Bede (1859)
The Mill on the Floss (1860)
Silas Marner (1861)
Romola (1862)
Felix Holt (1866)
Middlemarch (1872)
Daniel Deronda (1876)
Impressions of Theophrastus Such (1879)

EMILY DICKINSON
Poems (1890 *p*)
Poems, second series (1891, *p*)
Poems, third series (1896, *p*)

BEATRIX POTTER
The Tale of Peter Rabbit (1901)
The Tailor of Gloucester (1902)
Squirrel Nutkin (1903)
Benjamin Bunny (1904)
Two Bad Mice (1904)
Mrs Tiggy-Winkle (1905)
The Pie and the Patty Pan (1905)
Jeremy Fisher (1906)
Tom Kitten (1907)
Jemima Puddle-Duck (1908)
The Roly Poly Pudding (1908)
Ginger and Pickles (1909)
Flopsy Bunnies (1909)
Mrs Tittlemouse (1910)
Timmy Tiptoes (1911)

Mr Tod (1912)
Pigling Bland (1913)
Apply Dapply's Nursery Rhymes (1917)
Cecily Parsley's Nursery Rhymes (1922)
Little Pig Robinson (1930)

VIRGINIA WOOLF
The Voyage Out (1915)
Night and Day (1919)
Monday or Tuesday (1921)
Jacob's Room (1922)
Mrs Dalloway (1925)
The Common Reader, first series (1925)
To the Lighthouse (1927)
Orlando (1928)
A Room of One's Own (1929)
The Waves (1931)
The Common Reader, second series (1932)
Flush: a Biography (1933)
The Years (1937)
Three Guineas (1938)
Roger Fry (1940)
Between the Acts (1941, p)

Bibliography

I FANNY BURNEY
Barrett, Charlotte Frances (editor), *The Diary and Letters of Madame d'Arblay, 1778–1840* (1842–6)
Ellis, Anne Raine (editor), *The Early Diary of Frances Burney, 1768–78* (1889)
Hemlow, Joyce, *The History of Fanny Burney* (Oxford University Press, 1958)
    (editor), *The Journals and Letters of Fanny Burney* (Oxford University Press, 1972–81)
Lonsdale, Roger, *Dr Charles Burney* (Oxford University Press, 1965)
Simons, Judy, *Fanny Burney* (Macmillan, 1987)

II MARIA EDGEWORTH
Butler, Marilyn, *Maria Edgeworth, A Literary Biography* (Oxford University Press, 1972)
Edgeworth, Frances, *A Memoir of Maria Edgeworth* (Joseph Masters, 1867)

III ELIZABETH BARRETT BROWNING
Berridge, Elizabeth (editor), *The Barretts at Hope End: The Early Diary of Elizabeth Barrett Browning* (John Murray, 1974)
Irving, William, and Honan, Park, *The Book, The Ring and The Poet: A Biography of Robert Browning* (The Bodley Head, 1974)
Kaplan, Cora, 'Wicked Fathers: A Family Romance' *in* Owen, Ursula (editor), *Fathers: A Reflection by Daughters* (Virago, 1983)
Karlin, Daniel, *The Courtship of Robert Browning and Elizabeth Barrett* (Oxford University Press, 1985)
Kelley, Philip, and Hudson, Ronald (editors), *The Brownings' Correspondence*, four volumes (Wedgestone Press, 1984)
Kintner, Elvan (editor), *The Letters of Robert Browning and Elizabeth Barrett, 1845–1846* (The Belknap Press of Harvard University Press, 1969)

IV CHARLOTTE BRONTË
Chapple, J. A. V., and Pollard, A., *The Letters of Mrs Gaskell* (Manchester University Press, 1966)
Gaskell, Elizabeth, *The Life of Charlotte Brontë* (Smith, Elder, 1857)

Gerin, Winifred, *Charlotte Brontë, The Evolution of a Genius* (Oxford University Press, 1967)

Hopkins, Annette B., *The Father of the Brontës* (Johns Hopkins, 1958)

Lane, Margaret, *The Brontë Story* (Heinemann, 1953)

Lock, John, and Dixon, W. T., *A Man of Sorrow: The Life, Letters and Times of the Reverend Patrick Brontë* (Nelson, 1965)

Wise, T. J., and Symington, J. A., *The Brontës: Their Lives, Friendships and Correspondence* (Shakespeare Head, Blackwell, 1932)

V GEORGE ELIOT

Haight, Gordon S., *George Eliot* (Oxford University Press, 1968)

   (editor), *The Letters of George Eliot* (Yale University Press, 1954–5)

Pinion, F. B., *A George Eliot Companion* (Macmillan, 1981)

Purkis, John, *A Preface to George Eliot* (Longman, 1985)

Uglow, Jennifer, *George Eliot* (Virago, 1987)

VI EMILY DICKINSON

Dickenson, Donna, *Emily Dickinson* (Berg, 1985)

Duncan, Douglas, *Emily Dickinson* (Oliver & Boyd, 1965)

Ferlazzo, Paul J., *Emily Dickinson* (Bobbs-Merrill, 1976)

Johnson, Thomas H., *The Letters of Emily Dickinson*, four volumes (Harvard University Press, 1958)

McNeil, Helen, *Emily Dickinson* (Virago, 1986)

VII BEATRIX POTTER

Lane, Margaret, *The Tale of Beatrix Potter*, revised edition (Frederick Warne, 1985)

Linder, Leslie (editor), *The Journal of Beatrix Potter from 1881 to 1897* (Frederick Warne, 1966)

Taylor, Judy, *Beatrix Potter: Artist, Storyteller and Countrywoman* (Frederick Warne, 1986)

VIII VIRGINIA WOOLF

Bell, Anne Olivier, *The Diaries of Virginia Woolf* (Hogarth Press, 1977–84)

Bell, Quentin, *Virginia Woolf* (Hogarth Press, 1972)

Gordon, Lyndall, *Virginia Woolf: A Writer's Life* (Oxford University Press, 1984)

Nicolson, Nigel, *The Letters of Virginia Woolf* (Hogarth Press, 1975–80)

Poole, Roger, *The Unknown Virginia Woolf* (Cambridge University Press, 1978)

Schlack, Beverly Ann, 'Fathers in General: The Patriarchy in Virginia Woolf's Fiction' *in* Marcus, Jane (editor), *Virginia Woolf, a Feminist Slant* (University of Nebraska Press, 1983)

Schulkind, Jeanne (editor), *Moments of Being: Unpublished Autobiographic Writings of Virginia Woolf* (Hogarth Press, 1985)

Spater, George and Parsons, Ian, *A Marriage of True Minds* (The Hogarth Press, 1977)

Stephen, Leslie, *Mausoleum Book* (Oxford University Press, 1977)

Index